Praise for J. David Kuo's

dot.bomb

"A savagely funny account of the rise and fall of Value America, one of the many dot-com ventures once so beloved of investors. . . . Mr. Kuo's compulsively readable book captures the creative powers of an entrepreneur like Craig Winn, who by sheer force of personality managed to corral investment bankers, executive talent, and business luminaries, however briefly."

—Daniel Akst, *Wall Street Journal*

"If you ever wondered what it was like to work in a high-flying dot-com company during the height of the Internet bubble, you're bound to love J. David Kuo's *dot.bomb.* . . . It reads like pure farce. . . . At times I laughed out loud at how zany things became. Other times, I wondered why so many of us, particularly investors, analysts, and the media, were so clueless." —John A. Byrne, *Business Week*

"Riveting. . . . Craig Winn cavorted in dot.com excess, and the book is peppered with examples of his whimsy. . . . Kuo writes with journalistic precision and has a knack for colorful detail. . . . Unlike many corporate memoirs, *dot.bomb* is an easy read, even for those without the slightest knowledge of business fundamentals. It is partly a comedy of errors, to be sure, but it is also a lesson in business survival."

—Kim Peterson, *San Diego Union-Tribune*

"Intriguing. . . . Kuo's book captures the inane atmosphere of the Internet era. It pours cold water on the great axioms, such as the one that profits don't matter."

—Peter Galuszka, *Virginia Business*

"A cautionary business tale for readers of *Forbes* and *Fortune*."

—*Kirkus Reviews*

"Kuo's story of boom and bust may be all too familiar to many web pioneers, but it's entertaining reading."

—*Atlanta Journal-Constitution*

"An informative and sometimes entertaining insider's view of the e-commerce world that was. . . . The book is at its most compelling in the final fifty pages or so, when Value America is collapsing."

—K. Daniel Glover, *National Journal*

"Mr. Kuo describes his experiences as a dot.com spinmeister in a very readable book."

—Alan Goldstein, *Dallas Morning News*

"Kuo expertly grafts a dramatic sensibility onto this familiar boom-and-bust story, drafting exchanges between Value America's major players like scenes in a novel. Craig Winn, the company's charismatic, ambitious, fatally flawed hero-founder, seems worthy of a Greek tragedy. . . . Those vicariously seeking the thrill of the twentieth century's most dynamic business period will find Kuo a good storyteller and an engaging guide."

—*Publishers Weekly*

dot.bomb

MY DAYS AND NIGHTS AT
AN INTERNET GOLIATH

J. David Kuo

BACK
BAY
BOOKS

LITTLE, BROWN AND COMPANY

Boston • New York • London

For Kim

Originally published in hardcover by Little, Brown and Company, October 2001
First Back Bay paperback edition, November 2002

AUTHOR'S NOTE: The reconstruction of critical events and dialogue has been based on extensive interviews, news reports, document research, and my personal experience as senior vice president of communications at Value America. Only the name of Greg Dorn has been changed.

Library of Congress Cataloging-in-Publication Data
Kuo, J. David.
Dot.bomb: my days and nights at an internet Goliath/by J. David Kuo. — 1st ed.
p. cm.
ISBN 0-316-50749-0 (hc)/0-316-60005-9 (pb)
1. Valueamerica.com   2. Electronic commerce — United States.   3. Internet marketing —
United States.   I. Title: My days and nights at an internet Goliath.   II. Title.

HF5548.325.U6 K86 2001
381'.1 — dc21
2001038027

10 9 8 7 6 5 4 3 2 1

Q-FF

Book design by Fearn Cutler

Printed in the United States of America

Contents

dot.bomb

Prologue

It was the height of the Internet gold rush — though I didn't know it at the time. I just wanted to cash in on some easy and plentiful money. Everyone was doing it.

It was April 8, 1999, and I was busting my ass to get a little VUSA, the ticker symbol Nasdaq had assigned to burgeoning Internet retailer Value America. I was in my second day of furiously trying to get some of its IPO stock. It was going public with a little more than 5 million shares. I just wanted 500 — how hard could that possibly be?

The breakthrough came the day before, when I discovered that on-line trading giant E*Trade had a VUSA share allotment. Not knowing much about IPOs, or the stock market for that matter, I just assumed E*Trade would have hundreds of thousands of shares available. While I knew I wouldn't get that many — I wasn't an Internet billionaire *yet* and therefore couldn't afford them anyway — I figured I could probably get a few hundred, or enough to make a positive difference in my bank account when I sold those same shares at a ridiculous profit in the very near future.

Investing in stocks wasn't something I'd ever done before. I hadn't done it because I'd never had any money to invest. The past decade of my life had been spent in the political and not-for-profit worlds. The psychic rewards were great — I'd idealistically tried to make America a better place by starting an organization that would fund the best social service programs. The financial ones less so — I'd poured my own money into the now-failed venture and was still licking my wounds. But that was OK because, like every conscious American, I had heard about the quick riches that e-commerce IPOs offered. They went public in the high teens or the low twenties and then traded in the hundreds by the close of the first week of trading — sometimes on the first day of trading. It didn't matter what the company did, it just mattered that they had a dot.com after their name. Those little letters spelled out the secret password to riches. It was my last $10,000 in savings.

I did the math in my head: 500 Value America shares at the projected $21 offering price sold within the week for, conservatively, $100 a share. I'd clear nearly $40,000 for my efforts. Little did I know I was competing with every other little guy for E*Trade's entire allotment of . . . 1,000 shares divvied out in 10-share increments.

What I did know was that Value America was going to be big. Unlike a lot of other e-commerce companies, Value America wasn't a niche play. It wasn't selling just books or CDs or Chilean sea bass to Inuits. It sold *everything* in one place without holding any inventory — the manufacturers sent stuff directly from their warehouses to consumers. No one else was doing that, and it seemed like a very powerful concept. Even better, it had unbelievable backing. High-tech heavyweight Paul Allen, co-founder of Microsoft, was in for $50 million. FedEx chairman and founder Frederick W. Smith, who was in for $5 million personally and $5 million through FedEx, publicly called the company's business model the "best I've ever seen." That was all public information. The private news was even more encouraging. A friend of mine had started working there the month before the IPO, and she chattered to me regularly about the amazing stuff happening internally. The company's chairman and founder, a retail genius named Craig Winn, was constantly on the move, negotiating deals and alliances that were going to drive hundreds of millions — maybe even billions — in revenue. They were apparently close to signing Tom Hanks to be their celebrity spokesman. The management team, led by a *Fortune* 500 CEO personally recruited by Fred Smith, was absolutely first-rate. It was clearly a sure thing. Every time I really analyzed the company, I got a little short of breath. It was pornography for my greed.

This inside information fueled my moneymaking passion. I logged onto E*Trade's site every few minutes, furiously clicked the REFRESH button on my Internet browser, and waited for the chance to grab VUSA's stock. Compared to a lot of other retail stock traders, I knew a lot about the company. Many of the people out there competing with me for the stock knew nothing about what the company did, who worked there, or what would likely happen. They knew only that the stock was going through the roof. I thought that should disqualify them. Sure, I

wanted the money, too. But I also *believed* in what the company was trying to do. It was cool. That alone should have put me first in line. For
unknown reasons it didn't seem to matter.

The hours rolled by and nothing changed. I still couldn't apply for
my cut. Finally, breaking for dinner, I retreated and mulled over my options — or, as I thought, my lack of stock options. My friend didn't get
me any of the so-called friends and family stock that is typically set aside
so that close acquaintances of the company brass can get in on the action
and make a killing, too. My stockbroker couldn't get his hands on any,
since his firm, Lehman Brothers, hadn't been one of Value America's
backers. My only real option was E*Trade. I counted my blessings that
I'd at least discovered their bounty.

Returning to my room and overheated laptop, clicking around trying to register my name for shares, I met my doom. I was too late. The
message on E*Trade's IPO offerings page had changed: "E*Trade is no
longer accepting applications for shares of Value America's IPO. Thank
you for your interest." Thank me for my INTEREST?! How the hell
had I missed out? What did they have, like 10 shares available? Or had
a hundred thousand people suddenly shown up in the few minutes that
I was downstairs eating my Chef Boyardee?

I tried to calm myself by breathing deeply and regularly. I resigned
myself to my preordained fate: I was going to have to compete with the
masses to get some shares. Gone was any chance of $21-a-share stock. I'd
probably have to pay $30 or maybe even $40 a share. I tried to console
myself by remembering that even at $40 a share, I'd still make a killing.
It helped me sleep that night.

That brought me to Thursday morning, April 8. I woke up, grabbed
my laptop, and went to work. I must have been quite a sight — a six foot
five inch half-Asian guy sitting on his bed in a T-shirt and Winnie-the-
Pooh boxer shorts furiously pounding his laptop, trying to place electronic orders every 2.1 seconds. The stock was scheduled to begin
trading at 9:30 A.M., when the markets opened. But by 10:30, there still
wasn't any news. My broker wasn't having any more luck than I was. He
told me that unfortunately, the longer it went without trading, the
higher the price was likely to be when it did start trading. On top of that,
by 11:00 A.M., E*Trade sent me an e-mail to stop clogging up their system. It was probably a federal offense, I figured. But screw the law; I'd

have hopped on my left foot carrying raw meat through a den of ravenous lions to get some shares. With every passing minute I knew I'd have to pay a little bit more — actually, a lot more. But with all the news and all the deals and all the big backers, Value America was a great investment no matter how much I was forced to pay.

Finally, around 11:30 A.M., supply and demand equalized and the first figure popped up: $69 a share. It quickly rose to $74. I finally bought at $72. Success! All my hours of work had paid off, and I'd gotten in before it had really taken off. Assuming it was still going to go to $100 a share that week or the next, I wasn't going to make as much money, but I'd do well enough. I had nothing to complain about. I'd just made the most brilliant financial move of my life. It was like getting IBM or AT&T shares on the first day they went public. Value America couldn't miss. I shut my laptop, satisfied at my persistence and brilliant insider knowledge of Value America's impending success. I called my fiancée, Kim, and announced that we were going to have a celebratory dinner. Obviously, I'd be paying.

A month later I was working for the company, flying on a private jet, and cruising on a ninety-foot yacht — all care of a southern California law school dropout who got his retail start selling fly swatters.

Part One

YOU SAY YOU WANT A REVOLUTION

CHAPTER ONE

Dream Weaving

The twin-engine puddle jumper circled once above the single-strip air-field, turned its nose down, and dove for the ground below. In seat 3A, Craig Winn gazed out the window at the rich green carpet of maple trees undulating into the distance of the Shenandoah Valley. Seconds later the familiar thump, thump of landing gear meeting runway welcomed the little plane's passengers to Charlottesville, Virginia. It was Independence Day 1996. Craig Winn was arriving at not only his new home but also the new home of his newborn Internet retailer, Value America.

The dense heat and humidity of Virginian summer life socked Winn as he got off the plane. He'd left 70-degree temperatures that morning when he said good-bye to his recently former home — a multimillion-dollar estate in Palos Verdes, California, sitting atop perfectly manicured grounds overlooking the Pacific. Now he was panting and sweating as he gathered his bags from inside the three-gate terminal, looking for the familiar fair-skinned round face of his sandy-haired comrade in computer code, Joe Page.

Each man had something the other needed. Page had a car; Winn didn't. Winn had a home; Page didn't. Winn was therefore confident that Joe would be there to give him a ride, but he wasn't too confident about how Page would react to what he was about to tell him: The moving vans were days away. They were going to have to stop at Wal-Mart to buy camping mattresses, sleeping bags, towels, and kitchen utensils for Winn's vacant McMansion in the Glenmore section of Charlottesville.

Curbside, Page leaned against his old black Jeep and waved to Winn.

"Man, I'm sure glad I've got a real bed to sleep in tonight," Page, who had driven out from California, said with genuine relief. "The Jeep hasn't been too comfortable!"

Winn tacked on a big, impish smile and shrugged his shoulders dramatically. He did that at "gotcha" moments like these.

Page, who had been working with Winn on Value America's early programming for several months, *knew* that look. "What?" he said with alarm.

Winn explained. Page listened, cranked the wheel hard to the left, and headed for the shopping center. The two men plowed through Wal-Mart getting the bare necessities for Winn's house and also for the office they would occupy the next day.

After a night of camping in Winn's new home, the two men headed for State Farm Road and the fine offices of Commonwealth Clinical Systems. Double-fisting bottles of Formula 409, they marched through the front door, climbed up the center stairs and then one more flight of stairs to greet Value America's new world headquarters — an attic full of wires, cables, dirt, strewn files, and upended furniture, all sitting on a carpet Winn preferred to think of as rich burgundy, but everyone else thought was blood-red.

For the next six hours Winn and Page wiped down every square inch of the discarded furniture that would be theirs and the 500-square-foot space that would serve as the office for them and three other men currently inbound from California. As Winn and Page wiped and sneezed and wheezed and vainly tried to open windows to get fresh air into the space, they talked excitedly about the future — about Value America and about how it was going to revolutionize retail, creating a "living store" that would be the "marketplace for the new millennium."

In mid-1996, Winn's Value America vision was arguably the most ambitious Internet retailing vision in existence. While other Internet retailers of the day were building online specialty shops selling books, CDs, and zithers, Winn's goal was not just to sell a lot of one kind of stuff or another. He wanted to use the Internet to revolutionize every facet of retail, creating a one-stop Internet shopping site of unparalleled selection, product information, and efficiency. It would be for the Internet age what Harrods was for the entire British Empire at its height: the shopping source for *all* things. Winn knew it was an *inspired* — and possibly psychotically lucrative — vision.

The mid-'90s were an age that no one really knew, but many were beginning to suspect, would be an Age. The Internet and the World

Wide Web were without definition but full of wild expectations. While few Yahoo!'d, America Online was just a dorky company in a bland Virginia suburb, and the expression *dot.com* sounded odd in conversation, there was an expectant sense that those were just temporary realities — that the Internet was going to change the world, and the retail conducted over it would be the engine. What that *meant* wasn't exactly clear. Only the visionaries could describe the future for everyone else. And few revealed the pixels of the unknown future as well as the brilliant salesman with Ted Koppel–like brown hair, darting brown eyes, slightly doughy cheeks, pudgy hands, and a self-illuminating grin.

Craig Winn had been waiting for a revolution like this almost his whole life. He'd predicted it in the early 1980s, while a young manufacturer's representative in southern California selling household goods. Someday, he'd said, technology would change retail forever. It was, he argued, a historical inevitability that retail underwent a revolution every decade or so. During the Eisenhower era in the 1950s, department stores took off, replacing mom-and-pop shops. Then the *real* '60s revolution came, in the form of discount chains, which were amazingly efficient retail outlets. In the '70s, enclosed malls gave consumers unprecedented convenience, and they reigned supreme. The warehouse concept popularized by Price Club and Wal-Mart took over in the 1980s, again by selling quality goods en masse at a value, effectively transforming warehouses into stores and collapsing costs.

At some point in the future, Craig Winn had prophesied in those years before the Internet, retail would be dominated by technology, obviating the need for traditional retail stores or warehouses. Someday, Winn *knew,* there would be a single device that combined the information-conveying potential of television and the communication-efficiency of the telephone, allowing consumers to shop for everything from the comfort of their homes or their offices and manufacturers to ship the products directly to those consumers. This device and the retail world it ushered in would be the *ultimate* retail solution.

Winn knew his life had been created to make this inspired vision real. His father had been a manufacturer's representative with an office in their southern California home — right off the kitchen. Dad used to bring home new products, put them on the couch, and ask his son to critique them. After graduating from the University of Southern

California in 1977 and spending a single day in law school (it occurred to him in the middle of the first day of classes that he'd never met a lawyer he really liked, and therefore he probably shouldn't become one), Craig Winn started selling for a living. His father was still a manufacturer's rep, and he gave his son the chance to call on his worst accounts. The stores to which Craig tried to sell his plastic cups, fly swatters, smoke alarms, toaster ovens, and other housewares had either already turned down the Winn Company or demanded under the table payoffs to take products. They weren't exactly blue-chip prospects. After those stores rejected him in his first week of work, Craig had to find new sales targets. By combining a list of all the retail stores that sold housewares and a very good map, Winn plotted stores by geographic location and started making cold calls. His efficiency didn't lead directly to success. His first year, he worked eighty-hour weeks, got rejected more than five hundred times, sold two accounts, and made $12,000.

The next year, Craig Winn earned nearly $300,000. The year after that, he made $500,000. The sudden success wasn't the result of better products, a dramatically better economy, or being given much better accounts. The difference was Winn. He'd done what he discovered he liked to do best — invent an entirely new way of doing business.

Winn's father was the consummate salesman — gregarious, a back slapper, smooth, and polished. Craig Winn was shy. He couldn't sell simply by the force of his personality or through the strength of lifetime relationships. So he decided he wasn't going to *sell*. Instead, he was going to *present* people with what he knew they wanted. This could work because, after his failed first year, Winn realized he had an otherworldly intuition about what other people needed and wanted. That insight, combined with his own painstaking research into the products he offered for sale and the stores he wanted to buy his products, made it exceptionally easy for Winn to craft his *presentations* — he stopped using the term *sales calls* — to his audience. And it worked. Between 1977 and 1981, Craig Winn helped the Winn Company grow to a $40-million-a-year business. A nice life accompanied his business success — a house on the Pacific coast, a sailboat, country clubs, nice cars, a family. In 1983, the younger Winn bought out the older Winn and grew the company even faster. But even as he became a better and better rep, learning more and more about the products he represented, the brands that paid his commissions, and the retail market in general, he was restless for the next thing — the new arena he could revolutionize.

In mid-1986 he found his next something — lighting. In a casual conversation with two Price Club buyers, he discovered retailers' frustrations with their lighting suppliers. Their complaints, he was told, were that prices were prohibitively high and quality was embarrassingly low. In addition, lighting products were merchandised poorly — their containers were bad, their packaging was bad, their displays were bad.

Within weeks, Winn had $1 million in initial funding for Dynasty Lighting Classics, a company that would create and sell high-quality lighting merchandise for less. Instead of plain brown boxes, Dynasty's boxes would be white, with four-color pictures and lots of information about the lamps on the *outside*. There would be in-store displays highlighting his products. And in this business such things were revolutionary.

Dynasty's fundamental business insight centered on Winn's favorite word, *value*. There were, he believed, two kinds of value. First was what he called perceived value. That is what causes a consumer to buy a product in the first place. It is what the consumer *thinks* he or she is buying. Perceived value is enhanced by packaging and display and underscored by a reasonable price. If consumers think they are getting a great product and are surprised by the low price, they are going to be happy consumers. The second type of value was actual value. There were, he knew, a lot of things initially transparent to consumers that, in fact, were very important to them in the long run. Actual value was about creating the best possible product, engendering the best possible feelings from consumers who used that product, and believing that positive feeling would translate into future sales.

All of Winn's innovations — packaging, easy access to information, high-quality products at reasonable prices — were about driving *value*. And value paid him back. Dynasty's sales rocketed to $30 million by the end of the second year. By 1989, sales hit $65 million.

In the early 1990s, with the help of Morgan Stanley and Salomon Brothers, Dynasty went public at $12 a share and started expanding. The stock went up 44 percent right after the offering. Winn then expanded into Christmas lights, wall art, mirrors, and ceiling fans. But the expansion ate up money, and sales were slow, and by early 1995, Winn was discovering all the things about retail that manufacturers hated. Increasingly, his products were displayed only by massive retailers like Wal-Mart. Those retailers, he felt, tried to rape manufacturers with burdensome rules and regulations about how they could ship and label products, take returns, and the like. It became clear to Winn after one particularly financially devastating run-in with Wal-Mart that it was time for him to leave the manufacturing business.

So in November 1995, after bringing in others to run the now foundering Dynasty, Winn left the company and looked to a future with a lot of questions. He was in his early forties, with millions of dollars, a beautiful wife, and two great little boys. But beyond that, life was not promising. Unless the world somehow changed, he was done with business forever. Value, he now believed, was a lost business art.

Then a former lighting colleague called him. Like most people in the housewares industry from the '80s to the '90s, Linda Stevens had heard Craig's retail revolution pitch. She wanted Winn to help her build something she called an Internet store. It was, she assured him, his ultimate retail vision. Winn listened as she described how new companies were popping up to sell things "online" over the "World Wide Web."

Winn hung up the phone, spun around in his chair once, and looked out at the Pacific Ocean stretched out before his home office. Maybe, he thought, the world *had* changed.

Thus, in late 1995, Winn dug into what little Internet research existed and began exploring whether the Internet *was* the missing link for his retail revolution. The Internet, he learned, had the potential to wire and interconnect the entire world. It was already a communications device and an entertainment device, but its potential as a retail device was untapped.

Winn found that Jupiter Communications, one of the world's first Internet research firms, forecast online consumer sales would grow from about $90 million in 1995 to more than $4 billion by 2000. In 1995, about half of all Internet sales were from airline tickets. Another 10 percent came from a pair of fairly successful online grocery delivery companies — Peapod, based in Chicago, and Harvest America, in Las Vegas. The rest of the market was fragmented into stores where shoppers could buy clothes, shoes, CDs, books, pens, pizzas, and Amish quilts. The online Amish quilt shop was especially delicious — a technophobic religious sect from central Pennsylvania selling their wares on-line. It was precisely this kind of incongruity that was getting people hot and bothered when they contemplated the Internet's future.

But Winn saw nothing on the Internet retail landscape that would *dominate* the retail market. Sure, there were Internet malls. There was I-mall. Internet Gallery. Internet Plaza. Internet Shopping Galleria. InterShop. Net Mart. Net-Galleria. There was NetMall. Web Mall. Webmart. CyberMall. eMall. eShop. Each grouped together smaller Internet shopping sites, the places that sold the Amish quilts and zithers and things. But to Winn the idea of an Internet mall was madness. It was clear to him that no one would succeed in Internet retail by taking traditional models and putting them online. A new medium required something totally and completely new, something no one had ever done before. Something stunningly radical. Winn knew the next retail revolution had arrived. He also knew *he* was just the revolutionary to lead it. So, tentatively at first and rabidly thereafter, Craig A. Winn set about putting on paper the perfect company. There could be only one name for it: *Value* America.

It would be the perfect store, the ultimate one-stop shopping destination — the one online spot where people could furnish a house, buy a car, get groceries, find a dress, do Christmas shopping, make vacation plans, equip an office, or die. Well, not die exactly, but get the stuff necessary to die — caskets, flowers, a nice suit.

It would offer not only unparalleled selection but also state-of-the-art multimedia product demonstrations, so that consumers could virtually touch the products, learning more about them than they could in any "normal" store. There would be an animated personal shopper on the site to guide people. There would be voice recognition, rendering a keyboard and mouse moot. Purchases would be delivered straight to consumers' doors. It would be perfect.

As much as Value America would appeal to consumers, however, Winn's real targets were manufacturers. From all his business experience Winn knew *exactly* the problems they faced. The warehouse superstores had squeezed them dry, forcing them to sell quality products too cheaply. All the manufacturers Winn knew wanted a new place to sell their products. Second, they wanted more consumer feedback. Third, they wanted to be able to market their products on the basis of quality, not just price, and increase the perceived value of their products. Finally, they wanted to operate more efficiently. Winn's Value America would meet every one of their needs. It would be a vast new retail outlet. It would gather information about consumers' needs and behavior and share that information with manufacturers. If consumers saw that for a few dollars more they could get something far superior, they would pay extra for it. It would make selling much more efficient. It was the return of value.

Perfection came at a price. In return for giving the manufacturers everything they needed, Winn had two requests. First, the manufacturers had to pay for the multimedia product presentations featuring their products. That wouldn't be too hard, Winn figured, because they could highlight the merits of their products rather than just the prices. Second, the manufacturers had to ship *directly* to the consumers. Value America would pay for the shipping but never hold any inventory at all. With no inventory, Value America would never concern itself with warehouses, shipping, insurance, theft, damage, returns, or anything else. Bottom line? Whereas inventory ate up 10 to 20 percent of revenue in overhead, Winn's store would enjoy overhead in the low single digits. Value America was going to charge less and make more than anyone else.

The challenge, he knew, was how to get there first. Within a week Winn had completed a 250-page business plan. Shortly thereafter, he picked up the phone and dialed his buddy Rex Scatena in his San Francisco law office. "Rex," Winn said in a breathless monologue, "you've been telling me for three years to help you get out of your boring law practice. Well, I've got a proposal for you. We're going to start a technology company. I know you don't know a thing about technology. On top of that, it is going to be a retail company. I know you don't know a thing about retail — in fact, I'm not sure you shop . . . except for Ferraris . . . we won't have those . . . well, at least not right away. It can't be based in California. I refuse to base anything in California. It will, probably, be based somewhere in the South. You don't like the South. You won't make a salary for at least the first two years. In fact, not only won't you make any money, you'll actually be dropping several hundred thousand of your own dollars on the deal. Oh, and by the way, we may not make it."

Rex Scatena was no dummy. He was an accomplished lawyer. He

lived in San Francisco. He'd heard the rumors about Internet riches. He'd even watched as a company called Netscape had gone public in August. The stock went up 150 percent its first day of trading. If his old buddy was onto something hot in the Internet space, Scatena knew this could be a once-in-a-lifetime deal. He also knew that if there was any-one in the world who could sell a story, it was his buddy Craig Winn. He said immediately, "I'm in."

With one phone call, Craig Winn had his founding partner and president. Next in were two other friends, Ken Power and Joe Page, to help with creative design and technology. Winn and Scatena each plopped down $150,000 to get the company started. Winn owned about 70 percent, Scatena about 25 percent, and Power and Page each shared a few percent. Within months they had all relocated to the sleepy little town Thomas Jefferson had called home — Charlottesville, Virginia.

By Labor Day 1996 — two months after the exodus from southern California — the Value America team was up and running. Much was good. Winn had a great CD-ROM to present his vision, early support from a few key housewares brands, a powerful business strategy, and the programmed beginnings of an online storefront. One thing was bad — there was nothing *behind* the store. There was *no* technology infrastruc-ture. None of the Web companies of the day — Netscape, Oracle, Broadvision, or Open Market — had anything to support Winn's inven-toryless retail solution in the manner Winn wanted.

As much as he wished otherwise, Craig knew he and his Value America team would have to write the code for the entire store — or find something else to do in rural Virginia. Winn gathered his team, told them the facts, and let them make the decision. They looked at each other, wrinkled their noses a bit, shrugged their shoulders, and said, "OK, let's write the code!" That several of them didn't exactly know how wasn't too important.

Writing code didn't mean just deciding what the store was going to look like. First it meant writing the software they would eventually pro-gram to create the store. Then it meant writing the technological sup-port structure to make the store run. They had to do it all. The upside was that they could use a commercial Microsoft program as a foundation for some of the work, but for the inventoryless system to succeed, they had to program everything consumers needed to complete an order:

take credit-card information, provide digital receipts, route orders to the appropriate brand manufacturers, arrange for shipping — *everything*. In addition, the technology had to handle everything that could possibly go wrong: partial orders, back orders, mismatched orders, shipping delays . . . The list of problems, it seemed, was almost limitless. Programming and planning consumed their lives for the rest of 1996 and early 1997.

Almost every day at State Farm Road from September 1996 through spring 1997 began with a bunch of apples (Winn had heard they were power brain food) and ended with a gaggle of comatose men stumbling out of the cramped attic, hoping they had enough brainpower left to find their way home. In between the apples and the stumbling were blurry interludes of light and dark when Joe Page and a small techy team would "sling code" — write the store. Winn, eyes shut, leaned back in a chair, dictating every pixel of his vision to them. Winn described not only the Value America world; he drew from his retail memory to describe every scenario the code needed to address. Then all hands worked furiously to make it come to pass. Winn *knew* this was going to work — there was no other option. It was ironic to him, however, that the Internet he thought was his silver bullet the year before, when he wrote the plan, now was his Achilles heel.

In the momentary breaks they took during their days, the little team let themselves dream of the future. Craig tried to bolster the sometimes flagging crew by describing what it felt like to build a company from nothing, to sell part of it to the public, to watch the stock get traded, and to see your net worth fluctuate daily. It was a high. It was a *rush*. It was the businessman's Super Bowl. The other men sat intently listening, inspired by the man who saw the future they wanted. Then, full of adrenaline and excitement, they roared back to work.

As Value America was being built one line of code at a time, Craig's mind wandered to his other near-term challenge — getting more household brands into the store. His original plan called for a systematic rollout of key categories, beginning with items used most often by small businesses and home offices. That was the niche Sol Price exploited with Price Club and Fedmart and where Winn figured he needed to begin as well. But what Winn discovered in late 1996 was that getting computer, electronics, and office-supply manufacturers to pay him $15,000 to

$50,000 a pop for online multimedia product demonstrations for a store that didn't exist was . . . challenging. The near universal response from everyone from Apple to Zenith was, "No." Many times, "Hell, no." Winn didn't believe he was wrong in his fundamental business proposition — manufacturers did want what Value America offered, hypothetically. They just had a hard time trusting that an anonymous company operating out of rural Virginia was their retail Messiah.

Winn knew he needed a big break. After diligent research he acquired his target — Hewlett-Packard. HP was the leading maker of home and small-business PCs, one of the most respected brands in the world and eager to increase its market share. Winn's meetings with low-level regional sales reps began in November 1996 and extended into winter and eventually spring 1997. His pitch was always the same: HP and Value America would be perfect partners. And HP's response was always the same: Possibly, but not right now. Winn closed every meeting by asking if there might be someone else in the HP family to whom he should speak.

In April 1997, after more than thirty meetings, Winn and a couple cohorts were sitting in a Las Vegas hotel room with a group of HP's sales, marketing, consumer products, and development managers. Winn once again walked them through the seven things consumers wanted from an online store, the five things that brands needed, and the five key principles of *e-commerce,* as Internet retailing was now widely known.

And suddenly he could see it in their eyes. For the first time in an HP meeting, Winn saw he had made *the* connection. HP's general manager told Winn he'd hit at the core of HP's nascent e-commerce strategy — the need to reap the benefits of selling directly to consumers via the Internet without taking the Internet risk all on its own. For HP, the risk in selling directly to consumers online wasn't so much the financial risk of building an online store as it was the danger of pissing off current vendors and hurting bottom-line sales. After huddling for a few minutes, the HP team offered Value America a big prize — HP would grant Value America a test program to sell printers online. Rex Scatena started bouncing ever so slightly in his chair, beaming. Another colleague, Bill Hunt, saw success unfolding before them.

Craig Winn looked sadly at the sales manager and apologized he hadn't communicated better. What Value America wanted, he informed them, was the *whole* line of HP products. HP, he told the assembled team, gave Value America the credibility it needed to succeed. The HP team looked at each other and then at Winn. No way were they giving over the entire line of products to a store that wasn't even a store yet.

Winn left without a deal. Scatena and Hunt waited until they were inside the elevator to berate Winn. Then they both pounced. How could he have done that? HP was giving Value America what it wanted! It would have meant credibility! It would have meant more money! Instead, the team was going home empty-handed.

Winn didn't even hear them. He had just seen the promised land. He knew, he just *knew,* that HP would agree to his terms. He had seen what they wanted to do, and he knew Value America alone could give them what they wanted. He also knew Value America had a solution unique to the entire Internet space. If HP was as smart as Winn believed them to be, they'd be back. They wouldn't have a choice.

Within a month, HP sent out a team to do due diligence on Value America. By the end of that trip, HP agreed to sell its entire line of consumer and small-business products through Value America — even though Value America didn't have a store. Winn had his break.

Because HP recognized Value America didn't have a store and wasn't likely to be driving millions of dollars of sales right away, it gave Value America the option of purchasing HP products through any one of five major distributors instead of having HP ship directly. It wasn't *exactly* what Winn had envisioned, but it presented him with a new opportunity.

Each of the five big distributors — Merisel, Tech Data, United Stationers, New Age, and Azerty — wanted the HP contract. As with all things Internet in mid-1997, it wasn't about the actual dollars the contract represented, but rather the dollars it would represent once things got rolling. Winn knew this. He contacted each of the distributors, telling them he'd won the contract to sell HP online and he must choose one of the five distributors HP used. There was, Winn told each company, an easy way for Value America to make up its mind. Whichever distributor did the most to help Value America get more brands in the store Winn would select for the HP contract.

Azerty stepped up to the plate first. Within a week of Winn's call to them in May 1997, they had arranged for more than fifty brand partners to come in to hear Winn's Value America presentation. By the end of that day, more than twenty new brands, including Canon and Zenith, came on board, each plunking down between $15,000 and $20,000 for the multimedia product demonstrations and committing to placing their products in the Value America store. United Stationers was next, renting out a ballroom in one of Chicago's grandest hotels and filling it with their vendors. Winn left that day with more than thirty brands and more than $400,000 in financial commitments. Ultimately, however, he didn't choose either Azerty or United Stationers. He chose New Age, the smallest and least connected but, Winn thought, the most responsive to his vision. And while using distributors wasn't part of the original Value America plan, Winn placated himself by emphasizing that distributors might ship more quickly and be more responsive until Value America scaled to an appropriate size. Besides, distributors were bringing more brands. Winn had never built an Internet company before, but neither had anyone else. Everyone was winging it.

Meanwhile, the technology was progressing. Value America still didn't have a functioning store, but Ken Power's graphical efforts combined with Joe Page's technology prowess provided Value America with a rough draft of a store by early summer of 1997. On the functionality side, Page couldn't figure out a way to do a lot of what Winn originally wanted. There wouldn't be, for instance, an animated shopper to guide customers through the store. No voice-recognition capacity had been built in either. Significantly more important technically, the system couldn't process credit-card orders, and it had more bugs in it than a New York City sewer. But it was a start.

As Value America gained brands, added staff, and scrambled to finalize its storefront and technology in the middle of 1997, the world around them was ablaze with Internet and especially e-commerce wonder. People who didn't know a thing about the Internet, the World Wide Web, or the difference between the two were driven to the dot.com world by the voices they heard around them whispering — or for that matter shouting — two words: "easy money." It was not too different from the mid-nineteenth century, when a bunch of scraggly guys were hanging out at a creek near a place called Sutter's Mill. There they stood, probably jabbering about new advances in horse-manure technology and railroads while betting who could piss further into the river. Suddenly one of them pipes up, "Hey Ned, you pissin' glitter, or is that thar' gold in the water?" *Kabam!* The California gold rush.

By mid-1997, the Internet gold rush was under way, rapidly rejiggering the entire U.S. economy. Suddenly the business world was being divided into the old (people who manufactured tangible products or offered traditional services) and the new (anything that used the Internet for any part of its business). It was becoming a winner-take-all search for alchemy, as young and old, rich and poor, educated and uneducated raced to turn sand into gold. The growing conventional wisdom was that anything Internet gave huge payouts and was therefore worth huge risks. That year *Forbes* issued its list of the hundred richest people in technology. The entry point for the list was a net worth of $49 million. Several people on the list had had net worths of maybe $49,000 the year before.

Taking advantage of Internet mania, Winn raised nearly $1.5 million in private investments from some Richmond friends, including Value America's lawyer, Gary LeClair, a whippet of a man with a perpetual sunlamp tan, thick black hair, and a penchant for thin Ferragamo ties with stylized leopards, elephants, and such. The Richmond contingent bought nearly 100,000 of the Value America shares (for $1.50 a share) — though they wouldn't be able to sell any until and unless Value America went public.

At about the same time Winn was raising his first outside money, he began hiring the core components of an executive team. The biggest addition was the new CFO, Dean Johnson. Johnson was a grown-up version of *The Andy Griffith Show*'s Opie — but with an attitude and wild blue eyes. He'd received his M.B.A. from the University of Virginia, worked at Lehman Brothers doing corporate finance, helped found a successful wireless cable-television company, and done business development for a semiconductor manufacturer. As soon as he sat down with Winn, he saw the entrepreneur's wild-eyed vision and bought in . . . literally. Johnson invested $100,000 in the company (also for $1.50 a share) at the time of his hiring.

Winn's second Internet funding experience came in early October '97 when he toured Goldman Sachs, Morgan Stanley, Alex Brown, Union Bank of Switzerland, and several other large investment banks.

Winn's funding desires were simple. He wanted about $10 million to help launch Value America into the Internet big leagues. Winn was operating by the same business rules he'd learned when growing his manufacturer's rep firm and lighting company in the 1980s: aggressive but manageable growth capped off by a public offering to elevate the company to the next level of growth. He foresaw profitability in a year or two.

Wall Street in the early stages of its Internet love affair had a different perspective on how all Internet-related businesses should grow. The Internet business world was first defined by the success and public offerings of Netscape, Yahoo!, and AOL — companies that were either Internet service providers or portals to the Internet and that accrued value based primarily on how many people they attracted to their sites. In the equivalent of Nielsen ratings for the Internet age, Wall Street kept track of how many people visited each particular site. The higher the "Web traffic," the more valuable a given piece of Internet property was. The nascent e-commerce industry based evaluation of a company's growth not on traditional retail metrics of advertising-to-revenue ratios or gross sales or even profits but on Internet media terms — page views, unique visitors, and customer-acquisition costs.

Winn discovered during his New York funding trip that Amazon. com, the first big Internet retailer to go public, had used the same metrics to measure its progress. Since Value America wasn't built for those metrics, the Wall Street community wasn't very interested in Value America. The bankers at Goldman, Morgan, and elsewhere loved the vision. They just didn't think Value America understood it needed to be grabbing Internet land as fast as possible, staking its claim to cyberspace and becoming the leading brand in the electronic retail space. To grow like they needed to, the bankers informed Winn, Value America would need hundreds of millions of dollars, not the ten million Value America was purportedly looking for.

Instead of valuing his company based on actual or next-year revenues as Winn had been planning, the Internet experts demanded the company be valued based on revenues *two* years out, assuming the appropriate funding had already been secured. In other words, if Value America got $50 million of funding in 1997 and believed it could use that money to get $100 million in revenues in 1998, which would in turn allow it to raise another $50 million and therefore generate $200 million in sales in 1999, the company would be valued at at least two times those 1999 forecasts — or, according to this scenario, at $400 million. With the new Internet math, companies were valued at a *multiple* of *forward* revenue. To Wall Street's thinking, this was the only way to value unprofitable but potentially revolutionary companies.

The single goal was to build scale, build the brand, and become the Internet behemoth . . . overnight. Winn had more competitors than he had imagined. In Silicon Valleys, alleys, and corridors, retailers, technologists, and bankers were creating dot.com companies that would sell pet food, lingerie, books, electronics, discount items, luxury items, home-improvement items, furniture, and everything else imaginable. All *those* companies were already operating on new Internet math. Winn had to catch up.

Shaken and stirred, Winn went back to Charlottesville, looked at numbers that called for profits at the end of 1998, and scrapped them. Instead of relying on direct marketing to attract customers, Winn decided to refocus his firepower on both online advertising and offline print and broadcast advertising. He increased his marketing and ad budget 200 percent, projected greater quarterly revenue, and decided for the first time in his business career to not even think about achieving profitability. He had to get Value America to more than a billion dollars in revenue as quickly as possible, damn the losses. Value America couldn't be an attic operation anymore. It had to be huge *immediately*.

Winn gathered the team of fifteen or so employees around him and told them what he'd discovered. "The New York banks," he relayed to an increasingly wide-eyed team, "want to take us public . . . soon. They think we'll be huge — that Value America will be worth hundreds of millions of dollars very, very soon. Everyone here . . . everyone here . . . will be a millionaire!" Everyone was well pleased with the news.

As Winn assimilated these new realities, Value America opened anonymously in early October 1997. As Winn had been forced to accept, the site wasn't the store of his dreams. It didn't have all the bells and whistles — definitely no animated personal shopper, no ability to have consumers talk to each other or even write reviews, and no voice-recognition software. Customers entering www.valueamerica.com into their Web browsers were greeted by a clean, crisp storefront with a column of little square buttons, each representing one of the approximately six product categories Value America offered. Customers who clicked on the desired button would be taken to another screen, featuring the products. As Winn had always envisioned, users could rearrange the store according to their tastes. If they wanted to shop by brand, they clicked on a SHOP BY BRANDS button on the left side of the screen, and the list of a hundred or so brands popped up. Likewise, if customers wanted to shop by best buys, they could click on a BEST BUYS button, and the greatest deals popped up.

Now all Winn needed were customers and investors, and not in that order. And as if in answer to his prayers, almost out of the blue came the union boys.

ULLICO, the Union Labor Life Insurance Company, was a $4.5 billion financial-services powerhouse owned by the AFL-CIO. Originally created by the American Federation of Labor to provide death benefits to the families of union members, ULLICO had gradually grown to become a holding company for a panoply of financial services ranging from life insurance to medical insurance to financial planning. Mike Steed, brilliant, shrewd, and quietly known inside ULLICO as "the screamer," was a redheaded financier brought onto ULLICO's team with a mandate to go where the unions had never gone before — into aggressive capital investing. Steed understood the world was sprinting toward the Internet and believed ULLICO needed to get running. On November 13, 1997, he met with Winn. To Steed, who had heard hundreds of pitches in his life, this one seemed perfect. He couldn't find any apparent flaws.

Right there, Steed offered Winn a deal. ULLICO would invest $10 million for 10 percent of the company. Never mind that Value America had a grand total of about $10,000 in revenue at that point. Winn's perfect company was suddenly valued at $100,000,000 — ULLICO was doing Winn's Wall Street math for him. By new math standards it made a hell of a lot of sense. In the preceding eight months, Amazon's stock had increased in value nearly five times. Yahoo!'s ten times. Value America's story beat Amazon's and Yahoo!'s with a stick. Why *wouldn't* it be worth that much money?

Craig thought it was stunning. A company with no revenue was now worth more than Dynasty Lighting Classics ever had been.

For Winn, however, the $10 million investment wasn't the best part.

Steed also wanted a sixty-day option to purchase an additional 75 percent of Value America for $250,000,000. Considering Winn and Rex still owned about 85 percent of the company, it would be a hell of a payday (especially for Winn — Rex owned only about 19 percent).

At virtually the same time ULLICO became a player, another financial institution stepped up and wanted to become an important part of the Value America world — Union Bank of Switzerland. UBS wanted to take Value America public in early 1998. At the end of one of their meetings, one of the bankers looked Winn in the eye and said, "I will crawl on my hands and knees over shards of broken glass to get this deal." Everyone at Value America took that to be a very positive sign.

Going public was a fairly cut-and-dried process. Assuming Value America's S-1 registration statement with the Securities and Exchange Commission went through in late December, they'd have their road show for investors in early February 1998. They would go public in March.

Realistic valuation expectations were between $160 and $190 million, with an anticipated increase of 20 percent within three months — conservatively. That would mean a trading valuation of $225,000,000. So, whether it was the union boys from ULLICO or the Union Bank of Switzerland, Value America was going to be a quarter-of-a-billion-dollar company before the crocuses broke the spring ground in Charlottesville.

Craig Winn was getting very comfortable with the dot.com world.

CHAPTER TWO

Bowling for Dollars

On December 16, 1997, almost two years to the day after he finished writing his business plan, Craig Winn took the stage in Washington, D.C.'s National Press Club. To a medium-size crowd of interested parties — ULLICO union boys, assorted brands, and a few reporters — Winn described his company. Face beaming, hands waving about, decked out in a custom-fit suit and rich blue shirt, Winn proclaimed, "This is the first completely automated paperless commerce application. It costs the manufacturer less to ship orders to customers than to ship to a store." Value America was, he told those arrayed before him, "the next revolution in retailing." It was, he continued, going to change Web-based retailing by spending more than $150 million in advertising from January 1998 through the middle of 1999. By that time, Winn said, it would have millions of loyal members drawn by top-quality products and incomparable prices.

When his presentation finished, Winn bounced among his guests like a puppy, clicking them through the store at computers arrayed across the ballroom, helping them spend the $250 in credit he'd arranged for each to buy products for their favorite charities.

Winn did everything with vigor — shake hands, nod his head, talk, smile, breathe. Inside, however, he wasn't happy. Yes, there were some reporters here. But there was no CNN, no *New York Times,* no *Wall Street Journal.* His research showed Amazon.com was getting mentioned in more articles than this guy Bill Clinton. To Winn, neither Bill Clinton nor Amazon deserved that much attention — both were remarkably ordinary at best. Value America, however, was going to be the most spectacular, most powerful, best-funded e-commerce store in the world!

Winn's frustration increased in late December, a few weeks after the ULLICO meeting and shortly after the official launch, when UBS changed its mind about taking Value America public. Their excuse was that the IPO market was getting too backed up with new offerings, so they weren't sure investors would accept such an early-phase company. Privately, however, they got cold feet. Company insiders viewed Winn as too volatile and thought he still didn't *really* buy into Internet metrics. Besides, there were too many other good opportunities out there for UBS to take a risk on Craig Winn and Value America.

Winn's optimism, as well as that of eager employees, was promptly redirected toward ULLICO's potential purchase of Value America. Even though Winn and Scatena obviously had the most to gain in a potential sale, they made sure every one of Value America's thirty employees had some stock. Stock was the currency of record in the Internet age, and Craig deftly used it to create extreme loyalty, hard work, and dedication. Even the lowliest Value America plebe stood to make good money if ULLICO exercised its quarter-billion-dollar option.

As ULLICO sent a due-diligence team to kick the Value America tires and determine whether or not the company would meet the targets Winn set, Value America was busy buying ads to push revenue. December's *USA Today* jewelry ads were quickly followed by a spot pushing HP Pavillion PCs and monitors. Unlike the jewelry ads, which had produced a tepid response, the HP ad was a smash. Value America's HP distributor quickly sold everything it had, while Value America recorded its largest single day of sales ever — nearly $100,000. Hewlett-Packard was ecstatic.

Also in January, Value America got a break when IBM authorized Value America to sell some of its computers online. In early February, Value America ran a full-page color ad for IBM business PCs in the *Wall Street Journal*. Under the banner "It is cool to be Blue: No one ever got fired for choosing IBM," Value America made its first splash into the business big leagues. Not too long after the ad ran, one of Winn's business contacts told him Andy Grove of Intel had called IBM chief Lou Gerstner to find out who Value America was and what they were doing running an IBM ad. Gerstner had not seen the ad, nor did he know the store's name. But he promptly tasked his lieutenants to find out. The story became an anecdotal highlight of Winn's Value America presentation.

As ULLICO's sixty-day option neared a close, Winn and everyone else inside Value America were frantic, wondering whether they would be purchased or left dangling on the edge of an unfunded Internet abyss. The company was hitting its targets. Consumers were visiting the store and buying, new products were briskly being added, the company was taking shape. But as the option period expired in February 1998, ULLICO elected not to buy. ULLICO still backed Value America; they said they would invest more cash and even help bring other investors to the table. They just didn't want to own the thing.

Suddenly, those at Value America who had been banking on either an imminent purchase or an imminent IPO had neither. Even worse, Winn was left with the dilemma of how to generate tens of millions in revenue without the necessary tens of millions to spend on ads.

Tim Driscoll didn't worry too much about the lost option. A threatening precancerous throat condition had given him valuable perspective on life, even Internet life. When ULLICO didn't work out, it was simply time to resort to Plan B — or C or D or whatever the case might be. He honestly couldn't remember which alternate plan he was up to.

Driscoll was Value America's money-raising agent. He scoured rich neighborhoods and cornered potential investors. He had brought ULLICO to the table the previous fall and set up dozens of meetings with other possible investors. Driscoll was unique in the money-raising world. He was, arguably, the only union longshoreman ever to turn venture capitalist. He wasn't really a longshoreman. He went to high school in Wausau, Wisconsin, and was educated at Georgetown University. His dad had been a union guy. When his dad died, the union took care of young Driscoll — put him through college, actually. Now, though he didn't work for ULLICO, he helped look out for the union's money. That meant if he screwed up, he'd have the International Brotherhood of Barroom Brawlers and the International Association of Wrench Manufacturing Dwarves on his ass. That was motivation. Perhaps it also explained the relentless nervous energy and expletive-laced gusto. Regardless, Value America was his ticket to stardom — or at least to early retirement. As a forty-year-old single father with serious health concerns, he thought retirement — even if it was temporary — would be nice.

On a conference call with Winn, Dean Johnson, and Rex Scatena, Driscoll calmly — or at least calmly for Driscoll — said he understood ULLICO's decision even if he didn't agree with it. It's not a big f——ing deal, he scolded the trio. Value America needs to get in with some other, bigger fish who understand technology and the Internet better than a bunch of union guys do. Then it hit him. Driscoll knew *exactly* whom he was going to get. Paul F——ing Allen, the co-founder of Microsoft. He knew people who knew people who knew Allen. He'd attended a couple of Allen's high-tech conferences. This was a no-brainer. Winn looked at Johnson, who looked at Scatena, who shrugged his shoulders. No one in Charlottesville knew whether Driscoll was just trying to make them feel better or whether he could deliver this miracle.

Winn had been working hard to find a lead banker after UBS's desertion. In March 1998, Winn anointed BancBoston Robertson Stephens to lead Value America into the promised land of the public markets. Robbie Stephens, as the company was known, fancied itself the epicenter of the Internet gold rush. Though technically part of the "Four Horsemen" of U.S. high-tech investment banking — along with Hambrecht & Quist, Montgomery Securities, and Alex Brown and Sons of Baltimore — Robbie Stephens was intent on becoming head horseman. By 1998, it had participated in taking public such companies as E*Trade, Excite, and a host of others. The previous year, it had raised north of $20 billion for the 120 companies it took public and the 50 for which it helped raise private funds. Winn wanted to go public by summer. Robbie's job was to make it happen.

Winn's other concern was a call he'd received from IBM. His presence was requested immediately in Raleigh-Durham at IBM's PC headquarters. Worried that perhaps something had upset IBM, Winn sheepishly headed south for the meeting. He was escorted into one of the many identical conference rooms at IBM headquarters. Big Blue was no longer the wholesale manufacturer of the famed corporate automaton known as the IBM man, but there remained a certain sameness to the place, its people, even its conference rooms. IBM executives gathered around Winn, shaking his hand, pleasantly greeting him in an official IBM way — something like Jehovah's Witness evangelists knocking on doors on a Saturday morning . . . smiling, dressed nicely, and somehow not quite *there*.

Just as the meeting was about to begin, a short woman of indeterminable middle age with cropped blond hair parted on the side scurried into the room, picked up a copy of a newspaper lying on the table, and started scolding someone Craig Winn feared was him. "You didn't have permission to use the IBM logo. You didn't have permission to use the IBM logo."

Winn glanced up with a measure of alarm at the pixie-ish woman. He hadn't met her during his earlier IBM visits and wondered if she was a powerful executive or a worker bee.

Eventually the woman marched straight into his face, waved the

"It's cool to be Blue" ad at him, and said, familiarly now, "You didn't have permission to use the IBM logo."

The other men and women in the conference room didn't utter a word — they didn't actually move. That was a bad sign, Winn figured. This woman couldn't be good news for him or for Value America.

After a few insecure seconds, Winn decided he didn't give a shit. As much as he wanted to kiss IBM's corporate ass, he wasn't going to snivel and beg and plead — at least not unless Lou Gerstner himself wanted him to. He was smarter and stronger and richer than these IBM lackeys.

"It is *my* ad, *I* paid for it, it sold IBM products," he fired back. "Sorry if I didn't fill out the proper forms."

The woman looked stunned. She tried to smile, awkwardly glancing around the room at her colleagues. When she did finally eke out a smile, Winn was surprised to find it a very pleasant smile — though it revealed very English-looking teeth, a bit darker than white and a bit more crooked than perfect. Suddenly, she stuck out her hand — rather like someone drawing a gun — and said, "Hi, my name is Glenda Dorchak. I'm sorry for any inconvenience. I just thought you should know we are very sensitive about IBM's logo — we care about our brand."

Winn squinted back at her, shook her hand heartily, and made a mental note to find out more about this woman. He liked her. She was clearly tenacious. He liked tenacious. She had iron balls. He liked women with iron balls, and they were hard to find.

As Dorchak walked away, Winn flopped back in his seat, and the meeting began. IBM was *excited* about the response to the ad Value America had run. They had also heard HP was doing a lot of business with Value America. IBM wanted to know just how intimate Value America was with HP and whether IBM could forge a similar relationship.

Winn bit the insides of his cheeks and tried to control his smile. He liked the idea of threesomes — all the more so since the other two partners were *Fortune* 100 corporations. His eyes brightened as he leaned back in his chair and assured the IBM team that such a relationship was very, very possible.

Craig Winn left North Carolina with a thrilling task: to develop a strategy IBM and Value America could pursue together that would be beneficial to both companies but would also achieve something "important." Winn lived for these moments. By the time he touched down in Charlottesville, the full, detailed plan was developed in his head.

Value America would create a business approach designed to increase IBM's market share with consumers, small and medium-size businesses, governments, and alliances by properly presenting the merits and value of IBM's products and by bringing IBM and its customers closer together. It would, in short, position IBM to directly compete with Dell's customized-computer-building niche. It would be called the 8th Channel because IBM had traditionally believed there were seven primary channels it needed to cover in sales. It would include everything from a dedicated IBM e-commerce site powered by Value America to actual bricks-and-mortar stores that Winn referred to as the "unstores." There, businesses and consumers could get IBM service as well as access all of Value America's brands under one roof.

No sooner had Winn sent the strategic plan to IBM than Tim Driscoll called to announce he'd done exactly what he promised — set up a meeting in Seattle for Winn to pitch Paul Allen on the virtues of Value America. The first week in April, Craig and Dean were bustling to the airport, headed for the Internet mecca of Seattle. The problem on that particular day, however, was getting to the plane on time. They were very, very late for their plane out of D.C. That was a big problem, because unlike the man they were supposed to meet in Seattle, they didn't yet have a customized Boeing 757.

Pacing around the gate area, Driscoll steamed. Where the f—— are they? he wondered. I've put my ass on the f——ing line for these f——s and they aren't f——ing here. . . . F——! He was working himself into a lather. How could anyone be late to meet Paul F——ing Allen? If this were his company's meeting, he would have camped in front of the door an hour ago, not eaten anything for two days to reduce the risk of food poisoning, and been the first person on the plane. Driscoll would have had four backup flights and six excuses ready if anything went wrong. Damn, this f——ing money-raising business was going to kill him.

"Where the hell have you been?" he shouted at the dynamic duo as they raced in ten minutes after the flight's scheduled departure time. "I've had my ass wedged in the airplane door to keep them from shutting it."

Dean glared at Tim, rolled his eyes, smirked, and headed for the plane. Winn just smiled and blamed traffic. Driscoll dismissed them both with a shake of his head and shoved them onto the waiting plane. The trip's goal was simple. Paul Allen was investing hundreds of millions in dot.com companies in hopes of creating a broadband web of virtual businesses that would make the Internet the most ubiquitous medium in the world. Allen's vision was to make global information-, commerce-, and data-exchange effortless. Allen liked big ideas like Value America. It was a love fest waiting to happen.

Put more crassly, Paul Allen was a kingmaker. An Allen investment gave a company instant legitimacy. Because Allen was with Microsoft before it was Microsoft, the business world recognized him as a real seer, not just a wannabe. There were few accredited visionaries, and Allen was one of them. If he blessed your company, you were anointed indeed.

The trio arrived at Allen's expansive Seattle offices and was escorted into Allen's conference room, where they were told to plug in their laptops and wait for Allen to arrive. Suddenly the door burst open, and Allen and his boy genius, Bill Savoy, burst in. "Hey, so what do you boys got for us?" Allen asked as he plopped into his chair, looking and sounding much like Jabba the Hutt. Allen had been called the "luckiest fat man alive" for years by friends and foes alike. The reasoning was that he was lucky to be alive after his bout with cancer. He was lucky to be rich because he had the good sense to become best buddies with one of the biggest nerds Harvard ever produced — a weasly little guy the world would come to know as billionaire Bill Gates.

Winn assumed Allen didn't believe in funding foreplay. He was right. Allen wanted to get the thrust of a deal right away and figure out whether the thing had any "ups." He also sighed a lot. It was part of the performance, to show all potential suitors he was bored. He was busy and he was bored. So he sighed. Big, long, heavy sighs.

Clicking along with his laptop, Craig described the grand concept of the ultimate online superstore, expounding on how Value America was the solution to the intractable, bitter problems with which manufacturers had struggled for years. He told Allen and Savoy that Value America was the answer to everything consumers wanted most. Allen didn't sigh. In fact, the more Winn talked, the less Allen resembled Jabba the Hutt and the more he was transformed into an excited kid with bulging eyes who believed he could wire the world and change it forever. Winn dissected the problems manufacturers faced and then described *his* vision for a high-speed wired world that would break down borders and bring access to all, changing the world forever! Allen sat forward on his chair and bounced a bit, saying, "Yeah, yeah!" like a congregation member in an old-time gospel church. This, Winn thought, was the Allen who convinced Bill Gates that Microsoft's future lay in something called an operating system instead of just software applications. This guy got it. He saw what Value America could be — how its inventoryless model allowed it to make money on smaller margins; how the multimedia product demonstrations required better and faster Internet access to level the consumer playing field; how a one-stop superstore was the answer to shopping on the Web. Winn knew he held Allen in the palm of his pudgy little hand. The big fish was on the hook. And if Paul Allen was *really* impressed by Value America, what actual limits existed for his company? Value America, Winn increasingly realized, wasn't just going to become the Wal-Mart of the Internet, it was going to be the *Microsoft* of e-commerce.

Winn closed his presentation, dramatically slammed shut the lid on his laptop, smiled, and looked confidently at his hosts. There was silence for a few nervous moments. Then there was a huge sigh. With that, Paul Allen stood up, grinned awkwardly, rubbed some imagined stain off his belly, and said, "Boys, good job. You know your stuff. My seven-fifty-seven is waiting. Got to go see my Blazers [Portland Trailblazers, his NBA franchise]. See ya." That was that.

"We'll be in touch," said Bill Savoy, as he scurried after his Boeing jet–owning, NBA team–owning, rock-and-roll-museum–building, Microsoft-founding boss. Driscoll, Winn, and Johnson looked at each other befuddled, shrugged their shoulders, and figured they'd take the next plane back east.

A few days later, Savoy called Craig. Allen *really* liked the company and *really* liked the vision. In fact, he wanted to pick up ULLICO's lapsed option to buy the company immediately for $250,000,000. Cash. He liked Winn and loved the model. It was the best Internet shopping solution he'd ever seen. He wanted it.

There was only one problem. Craig Winn told Savoy he couldn't rationalize selling Value America. What Value America *needed* was to go public. The Internet world was *complicated,* he told Savoy. Only he, Craig Winn, *truly* understood how to guide Value America through Wall Street's new Internet maze. He wanted Allen's involvement, wanted Allen's money. But he no longer wanted to sell the company. Savoy told Winn to send him a memo.

Winn fired off a handwritten memo but didn't hear back from Allen or Savoy for weeks. That was bothersome, because Value America needed cash to buy more ads. Then, in early May, Savoy called back. Allen had lost interest in Value America. Winn was disappointed in the pair. They should know better. They were too smart to make such stupid decisions, he thought.

What was left unsaid to Winn but made very clear in a separate call from Savoy to Tim Driscoll was that Winn's handling of Allen's investment offer had given Allen and Savoy serious qualms about future involvement. "We have questions about your entrepreneur," they stated delicately. To them, Winn seemed a bit unstable, certainly arrogant, and alarmingly unpredictable. Value America wasn't Microsoft and would never be Microsoft. It may succeed, but Winn needed to understand it was just a store.

With a huge commission in severe danger, Tim Driscoll hopped the first plane to Seattle. He called Allen from a Seattle hotel the next morning and requested a meeting. Allen told him he wasn't planning on being out east anytime soon. Driscoll said that didn't matter. He was in Seattle. Allen blurted, "What are you doing *here*?"

"Trying to save a f——ing deal," Driscoll said, smiling back at the Portland Trailblazers' owner through the phone.

Winn, Driscoll explained to Allen and Savoy later that day, was just a high-intensity salesman. Everyone inside the company and an increasing number of people outside were coming to the conclusion he probably wasn't the best person to run the company day to day. Hell, Winn himself had admitted that to Driscoll days earlier. But that would be taken care of in time. Driscoll tried to focus Allen and Savoy on the beauty of the model. That, he reminded them, was the reason everyone would want this thing. The business model was just about perfect. Besides, Driscoll reminded them, he wasn't in this for a commission. He was in this as a believer; he'd be investing more than $1 million of his own money in the company. Plus, ULLICO was investing more and brought more investors to the table. Value America's success wasn't really in doubt, he told them. It was now just a matter of execution. Allen agreed to send someone to Charlottesville to do due diligence on the company — dig through the numbers, meet the management, check the systems. If the reality matched up with the story, then maybe he'd invest.

The man tasked with this due diligence had been part of the Allen team for about a year. Jerry Goode was a most unlikely technology consultant. He'd grown up in a small coal-mining town in Kentucky. He attended Southern Methodist University only because a family friend mentioned it was a good school and he could find work there to pay the bills. Computers were his first love, and a college — any college that got him out of coal-mining hell — was good enough for him. From there he traveled heady roads, working as part of the Apple team and then as part of Steve Jobs's subsequent adventure, NeXT Computers. The latter had assembled the brightest group of people he'd ever known. They were so far ahead of their time that their only lasting contribution was the NeXT Computer on display in the Smithsonian. Examining Value America's infrastructure was going to be the easiest job Jerry ever had. He was already in Charlottesville, having moved there for a quiet pace of life and a safe place to raise his new family.

Technologically, what he discovered at Value America impressed him. The company had created a software system that was tailored to its inventoryless needs. Folded into that software were options for users to organize the store according to their liking. Furthermore, the Electronic Data Interchange capabilities enabling Value America to place electronic orders with distributors and manufacturers were in place and functioned — not perfectly, but well enough to be hopeful. The hardware system was functioning, too, if not totally secure. Value America's tech team had cobbled together a system by expanding one server at a time. For a variety of reasons such a hardware system was more prone to crashing and less likely to operate at peak efficiency. But all in all, Jerry liked what he saw and was overwhelmingly impressed by the vision. Maybe, if Allen invested, he might even join this merry crew.

Winn had the exact same idea. He loved Joe Page and all Joe had done for the company. But there were limits to what Joe could do with the store. Perhaps Goode might complement Joe and create exactly the store Winn envisioned. Most important, as the company grew, Winn knew he needed skilled managers and experienced hands running the ship, and Goode fit that bill very nicely. Finally, and not insignificantly, as Value America prepared to go public, Winn needed seasoned executives he could sell. He tried to recruit Goode, and both parties agreed to table the offer pending the outcome of Allen's decision.

As the financing gyrations continued, Value America continued to grow. By mid-May 1998, it was a fledgling Internet retailer with almost

$6 million in total revenue and nearly one hundred employees. The company was now running regular full-page ads in the *Wall Street Journal, USA Today,* and the *New York Times* and also advertising in specialty and trade publications, radio, and even television in most major markets.

Value America stood apart in its emphasis on offline advertising. Every other Internet retailer advertised online using banner ads on Web sites, often pouring millions into those ads, despite the fact the results were completely unproven. These ads were touted as advertising's cutting edge, but to Winn they were a sham. The sites with the most traffic — Yahoo! and AOL — were charging obscene rates, and there was scarce proof the ads even worked. Winn believed they would never pay off. Whenever *he* looked at a Web page, he focused on the content and tuned everything else out.

Regular people were still deciding whether they trusted online stores at all. So, Winn figured, real live print ads in real live newspapers added an air of legitimacy. Appearing alongside GM, Ford, and GE let Value America bask in the reflection of their legitimacy. Plus, Value America wasn't just a Web catalog; customers could also order over the telephone. Online ads wouldn't reach that crowd.

The advertising was also a potential source of revenue. Scores of Internet retailers were spending their money online with no assistance from the brands, but Winn intended his ads to be paid, in part, by the brands. Just as traditional bricks-and-mortar stores often charged fees to stock particular products, so, too, did they make money from advertising. In an arrangement called co-op advertising, companies often paid key retail stores to appear in their advertising campaigns. For example, IBM would pay CompUSA to be included in one of CompUSA's ads — be it a Sunday newspaper filler, a magazine, or even a television ad. For major retailers, co-op advertising was a huge revenue source.

Meanwhile, Value America was working to close its B round of funding. Funding rounds are like bowling. There are a series of rounds, in which a company aims for a strike — an amount of money large enough to carry it to the next round. Value America's first round — or A round — had been ULLICO's $10 million investment. That cash would last until July if ad spending slowed and until June if things kept on pace. Either way, Value America was aiming for a meaningful B-round strike that would enable continued ad spending — $20 million in the bank by the end of May.

Jerry Goode's glowing report found its way back to Seattle, reminding Savoy and Allen why they had liked Value America so much in the first place. Now Allen sent word back through Tim Driscoll that he was officially in for $15 million in the next round of funding. Joining Allen, ULLICO signed on for another $1 million. Their brethren, the United Association of Journeymen and Apprentices of the Plumbing and Pipe-fitting Industry of the United States and Canada, did as well — also for $1 million. Even Allen's wunderkind, Bill Savoy, invested $500,000 personally. By the time the B round closed on June 26, 1998, Value America had netted more than $19 million, and every share of the company's still privately held stock was valued at $10.16. That meant Value America, now boasting about $6 million in total revenue, was worth more than $320 million — with about 75 percent of the company still owned by Winn and Scatena.

As part of the funding round, Winn managed to unload about $6 million of his stock on ULLICO and other investors. Though it was never discussed, ULLICO and others assumed all of the stock available in the round was newly issued stock, which directly benefited the company, even if it diluted Winn's and Scatena's shares. On the Friday afternoon the B round was to close, ULLICO discovered some of the "new" stock was actually Winn's stock. Winn was liquidating a few hundred thousand shares via the new investors. These investors were apoplectic, but the deal was done, and it was too late to scuttle.

Winn's move was, to the outsiders, supremely odd — and supremely troublesome. Typically, entrepreneurs don't touch their equity positions until much later. They usually give some equity to venture capitalists and other investors, but the money earned is reinvested in the company to help it grow. The entrepreneur's goal is usually a massive payday later, not small paydays along the way. But Winn felt he deserved a little financial boost. Plus, he needed the cash to build his dream estate, the lavish Winndom. Winndom itself was something of a mystery around Charlottesville. There were lots of rumors about what, exactly, Winn was building east of town on his 150-acre lot. Small-town rumors are never terribly reliable, but Winn didn't seem to care what people said. Revolutionaries didn't have time for that sort of thing.

CHAPTER THREE

Peddling Sand

With $19 million in cash in its bank account, Winn's Value America set about dramatically expanding its advertising, shifting from periodic appearances in major newspapers to a daily presence. From January through June 1998, Value America spent nearly $7 million on advertising, but from July through September, it budgeted more than $11 million in hopes of generating $15 million in revenue. Rather than budgeting $19 million to last the company through the end of 1998, Winn and his team budgeted the money for only three months — until the end of September. By that time, they figured, they would have an additional $80 million or so from a public offering.

The ads were strictly trial and error. Because Value America was the first and only Internet retailer to engage in substantial offline advertising, there were no rules for what was — or wasn't — going to work. The best responses came from Value America's computer offerings. Since that worked, Value America added more and more of them and focused less and less on consumer items like electronics or housewares.

To attract more customers, Value America also lowered its prices. In late 1997, the company had robust gross margins — the difference between how much it cost to buy a product and how much the company sold the product for — of about 40 percent, though on paltry revenue. But by the middle of 1998, Value America's gross margins slipped into the low single digits. It was, objectively, no way to run a retail business under normal circumstances, but Robbie Stephens, still managing Value America's spastic go-public plan, assured Winn the trade-off was acceptable. Profits weren't important. The *only* thing that mattered was driving substantial revenue quickly.

In late June, just as the B round was closing, Winn hit upon a potentially radical new way for Value America to generate revenue. From the beginning of the company, Winn believed Value America's virtual nature was its greatest strength. It gradually dawned on him that he could take Value America's back-end technology and brand relationships and offer them as an e-commerce infrastructure for others. The others he had in mind in June 1998 were charities, religious groups, and nonprofit organizations. Winn called this approach — which he quickly concluded would be Value America's secret weapon — the Value America custom store program. The charities would advertise the store and get their supporters to shop there. In turn, the charities would get a portion of all sales — 5 percent as originally conceived. For charities it was a way to use the e-commerce frenzy to increase their income. For consumers it was a way to support their favorite charities while shopping at a store where they could get high-quality merchandise at lower-than-expected costs. For Value America — which would get a cut from each sale — it was an easy and benevolent way to drive e-commerce revenue quickly and cheaply. The American Cancer Society, the American Heart Association, Habitat for Humanity, the United Way ... Winn could open custom stores for all of them. It would mean huge money for Value America.

Winn knew his idea was genius not only because it would increase revenue, but also because it would help Value America with the so-called customer-acquisition metric. One of the new metrics Wall Street had developed for Internet retailing, in addition to page views and stickiness (how long someone spent on a site), was customer-acquisition costs — the amount of money it cost a company to get a customer to actually purchase something. For early e-tailers like Amazon, customer-acquisition costs were relatively low. Imagine the Joe Blow Deli. JBD invents a terrific new sandwich: the roast beef sandwich. They begin with a bit of advertising to let people know the company exists. Slowly, the sandwich catches on because it is tasty, but also because it is novel. Word spreads. The lines get longer. JBD starts ringing up the cash. Their cost to acquire customers now is relatively low, because they are the only peddlers of roast beef sandwiches. That was Amazon in the early days. While they were losing money hand over fist on technology and shipping and product fulfillment, Amazon was a novelty. Shopping through an infinite selection of books without ever leaving your home, clicking on a few colorful icons, and finding your loot appear in your mailbox was original indeed.

But just like anything novel, Amazon soon faced competition. If Amazon could earn millions in seed capital just from selling books, the thinking went, I'll bet a bunch of people would invest in us if we just sold _____ [fill in the blank]. So shops like eToys, garden.com, Pets.com, furniture.com, and CDNOW were born. There was instantly Internet pet food, golf equipment, travel tickets, clothes, even used underwear. If you could sell it, someone would put a dot.com after it and hope to make a Bezos-zillion dollars. And as soon as there was one Internet pet-food company, there was another and another and . . .

So whereas Joe Blow Deli had charged $2.50 for its novel roast beef sandwich, once the competition started, it lowered that price to $2.40, and then $2.20, and then $2. And the fiercer the competition, the more these too-low prices would be augmented by increased advertising and marketing expenditures. If Joe Blow wasn't careful, the deli might soon find itself losing money on every sandwich sold.

That, in short, is what e-tailers faced in 1998.

The more Value America advertised, added brands, and pursued new projects, the more Value America's staff and budget grew. In addition to launching custom stores and bringing Jerry Goode on board to keep technology humming, Winn was determined to keep the advertising and product-presentation departments in-house. But as it added the necessary people to support those blossoming efforts, Value America was outgrowing its facilities. By July 1998, there were more than 135 employees. By far the largest department was product presentations. Winn often joked that Value America had more top-notch journalists on its staff than the *Washington Post*. He was almost right. There were more than fifty people researching the products and writing descriptions for inclusion in Value America's virtual store.

CFO Dean Johnson, meanwhile, was heading up the urgent task of getting Value America ready for the public offering. The cornerstone of the go-public effort was writing and filing the S-1 registration statement with the SEC, a document that basically requires a company to disclose everything it has ever done, ever hopes to do, and every remote reason the company might stumble. (A good idea in theory, but in practice, registration statements tend to be so mind-numbingly generic as to be practically devoid of meaning.) To Dean Johnson fell the challenge of satisfying the SEC's every convoluted requirement. This was a big job, since Value America had been run as a checkbook operation from its inception in early 1996 through the end of 1997. Not that there was anything illegal or improper about that. Anyhow, if anything not quite on the up and up had ever occurred, Dean figured there probably wasn't any record of it.

The first S-1 red flag went up when Value America's independent auditor, PricewaterhouseCoopers, noted that Value America proved unable to consistently determine product shipment dates and order statuses on a timely basis. This meant orders got misplaced, shipment dates slipped, and Value America wasn't always 100 percent on top of its accounting data. Actually, sometimes it wasn't 50 percent on top of its accounting and financial data, and PwC didn't think this was a good thing for an aspiring public company.

PwC determined these imperfections were a reportable condition, meaning that prospective investors would be warned about the problem. Winn, not surprisingly, disagreed. It was absurd, he decried, that such a small, trivial matter should amount to anything. Sure there were glitches, but PwC made it sound like there were systemic problems. This was retail, not microbiology. Things got lost and misplaced. So what?

But Dean Johnson knew Value America was lucky PwC wasn't making the reportable condition even more sweeping. PwC was right, and it was up to Value America to fix the problems before their fall IPO.

That IPO became paramount when Winn and team decided no more private money–raising would take place. Ever since Winn had become convinced of the all-encompassing need to drive revenue, his fixation was on the bounty of the public markets. But going public would certainly not solve all of Value America's problems. In fact, Paul Allen was generally against the IPO plan. Allen argued to Driscoll and to Winn that going public would cause more headaches for Value America than Winn could possibly imagine. In Allen's mind, Value America didn't have enough history to go public in 1998. It took at least a couple years of revenues to safely predict growth trends and to stabilize the business. So serious was Allen about delaying an IPO that he offered to buy more of the company to keep Value America off the public markets.

Having taken one company public, Winn was familiar with the pressure — and the rush. But, Winn was convinced, going public was required for media coverage and general buzz. With buzz, Value America wouldn't have to spend so much on advertising, which meant actually saving money in the long term. In addition, because the public markets were so hot for dot.com companies, raising *more* money after the initial offering would be easier. Winn's view was eagerly supported by the gatekeepers to the public markets — top-tier investment banks like Robbie Stephens. From their perspective, Value America was hot. If Paul Allen liked the company and invested in the company, the bankers supposed, then the rest of the world would want a piece of it, too.

The SEC, if it chooses, can make life very hard for a public company. If the regulators decide a company is not being up-front enough — is, for example, withholding important information or spinning its disclosures in a misleading way — they can withhold approvals, investigate, or sue, leading to plummeting investor confidence. As Value America awaited word on the SEC's rulings and a specified go-public date, Winn prepared for the road show, and the company worked on remedying the reportable condition.

A going-public road show is one part traveling circus, one part brothel. Seven or eight times a day, the executive team of the would-be public company visits high-powered bankers and investors to perform a highly choreographed routine. The preparatory work is enormous — SEC filings, multimedia presentations, logistics — but in the end it's all about the meetings. A road-show team wants every target investor to feel they are the single most important potential investor the team has ever met. And they want to be able to get through the pleasuring and the pillow talk in less than an hour so they can get up to do it all over again with the *next* "most important" investor.

The road show occurs in the weeks leading up to the prospective offering. After the executives have presented and left, the investors sit back, smoke a postpresentation cigarette, and huddle to decide how much, if any, stock they want to buy. They then contact the lead banker taking the company public to place their order. The lead banker keeps a running total of exactly how many shares are in demand, what people are willing to pay, and how the price of the shares needs to be adjusted to balance supply and demand.

There would be more than seventy potential investors across the country whom Winn had to persuade to desire VA stock. Robbie Stephens was calculating Value America should get $14 to $15 per share based on the state of the market in mid-August. Winn figured if he did his job, he could reach $17 a share. That didn't mean more money just for ads; that meant more money for Craig Winn.

One thing that would help, Winn thought, would be to have someone from a prestigious company on the management team. That sort of credibility Winn could sell with gusto. IBM had not yet embraced Winn's aggressive 8th Channel strategy, but it was becoming a bigger and bigger part of Value America's business. Winn and Glenda Dorchak had been in several meetings since their initial confrontation, and Winn rather enjoyed his dealings with the woman. She wasn't a Harvard Business School clone; she had the feel of someone who had learned business the hard way, from the bottom up. He'd learned from his dealings with her and a few questions to her colleagues that she was someone who knew both direct marketing and sales, two things that Winn knew Value America needed badly.

Winn picked up the phone. What would it take, Winn asked Dorchak, to get her to leave IBM and become senior vice president of sales and marketing at Value America? Value America, he reminded her, was on the verge of going public, and everyone with a pulse knew dot.com companies going public made a killing.

Dorchak couldn't believe her ears. Senior vice president? Glenda Dorchak had spent twenty-three years at IBM, starting as a secretary. Whereas most of her onetime secretarial peers were still secretaries — or executive assistants at best — Dorchak had risen above her circumstances and made the leap to IBM management. It was middle management, but it was still management.

Dorchak never graduated from high school, didn't go to college. Winn heard that her chosen path early in life was the Ice Capades. But after her skating career ended, she found herself working at IBM in Vancouver, B.C., as a secretary. IBM in the 1970s was famous for its assembly line of blue-suited, white-shirted, rep-tied middle managers. If you were a WASPy, Ivy League–educated, business-school graduate with iron balls, you had a bright future. If you were a high-school dropout from Canada, you were more or less around to fill a quota.

Glenda didn't want to be a quota. She chopped her platinum blonde hair, combed it flat against her head, and started parting it on the side. Her restrictive suits were button-up numbers that cloaked any feminine curves beneath with restrictive gray-and-blue flannel. She talked like a guy, laughed like a guy, cursed like a guy. Hell, she even drove like a guy. And she was promoted. She could be counted on to get a job done.

Now Craig Winn was giving her a chance to be part of senior management in a world-class Internet-commerce company on the verge of going public. Her life at IBM was secure; she and her husband, who consulted for IBM, had a nice retirement plan and enough stock to make for a nice life. But Value America gave Dorchak the chance to really run something — to build something new and make it last and get financially rewarded in the process. Like a lot of her colleagues, Dorchak had caught the Internet bug. She knew the story behind Yahoo! and Amazon and AOL. She agreed to meet Winn, tour Value America, and learn more about it.

There were more than 150 people working at Value America when she arrived, and more were being added by the day. It was the perfect opposite of IBM. There were kids in tattered blue jeans and two-day beard stubble drinking Diet Cokes and yabbering about slinging code. There were intellectual types writing pithy paragraphs on the virtues of Knorr's condensed soups. There was something else, though — a huge buzz and excitement. These people looked casual on the outside, but there was real wattage within. The kicker was that IBM had a little office in Charlottesville where her husband could work.

She called Winn back in late July and told him she was in.

That wasn't the only good news. Value America had reassured PricewaterhouseCoopers its systems were in fact up to snuff. Value America would have to report in the S-1 that its order-fulfillment system was not fully integrated with its accounting system, requiring "manual effort to prepare information for financial and accounting reporting," but there would be no reportable condition.

As Winn worked through his presentation during the month of August 1998, the stock market softened, and the Internet stocks that had risen like helium began to fall like lead. Hot technology companies like AOL, Amazon, and Microsoft suddenly lost 30 percent or more of their value. Even more disturbing, news was trickling back to Charlottesville that the IPO market was drying up. Company after company couldn't get the valuations they needed and cancelled their IPOs.

Value America had budgeted $19 million from the B round to last through the end of September. But by late August, because of the company's stratospheric growth and spending, it was clear the money would *barely* carry it through late September — and maybe only until *mid*-September. Value America now had more than 170 employees spread out in two buildings, contracts for new office space, commitments to buy or lease new computer servers, and ads to buy.

Value America *had* to go public — it needed the money. The company couldn't afford a quarter of declining revenues — things had to be moving ever skyward. By all appearances, as September dawned, Value America was going to come close to hitting its $15 million revenue target for the third quarter. That meant it needed to do *at least* $20 million in the fourth quarter of 1998 to show progress and justify higher valuations.

Winn finished honing his presentation during the first week in September and invited a group of forty business leaders and friends to Richmond, Virginia, on Friday, September 11, to hear the pitch and officially kick off the Value America IPO road show. While it was somewhat atypical to have such a big meeting, Winn liked the thought of kicking off the road show with a bang. Besides, it was e-commerce — *typical* hadn't been invented yet.

Winn felt no small measure of surprise when Dorchak told him there were issues they needed to address before Craig left for the road show. She had questions about her role within the company and whether it was the kind of place she could stay indefinitely. Sharing a ride with Dorchak to Richmond for the road-show kickoff, Winn looked at her quizzically. "Excuse me?"

Dorchak was operating without a contract, without any specific assurances, and it was making her nervous. Others in the company told her her concerns were more than valid. Plus, she was only included in the first part of the road show. There was, however, the possibility things could improve if certain items were "resolved."

First, she wanted more stock — a lot more stock, actually. Second, she wanted a significant raise in pay. Third, she wanted to be promoted — perhaps president and COO would be a possibility.

Winn suppressed the urge to throw her out of the car. Instead, he glared at her, got very red in the face, and tried to contain his anger. He wasn't sure exactly what came out of his mouth, but he feared it sounded something like, "Are you shitting me? We are going on a road show, we are low on cash, you just got here, and you are *blackmailing ME?*"

Winn quickly analyzed things. If Dorchak left, it would scuttle the IPO. He could survive a previous reportable condition, but how could he explain a former IBM executive — that's how Winn was selling her — departing two weeks prior to an IPO? He couldn't. Dorchak sat quietly in the passenger seat, waiting for his response. He didn't give one.

The lights fell dramatically in the quiet men's club, and the front wall of the room was filled with the Value America logo, a simple "Value America" in blue script set against a small, spinning blue-and-green globe.

Winn paused. He had put Glenda out of his mind. The IPO was out of his mind. He was totally focused on the crowd before him and the presentation he was going to make. It was important to let his audience grasp the magnitude of what they were about to hear even if they didn't yet know what they were about to hear. It was the art of salesmanship — the honed craft of entertainment as business. That is why the road-show presentation was so vital. A lot of people went out with standard Microsoft PowerPoint presentations. That was nauseatingly conventional. Winn's presentation had video, audio, moving graphics. It was representative of the mind that created this grand and sweeping vision.

"Value America is an online store for business and consumer products. We are a customer-centric and brand-centric solution, serving each better by serving both better. Our e-commerce model is built on five core concepts." Winn began his presentation slowly, almost cautiously. The speed — or lack of it — gave the audience a chance to absorb the pictures behind him, get used to his voice, learn to trust him. "We are comprehensive — selling products from one thousand brands in twenty industries. We demonstrate products so our customers become better buyers. Convergence allows us to integrate the convenience of online shopping with the benefits of real customer service. We use offline advertising to drive online revenues and are establishing our brand as the gateway to quality products. We are a new marketplace designed to bring people and products together. We have built an engaging and informative front end for the consumer and linked it to our own back-end transactional solution."

All this was the teaser. He wanted this audience — and every audience — to understand right away that Value America wasn't just some retailer. It was the answer to all of retail's problems. It wasn't a shallow, immature Web pipe dream. It was a real company run by real, grown-ups.

Manufacturers, he said, were pitted against the retailers who sold their products. Consumers, on the other hand, were growing increasingly tired of the traffic, hassle, and expense of conventional bricks-and-mortar shopping. They wanted an alternative. Home shopping through TV and catalogs had taken off, but that wasn't the future. Listening to Winn, the audience shook their heads sadly. They felt *bad* for the manufacturers. They *wished* there was *something* that could be done.

Winn looked sadly at his audience for those few seconds. Then, the clouds passed. Winn was smiling and radiating confidence. With a higher-pitched voice and a quick punch of the fist, Craig Winn, retail Messiah, promised that salvation was at hand. Value America, using the Internet to go direct to consumers, would save the day.

In late 1998, e-commerce was a vast strip mall of bookstores, even more adult bookstores, CD warehouses, and a mess of little boutiques. In this setting, Value America was to be *the* massive department store. It had north of eight hundred brands whose products it could sell — from Zenith televisions to Amana refrigerators and from Wilson sporting goods to Weber grills. All in all, Value America sold products in more than a dozen product categories, and it was growing daily.

"While it would be easier to develop systems to serve one industry," Winn explained, "we do not think — and this is *important* — that consumers will learn to navigate and purchase products at hundreds of different sites. They will not bookmark thousands of sites for each unique need. Nor will they share personal and financial information on a wide scale. We believe they will gravitate to the handful of comprehensive sites that provide most of what they need in one convenient place. The primary motivation for e-commerce is convenience. It is more convenient to go to one store than to twenty. And if competitive pressures rob one industry of profitability, another can be mined for margin. Plus, when one considers the enormous advertising required to break through and become a victor in this space . . . only comprehensive solutions work." The sentences caressed his audience. Winn's rich baritone dripped with this odd combination of confidence bordering on arrogance and a little boy's *gee whiz*. Members of the audience sat and watched him wide-eyed. They could all see zeroes being added to their net worths.

Winn's voice rose and dropped like a yo-yo, punching just the right predetermined words. Elmer Gantry had found the Internet gospel. He bobbed as he spoke, widening his eyes as his grin expanded like a balloon. This was his baby, and he knew this baby was going to be the greatest of all babies — ever.

One of the hardest parts of e-commerce was giving people the attention they wanted and needed online. If they went into a store like Nordstrom, Winn pointed out, there would be a swarming entourage tending to their needs and questions. In the online environment, it was exactly the opposite. You surfed and shopped alone — "in your bathrobe and bunny slippers." Winn loved that line. But sometimes people got lost and confused. Insecure, frustrated. They needed a guide, a dependable friend. Value America would be that friend. "We want our customers to have the choice between the anonymity of the online experience and the personal interaction and sense of community possible with customer service . . . the best of both worlds, high-tech and high-touch. Our people, empowered by technology, are able to sell and support quality products."

There was more, much more: the co-op revenue, the lack of any inventory, the multimedia presentations. As he presented each beautiful facet of his gem to the crowd, Winn still couldn't believe the genius of the whole thing. It gave him goose bumps. This was the epiphany. This was why Wall Street was going to make him a billionaire. This was the future, and he had discovered it before anyone else. Despite two decades of telling everyone about his retail vision, he was the only one to achieve it. "Our solution is proprietary and scalable. We have built a national brand. Value America brings the best people and products together and is *the marketplace for a new millennium!*"

The audience was silent for a moment after Winn stopped speaking. They wanted to be sure he was done. They waited. They waited. Finally they could wait no longer. They clapped and they clapped and they clapped some more.

Three days later, on Monday, September 14, the road show went airborne. That night, Winn called Dorchak and said her wishes had been granted. It was a short conversation.

Value America was in Boston on the fourteenth and fifteenth. At the end of each hour-long meeting, the investors were relatively enthusiastic.

But even before the Boston meetings were over, Dean Johnson became preoccupied with a new game, which he called vendor poker. All that spending had left Value America *seriously* low on cash. Between pitch meetings, Johnson was on the phone back to Charlottesville advising his staff on which companies to pay and which ones to put on hold. Johnson had already discovered that one of the biggest things Value America had going for it was a highly advantageous byproduct of Winn's business model. Because Value America was an inventoryless model, it never had to pay for the products it offered. It could and did, however, bill customers' credit cards the moment they placed an order. Since Value America didn't pay its vendors for thirty to sixty days, it survived on other people's money as it waited for more money to come in the door. It played the same shell game with advertising, too. Instead of buying ads directly from newspapers, its media consultant purchased the space on credit and then billed Value America. Dean could stiff the consultant for weeks!

By the time the road show was in its second week, the markets were still headed south, and virtually every other company had long since pulled plans for its offering. Remaining on the road during such a drastic market downturn posed many problems for Value America. Going lower than the $10.16 per share of June's financing round was obviously impossible — the private investors didn't want to *lose* money. Second and just as important was the perception factor. The longer they stayed on the road hawking their IPO, the louder the message that Value America was a company in desperate need of cash. That wasn't exactly the message they wanted to send.

Winn was particularly upset by this turn of events. What annoyed him most was how inconvenient the whole damn thing was. He had worked so hard with the very fine people at Robbie Stephens to value his company at nearly half a billion dollars. That meant a potential IPO stock price of at least $15 per share and a paper windfall for Winn of about $200 million. For Value America, it meant $80 million in cash to keep things growing.

But with the markets in the tank, there was no way to get $15 a share; maybe $12 or $11 a share would get the IPO done, but such a low figure was positively unacceptable to Craig Winn. Squeaking into the public markets wasn't good enough. The public had to be *clamoring* for the offering. It was crucial to drive name recognition and perceived value for Value America's other customers — Wall Street and the media.

On Thursday evening, September 24, Dean Johnson and his wife were relaxing in Richmond at a nice little B&B prior to Johnson's scheduled trip to London — via the Concorde — the next day. Value America had been planning an overseas trip to hit up more potential investors. He got a message from the front desk to call Craig Winn.

"Craig?"

"Dean, I've pulled the IPO."

"Excuse me?" Johnson knew it was a possibility, knew it made sense, but didn't really think Winn was going to pull the IPO, since Value America was nearly bankrupt.

"Dean," Winn said slowly, "I'm killing the IPO. I'm going to pull the registration statement tomorrow."

"Shit." That was about all Johnson could manage.

What Winn neglected to do, however, was call any of his other investors that night — like ULLICO or Paul Allen's Vulcan Ventures — to tell them the road show and the IPO were off.

Tim Driscoll was somewhat surprised, therefore, when he called Dean Johnson the next day to find out how the London leg of the trip was going only to find that Johnson wasn't *in* London.

"Where are you?" Driscoll grumbled.

"Richmond."

"Is Richmond near London?"

"Not last I checked," Johnson replied flatly.

"Then why are you in Richmond?"

"I'm figuring out what to do with the rest of my life." Dean Johnson saw no way back from this particular abyss. He didn't object to what Winn had done — there probably wasn't any choice — but Value America, he knew, was finished.

"Why aren't you meeting with investors?"

"Winn pulled the IPO."

"He did WHAT?!"

To Driscoll and all the other investors, the prospect of losing out on the IPO was a very bad thing. Without an IPO, everyone's money was locked up in a privately held company making no money and losing lots of it.

From the time Winn first hit the road hawking his company, he'd closed his presentation by saying that every so often a new company truly changes the world. The last such company came along when a returning Vietnam veteran finishing up his business degree developed a plan for a transportation company that would ship packages across the country overnight. That company, Winn told audience after audience, was Federal Express, and it had absolutely, positively changed the world. The genius behind that company was Frederick W. Smith of Memphis, Tennessee, who he considered to be the "Babe Ruth of American business." He would pause for a purposeful moment to punctuate his point, survey his audience, smile just a bit, and say with as much calm humility as he could muster that Value America had the potential to change the world more than Federal Express. Eyebrows invariably rose a bit and glances were exchanged, but Winn was so earnest, so confident, and so believable that audience after audience just nodded and wondered where the story ended and the truth began.

Now Winn sat in his office chair, fresh from killing the IPO, and forced himself to go through his voice mail. Suddenly, his chest constricted and his stomach felt queasy, as a slow, drawling voice almost mumbled, "Hello, this is Frederick Smith of Memphis, Tennessee. I would appreciate it if you would give me a call back at your earliest convenience. My number is . . ." The numbers were a blur.

Clearly someone was playing a joke; it wasn't really Fred Smith, and when he called the number, it would be some psychic hotline or something. Or maybe one of the hundreds of people who'd heard his presentation had told Fred Smith about his assertions, and Fred Smith was really, truly pissed off.

After a half hour had passed, Winn took a deep breath and slowly punched the numbers. It rang and rang and clicked into voice mail. A woman's slow southern drawl answered the phone. "Hello, you've reached the chairman's office at Federal Express. No one can take your call right now. Please leave a message." He did. "Uh, Mr. Smith, this is Craig Winn of Value America returning your call, I think. Please call me back at your convenience."

Winn hung up, feeling rather like a high school boy leaving his first message for that really cute girl in his biology class who might not even know who he was — or worse . . .

CHAPTER FOUR

Phoenix

Regardless of what Fred Smith wanted, Winn had other things to focus on. Value America had escaped a hundred deaths before the now-failed IPO. But this time Winn thought they were *really* dead — cold, stiff, and stinky. So did every other executive in the company. They had no money.

Late on Friday night after the Fred Smith call, Rex Scatena came into Winn's office. He walked over to his friend, grabbed Winn's shoulders in his hands, shook him just a bit, and said, "It has been a hell of a ride. We gave it all we had. I'd do it again with you in a second. It was a hell of a ride."

Winn looked at Scatena, smiled, shrugged his shoulders, and tried to grasp the cold, clammy sense of death that surrounded him.

The team took Saturday off to regroup, reflect, and rest. Then Johnson, Winn, and Scatena gathered at the 2300 Commonwealth Drive office on Sunday morning, September 27. Their task was to come up with the spin — and a go-forward plan. Regardless of what was going to happen in the next several days and weeks, they needed to buy themselves a little bit of time. They couldn't come back in from the road show that was supposed to be the appetizer to the IPO main course and tell employees and colleagues there wasn't enough money left to pay salaries — even though there wasn't. Telling the company there weren't enough people to buy the stock that was supposed to make them all rich — well, that was also too much of a heartbreaker.

As Winn and Scatena had done before, they pulled out their checkbooks. They weren't investing, they were "loaning" Value America money to meet payroll. Winn's $300,000 check and Scatena's $250,000 would cover the company for at least one pay period — maybe two. Then Winn got on the phone to friends and investors. He called them one and all — Mike Steed at ULLICO, Allen and Savoy in Seattle, Tim Driscoll, Gary LeClair, everyone. His story was the same: Value America had to pull the IPO because there was no market for the company to go public. Now, Value America had no cash, no ad budget, no money for trips — potentially no money for utilities. Things were bleak. Winn didn't ask a single person for money — he didn't figure it would be fair. The chances of his company succeeding at that particular moment in history were slimmer than they had ever been. If someone *did* want to invest, the situation spoke for itself.

Everyone supported Winn. There were no recriminations — no lectures, no should-haves or could-haves. Everyone wanted to help, no one more so than Mike Steed at ULLICO. He would, he promised Winn solemnly, get Value America money. It would probably take him a while, but he would get it done.

Winn thanked him profusely — still not holding out too much hope for the company — and went to address his employees.

It was a warm fall day, and the employees gathered out in the Commonwealth parking lot. The buzz was bad. People had noticed the go-public team was back in the office early. Everyone knew the markets were soft and money was short. Employees believed only three possibilities remained: the company was over, they were going to be laid off, or they were going to be asked to work without pay.

Winn walked slowly out the front door of the yellow Victorian house and followed the walk to the parking lot. He climbed up on a picnic table and looked at the nearly two hundred people before him.

He'd talked to the company from that table numerous times before. Those times, however, were exciting, visionary times. This time was anything but. It was, he realized from his small stage, looking out at the crowd, no time for spin. It was just time for the truth. He told them the truth.

"Dean, Rex, and I have spent the last two weeks on the road trying to take our company public." There was no sing-song quality to his voice. It wasn't flat, but it was faltering. "Our reception was tremendous. People loved our vision, loved our people, loved our company. Unfortunately . . ." — his voice broke just a beat — "unfortunately . . . the markets are tough right now. There is no way for us to go public right now."

The Value Americans who had seen their leader confidently grow the company now watched their leader stammer.

"We are going to fight for the company. But the situation is bleak. As we have in the past, we are asking everyone to pull together. We are short on money. Everyone will, however, get paid. We make that commitment to you. Oh, and if you know anyone who wants to invest a few million bucks, send them our way.

"We will succeed . . . or we will fail . . . together."

Winn jumped off the table and walked quickly back to the house, hands in his pockets. He scurried up the stairs and into the building, directly to his office.

He wasn't there five minutes before he heard a knock on the door. Winn, back to the door, looking out the window, spun around. He didn't know the young man's name but recognized him nevertheless. Winn stood up and looked at him quizzically.

"Craig, I've been thinking. I don't have a ton of money, but I've got some. I want to invest in Value America. I want to invest a thousand dollars."

Winn started to say something, when he saw Scatena in the door with a big smile on his face. He was pointing. Next to him and extending down the hallway were dozens of employees. All, apparently, wanting to talk to Winn. Value America's employees, it seemed, wanted the chance to become Value America investors.

Over the next two weeks, more than $500,000 in "loans" came from Value America employees to the company. For Winn, Scatena, and Johnson — and the outside investors — it was something they never thought they'd see — a company as a family.

Meanwhile, Steed and ULLICO, Driscoll, and LeClair were leading a fast "pass the hat" round to get Value America through the end of the year. Driscoll contacted Democratic super-fund-raiser and Clinton pal Terry McAuliffe to throw in a few hundred thousand. Patricia Kluge, former wife of multibillionaire Paul Kluge was also approached about throwing in a few hundred thousand. Heavyweights from the Carlyle Group, Pacific Capital, CIBC/Oppenheimer, and others all considered anteing up to claim a chunk of Value America.

By October 14, Johnson's vendor poker–playing days were over. ULLICO, Driscoll, and friends came through with a complicated convertible bridge loan that gave the company $34 million in instant cash and gave the investors the opportunity to own a bunch of stock at about the same price the B round investors got in June.

As the company regained its footing, Craig Winn began actively courting Fred Smith. Since Winn's initial return call to Smith, the two men had been playing a long-running game of voice-mail phone tag. First, Smith wanted the business plan. Winn sent it immediately. Winn actually considered whether or not to fly it to Memphis himself, using his little Cessna single-engine. Johnson and Scatena suggested simply sending it FedEx might work better. That in and of itself was no easy task, however. Value America had promised ULLICO it would use UPS whenever possible for all of its shipping. UPS was pro-union, and FedEx was decidedly not. So, as Winn prepared to send the business plan, no one could find any FedEx materials for shipping. Finally some were found at a nearby Kinko's.

A few days later, Smith called back and left another message, saying, "Craig, this is Frederick Smith of Memphis, Tennessee. I've read your business plan, and I think it is the best business plan I've ever seen. I'd be pleased to get together with you at your convenience." Winn, who was now convinced it *was* actually *that* Fred Smith on the phone, was giddy. He jumped around the office like a kid who hit the winning home run in the Little League World Series. By late October 1998, Smith and Winn got together, and Winn walked Smith through his business concept. The two men hit it off, and Smith said he wanted to invest both personally and through FedEx. Winn had no problems taking more money. Although he still had tens of millions in the bank, Winn wanted to close a C financing round in January 1999 of at least $50 million. If that round included investments by both Fred Smith and Paul Allen, then Value America would have serious momentum as Winn tried again to position the company for an IPO.

Due to its cash shortfall, Value America had largely gone dark with advertising for almost all of September and October, but miraculously, it had still made its $15 million revenue target for June through September. Having not advertised for all of October and part of November, however, meant there wasn't a chance in the world of hitting the $25 million fourth-quarter goal the IPO would have enabled.

But somehow, some way, the company had to top $15 million for the October–December quarter. Not only did it have to show progress, it had to show it was capable of translating the frenzied holiday shopping season into greater revenue — and hopefully get noticed as one of e-commerce's leaders.

Internet research firms like Boston Consulting Group, Jupiter Communications, and others were forecasting that 1998 holiday shopping totals would more than triple 1997's. Around Thanksgiving, Amazon.com reported its Web traffic had quadrupled from the year before. In mid-November, its cash infusion in hand, Value America ads returned.

Just three years earlier, when Craig Winn began writing his business plan, Internet retailing was a novelty. A few months before, the Nasdaq and IPO markets treated it like a losing idea. But in a matter of a season or two, e-commerce insanity was reaching psychedelic levels. Now it was nearly a national obsession. Suddenly there were shopping sites offering gift registries, gift suggestions, online Santas, and customer service. The companies selling online weren't just a bunch of technologically zealous Amish artisans. There were real stores now, too. Eddie Bauer, L.L. Bean, Victoria's Secret, Gap, and dozens of other established retailers were selling online. Joining their battle for Web traffic were ever more popular and ever more obscure sites.

If his timing earlier had been bad, now Craig Winn looked like a genius. As Value America was closing in on its C round, Winn had two investors — Paul Allen and Fred Smith — who wanted to invest $50 million . . . *each*. There was no way Value America needed $100 million and no way Winn wanted to dilute his stake in the company by issuing that much more stock to handle such a massive investment. But $100 million! It seemed too good to be true.

In fact, it was. The week after Thanksgiving, Winn got a short letter from FedEx informing him that neither Smith nor the company was going to invest in Value America after all.

Winn suspected the culprit. He believed FedEx's issues were actually Fred Smith's issues. Those issues, Winn surmised, were both personal and geographical. Just prior to Thanksgiving, Smith's son Richard was expelled from the University of Virginia. Richard Smith and two of his classmates brawled with another student the previous school year. Richard was convicted of a misdemeanor assault charge in the spring, but neither Fred nor Richard expected an expulsion.

When the news reached the elder Smith, he was furious. The University of Virginia, he believed, had turned against his son because of

Fred's high business profile. He wanted to wash his hands of Charlottesville.

Winn couldn't tell other investors FedEx or Smith decided not to invest in Value America for "personal reasons." The message all of the other investors would hear was FedEx or Smith had found something of personal concern in Value America. So he sat down and wrote a letter to FedEx's executive offices, cc'ing Smith. Smith and FedEx, Winn argued in his letter, had already committed to investing in Value America. Reneging on the investment now would cause a host of problems for Value America. That, Winn stated bluntly, "would be a regrettable state of affairs."

Winn watched the fax machine gobble up his letter and waited for a response. He sat in his Charlottesville office, knowing he'd be hearing *something* back from FedEx before too long.

Two hours later the fax rang with another letter from FedEx, this one proclaiming it would be pleased to invest in Value America.

A year earlier, Winn would have wanted to celebrate. But now he simply looked at the letter, breathed a sigh of relief, and went back to work finalizing the C round.

In Charlottesville, Virginia, despite the ad blackout in September and October, millions of dollars in orders had flooded in. Between Thanksgiving and Christmas they amassed more than $15 million in revenue, a monthly figure that annualized to a rate of more than $150 million. The orders were overwhelmingly for computers; together, IBM, Hewlett-Packard, and Toshiba totaled more than 90 percent of all revenues. Technologically, this was highly beneficial for Value America and its customers, because by now there were electronic-data-interchange (EDI) links between Value America's order-taking apparatus and IBM, HP, and Toshiba. That meant the orders worked exactly according to Winn's plans — the products sold never touched Value America's hands.

In November the technology and Internet markets had rebounded, and by Christmas they were hitting all-time highs. A single share of Amazon's stock traded at about $325 by mid-December, up more than 60 percent from Thanksgiving. Ebay, Onsale, CDNOW, and almost every other e-commerce stock were at all-time highs as well. No one could predict just how vast the market would grow, but observers generally agreed it was an old-economy-versus-new-economy battle for the future of retailing. No one, the argument went, could survive without a commanding Internet presence. It didn't matter if you were Wal-Mart, one of the largest companies in the world. If you didn't have E, you were like a woolly mammoth wallowing in a tar pit.

Value America roared into the New Year. By January 1, 1999, Value America had 227 employees — 40 in technology; 23 in merchandising and vendor partnerships; 33 in product presentations; 14 in advertising; 52 in sales and customer service; 38 in operations and fulfillment; 20 in finance and human resources; and 7 in the executive team and business development.

For many of those employees, getting to work meant navigating their way through hundreds of boxes every day.

When Winn created Value America, an important part of the model was not holding any inventory, anywhere, at any time. But a strange thing began to happen as the company sold more and more merchandise. When people didn't like a product or changed their minds, or when the product didn't work, they returned the product to Value America. Despite the fact they were *told* to send it back to the manufacturer, they did what shoppers everywhere do — they returned it to the place where they purchased it.

After the New Year, the returns only accelerated. Employees rummaged through the stuff, asking if they could take a box or two, only to be greeted with blank expressions from their bosses. The manufacturers refused to accept the returns. No one knew *what* to do with the stuff. It wasn't even supposed to exist. Maybe, some thought, it was a Value America perk — come to work, get a laptop. Come to work the next day and get a TV. It would certainly make for happy employees.

For Winn it was as if the stuff *wasn't* there. He'd walk into the 2300 Commonwealth Drive building, step around the packages like they were office plants, and move on to his destination. He didn't notice them, register their presence, or pay any attention to them. Finally, Dean Johnson approached Winn about the returns. The boxes weren't only a tripping hazard, they also counted against Value America's bottom line. Something needed to be done about that. With boxes disappearing daily and no one cataloging what had arrived, it would be impossible to reconcile the books. That was less important for a private company but highly important for the public company Value America aspired to be.

At first Winn dismissed Johnson, insisting it would take care of itself, because really there weren't too many returns; it was more of an anomaly. But when boxes hit the ceiling, Johnson and Winn met again. It was, they decided, a good idea to rent a storage locker to hold the returned merchandise. So a Value America crew gathered the mountains of boxes, shoved them into storage, and tried to forget about them. Value America now officially held inventory.

On January 20, 1999, Value America closed what it hoped would be its final round of private financing, with a $50 million investment from Paul Allen, $5 million from Frederick W. Smith (whose son Richard was now a Value America intern), and $5 million from FDX Corporation, Federal Express's parent company. Flush with $60 million in cash, Value America could raise its ad spending and revenue generation to a new level. Winn's goal for the first quarter of 1999 was $30 million in revenue.

As Winn evaluated his executive team in late January 1999, he liked much of what he saw. But Winn knew he needed someone at the top who was temperamentally and experientially different from himself, someone stable and steady and experienced in building and running what would certainly be a *Fortune* 500 company. It was the way Bob Pittman and Steve Case built AOL, and Bill Gates, Paul Allen, and Steve Ballmer built Microsoft. There was the visionary, and there was the manager — the one who executed. You needed a team. He also knew that having such an executive on his team would be another wonderful selling point for him — Value America was the Internet company run by grown-ups.

Six months earlier he'd met the man he wanted for the job — Tom Morgan, the newly appointed CEO of US Office Products, a *Fortune* 500 rollup of hundreds of smaller office-products companies. Winn predicted that US Office Products wouldn't amount to anything, but Morgan fit the personality and professional profile of a successful CEO. Morgan, Winn decided, was someone he could sell on the road shows, sell internally, and sell to the board, and someone who might just be able to make Winn's life a bit easier.

No-nonsense, deeply religious, detailed, and sartorially stylish, Tom Morgan was the kind of man who Q tipped the air vents in his Range Rover while wearing a Tommy Bahama linen shirt and humming a contemporary Christian melody. He was Clark Kent minus the Superman, with perpetually tan skin, a rugged, handsome face seemingly devoid of any facial hair — from eyebrows to stubble — and an athletic body. Most of Tom Morgan's business life had been isolated in the friendly confines of Genuine Parts Company. Genuine Parts wasn't sexy — it mostly made auto parts for GM cars. But it was a good, solid — multi-*billion* dollar — company full of great people. And to Morgan, Genuine Parts was the model for every other business. Integrity permeated the place. It was a handshake, a look-in-the-eye, and a pat-on-the-back kind of business. Throughout his tenure there, he'd never had an employment contract, never had to put anything binding in writing, and never really thought about those things — even as he rocketed up through the ranks. He knew one day he'd leave Genuine Parts, but he vowed he'd never leave the Genuine Parts lessons or culture behind. That culture of integrity would be his gift to whatever company he worked for next. At US Office Products he never really had a chance; the culture was already established — he couldn't mold it. But he liked the business and liked the people he worked with, even as the company's stock slid dramatically after he assumed control.

In the summer of 1998, at US Office Products's Georgetown offices, Winn had come by to explain how Value America and USOP could work together. Morgan wasn't too surprised, therefore, when Winn phoned him in late January and invited him down to Charlottesville to see what Value America was up to and "talk business."

Winn greeted Morgan at one of Value America's new offices on the north side of town, escorted him into his new office, shut the door, plopped down, and announced bluntly, "Tom, I'd like you to become CEO of Value America."

As it frequently was with Winn, any other agenda a person arrived hoping to adhere to was rapidly discarded. Morgan wasn't sure he understood what Winn was saying; he was still thinking about all the different ways Value America and US Office Products could work together. Morgan paused for a second, got a quizzical little smile on his face, tipped his whole body to the side, and said, "Excuse me?"

After Winn made his pitch, Morgan told him he was flattered, he'd consider it, but it really wasn't something he was looking to do. He was committed to USOP and what that company could become.

Within a few days there was a long phone call from Fred Smith, who told Morgan that Value America had the best business model he'd ever seen and that the best way for it to succeed was to have an experienced executive at the helm. Morgan shuttled back and forth to Charlottesville for more meetings with Value America's executive team. His decision impacted everything from its go-public strategy to SEC filings. (If he came on board, the latter would have to be amended to reflect Morgan and his new options. The former would be altered because Value America would no longer technically have Craig Winn running the company.) Finally, on Monday morning, February 22, Morgan phoned Winn. He really did want the job, he told Winn. It was the hottest industry in modern history, Value America was already set to go public, he could influence its culture, and if the whole thing panned out, he'd be able to comfortably retire and devote more time to sharing God's love with kids across the country.

Morgan told Winn there were four conditions that were inviolable. First, he wanted to nearly double the number of stock options. Typically, CEOs get a portion of the company in equity ranging from 3 percent to 10 percent. But because Value America was already within weeks of its public offering, his risk was substantially minimized. He was, therefore, willing to forgo equity but did want at least 400,000 options at $15 a share. Second, since he was making $1 million a year at USOP, he didn't want to take a $600,000 pay decrease to the $395,000 Winn offered. He wanted $495,000 plus minimum total bonuses of $166,667 for 1999. In addition, he wanted an incentive bonus that would pay him the lesser of $1 million or 1 percent of the amount Value America's stock increased during his first year. Third, he wanted a housing allowance for temporary housing, since he didn't know when he could move his family down from D.C. Fourth, he wanted a quick media announcement, because he didn't want a lengthy transition period. If this was going to happen, it was going to happen fast. Morgan expected there to be a lengthy debate after each issue. Instead, following each statement, Morgan heard "Done. Next?" At the end of the four requests, Winn simply asked, "Is that all?" Morgan, wondering a bit if he should have asked for more, said no. On the other end of the phone Winn glowed. "Welcome aboard."

Three days later, Morgan moved into the office once occupied by Glenda Dorchak, two doors down from Craig Winn. Dorchak moved next door. She wasn't thrilled at the prospect of a new CEO, but she did welcome the opportunity to get a little insulation from Winn. The two hadn't been getting along all that well.

This was Morgan's chance to give back — to show the new Internet workers exactly how an ethical, vigilant, and strong company can bless everyone it touches, internally and externally. He was CEO from the start — at least from the go-public start. Now he'd have to live up to the men who had guided him through his business career. He started building by learning.

Tom Morgan threw himself into learning about the technology, the vision, the marketing, the operations, and every other detail he could get his hands on. There wasn't any time to waste with pleasantries. Winn informed Morgan that Value America was going public in late March or early April. That left Morgan four or five weeks to learn everything. For Morgan it was a 5:30 A.M. to 7:00 P.M. workday race to get everything ready for the scrutiny they'd receive as a Nasdaq-listed stock.

Two weeks into his tenure, Morgan witnessed his first crisis. Value America was trying to finalize its IPO prospectus — a scaled-down version of all the information filed in the S-1 for potential investors to receive prior to investing in the company. At particular issue in mid-March was an old crisis in a new form — the brands debate.

To Winn and therefore to Value America, one of the most important things to tout was the number of brands in the store. The logic was simple. If Value America had a lot of brands, then Value America was succeeding.

Winn professed daily that there were more than one thousand brands in the store. The previous fall, when they were attempting to go public the first time, Winn claimed there were eight hundred brands. Since several months had passed, it only made sense that there would be more than eight hundred, and one thousand was a nice round number.

In a debate eerily reminiscent of President Clinton's Monica Lewinsky deposition, where he blustered over the definition of the word *is,* Value America debated the term *brand*. What, exactly, was a brand? It seemed obvious. A brand was a manufacturer recognized by consumers for making a particular product. IBM was a brand, Panasonic, Sony, Polo, etc. But to Craig and to other hard-core retailers, it wasn't that simple. To them a brand was closer to a product. IBM Aptiva was a brand. So were IBM ThinkPads and IBM NetVistas. These were brands, because the companies spent money making them recognizable to consumers.

The challenge, therefore, was to quantify Value America's brands. Before the prospectus describing the company could be finalized, everything had to be technically (read: legally) correct. That meant counting brands. So they started counting. The goal was to find one thousand.

With Winn skiing in Colorado with his family, Dean Johnson and Sandra Watson, the controller, started rummaging through the store category by category, product by product. Behind them, a row of lawyers verified what actually qualified as a brand. They went from Apple to Zenith, from Amana to Zebco. All the while, Johnson huffed and smirked, with his Opie haircut and blazing eyes, wondering how the hell he'd gotten to the point in life where his job was counting the number of brands in a virtual store without any product.

At about 5 A.M., when it was clear there were only about seven hundred brands, lightning struck. I don't need to be doing this! Johnson thought, recovering his stiff posture. I can find some other fool to do it!

Johnson thought for a minute, and then it dawned on him — Greg Dorn. Greg was a basset hound of a man who lived to please Winn — for good reason. Dorn had struggled through personal difficulties of his own and Winn had given Greg a job when no one else would.

Now, a day later, Greg slogged through the store, logging everything that could remotely be considered a brand. There were four different types of Crest toothpaste. Looked to him like those were four separate brands. There were six different types of Near East couscous — six more brands. Early on Saturday morning, however, he was still many brands short of one thousand. It was time to get creative. Greg had categorized all Mongol pencils as a single brand. That wasn't right. He needed to categorize Mongol #2 pencils as one brand and Mongol #2.5 pencils as a separate brand. They were, after all, completely different. Then there were the highlighters: HiLite Green highlighters were very different from pink or yellow or blue. Hey, that was four more brands. This was easy! Now Greg found hundreds of brands, sent everyone a memo saying he'd found *more* than one thousand brands, and dashed home to sleep for the first time in forty-eight hours. Winn and Value America now had the thousand brands they needed to sell the world on the wonders of the first inventoryless e-commerce company.

The brands debate solved, the company again prepared itself for the IPO onslaught. Unlike last September, however, Value America's go-public timing appeared to be ideal.

In mid-March, as the Value America road-show team was preparing to hit the road, iVillage, a conglomeration of news and information Web sites for women, went public at $24 per share. It was up $56 the next day, raising its market capitalization to nearly $2 billion. IVillage's financial statistics boded well for Value America. IVillage lost $43.7 million the previous year on a paltry $15 million in sales. But since AOL owned 10 percent of the company, and NBC owned another 7 percent, the buzz was tooth rattling. Across the country, Autobytel, with about $23 million in sales and $19 million in losses, saw its stock increase 75 percent on the first day of trading, while raising more than $100 million for its operations. Joining Autobytel and iVillage were a slew of companies like iturf, Healtheon, cheaptickets.com, MiningCo.com, and OneMain.com that raised a combined sum of more than $400 million from the dot.com-hungry public. Pity the fools who tried going public with businesses that actually made a profit. Korn/Ferry International, the world's largest executive search firm, with *profits* of more than $5 million on revenue of more than $300 million, dropped its first day of trading. Pepsi-Cola Bottling Company, the largest bottler and seller of Pepsi products, saw its stock slip from $23 a share to just over $21 on its first day of trading. If you weren't a dot.com, you weren't worth considering.

On March 19, the road show was about to commence for what was *certain* to be a successful IPO, and Craig Winn wanted to gather the company together, celebrate their success in beating death so many times, welcome all of the new employees — there were well over three hundred by that point in time — and prepare everyone for the journey ahead. It was his role now. With Tom Morgan on board running things, Winn wanted to inspire!

Value America was absolutely going public this time. As the employees gathered at a hotel a mile or so away from his office, Winn looked at the magazine splayed on his desk. *Chief Executive* was a new publication aimed at a high-end business clientele. There, on the cover of the latest magazine, was Winn's smiling face and widespread arms under the title "The Prince of E-Commerce."

A three-foot-high stack of magazines lay in Winn's office closet. Every so often, when no one was looking, he sneaked a peek inside that closet, picked up a copy with its glossy black cover, and got a tangible reminder this whole dream was real. He really had started a company with a clear plan to profitability, not been able to raise any money, revised his plan to eschew profitability indefinitely, and lost scores of millions of dollars driving revenue, and he was now about to become a billionaire as his reward. He was the *prince* of e-commerce at precisely the moment e-commerce ruled the world. Winn liked being prince. He was going to like being a billionaire a whole lot more.

Of course he wasn't technically a billionaire *yet*. But considering he owned nearly 15 million shares of Value America stock that would most certainly close above the $69.44-per-share figure he needed to be a billionaire, he was, for all intents and purposes, a billionaire. It was like a birthday. If you had a birthday coming in a week, you weren't yet a year older, but you certainly knew you would be in a few days. Winn was counting the days like a six-year-old. He was going to be a *billionaire*. Stunning. He shook his head in amazement. At this moment you could make gold simply by peddling sand. This wasn't the stuff of science fiction or even fantasy; this was the stuff of *mythology*.

Discussions with Robbie Stephens suggested the public offering could net Value America more than $100 million. That meant Value America could *really* start building now. There was a new campus to construct, for instance. The campus would have several buildings, walking trails, restaurants, a three-hole golf course, and a nice lake. There was a jet to buy so executives could get to meetings quickly and efficiently — and a bit stylishly. Value America could sponsor things, advertise things, and, hell, skywrite if that's what it took to make the company money and make Craig Winn a household name. The latter was a sacrifice he was willing to make.

At the DoubleTree Hotel, the site for all big Value America meetings, Winn's big copper-colored Suburban, with the customized VA.COM license plate, pulled around the corner and inched toward the parking lot. A bunch of people waved mightily, swinging their arms above their heads like stranded survivors on an uninhabited island signaling an airplane. He was a mystery to them, but they loved him. As the car drove by, he could see them stand a little taller. They smiled. Their countenance was brighter. It was stunning, really, that they loved him so much — he loved them for it. He really did love them all. They were fine, fine people. He was going to reward them all mightily. They were going to be *rich*. He just hoped he didn't have to talk to them *all* — or if he did have to talk, he could sound intelligent and not nervous. He was nervous. His toes felt kind of numb. They got that way when he was slightly nervous.

He forced his almost six-foot-tall frame with just a bit of middle-age paunch out of the car, ran his right hand slowly through his rich brown hair, and looked at himself in the truck's slightly tinted windows, flashing a quick smile. As much as he liked to present, happy talk with new people accentuated his latent shyness. What were they thinking? What did they want? What did they think about *him*? Most pressingly, what was he supposed to say? So Winn smiled and waved to all his people, patted a few on the back, nodded rhythmically, and made his way over the blacktop, then over the carpet, to the front of the ballroom. All eyes turned to him. Now, he was home.

The Value America presentation was riveting, inspiring. His team of programmers worked with him to make everything just so. He knew every word and could literally say them all backward. For fun, sometimes he did. He knew exactly which syllable in every word and which word in every sentence to emphasize. But before he got to those words, he needed to get his people going with these words, "Value America is poised for *greatness*. Soon, very soon, we shall be among the *biggest* companies in America . . . in the *world*. We shall stick to our plans to sell the *best* goods for the *lowest* possible prices. We shall *overcome* our doubters. We shall *win*. *Destiny* has brought us all here to the foothills of the American experiment, and destiny shall ensure our *stunning success*."

It was classic Craig, Dean Johnson thought. How does he do it? Where is he really from? Am I going to survive? Two years into his tenure, the CFO didn't know how much more was in him. The IPO was largely his doing. He'd overseen the prospectus drafting, answered all the tough questions, put his career on the line by advocating Value America's public offering. But there were times, usually in the middle of the night, when he was far enough removed from Craig's reality vortex to wonder if this was right. He loved the company; hell, he loved Craig. But did this thing deserve to go public? Could it survive going public? Well, he resolved, everyone else was doing it. Why not us?

Dean's wager was, to a degree, everyone's wager. Each Value American, at some point, had to answer this foundational question: Is it safer to believe in Craig Winn or not? Basically everyone in the DoubleTree ballroom had come to the conclusion that it was better to believe. If they believed in Craig and Craig was right, they would be superbillionaires — stunningly wealthy and admired the world over. They would buy small islands, unless of course they became Winn favorites — then they would buy large islands.

One could elect *not* to believe in Craig and eventually find that he or she was right. But in that case, said person would simply be unemployed. Finally, one could believe in Craig and find out later Craig was wrong. In that instance, said person would probably be like those who had believed in Craig's last failed company — well taken care of and perhaps given the chance to believe again in a future endeavor. Therefore, the only logical position was to believe. It was Pascal's Wager for the Internet age. Everyone from Fred Smith and Paul Allen down to Linda Harmon, receptionist, and India Hamner, customer-service technician, believed. Some, like Smith and Allen, had millions of shares. Others, like Harmon and Hamner, had fewer than 1,000 stock options. It didn't matter. They were all committed. They all believed.

As he walked through the presentation that was largely identical to the one he had given in September and was exactly the same as the one he'd give on the forthcoming IPO road show, Winn still couldn't believe the genius of the whole thing. It gave him goose bumps. Value America was the future. He had discovered it. Together, they were executing it. He loved them all so much. A smile started on the left side of his face and spread. He tried to control it. It wasn't just part of the show; the show, the sale, was his life. There was no separation between where life began and selling ended. It couldn't be contained. It was the smile that captivated Wall Street, mesmerized his sales prey, and motivated the hundreds who worked for him. It was the smile that set the prince aglow. "In time, if we do this right, you will all be *millionaires*." The $10-an-hour customer-service representative turned to the $19,000-a-year receptionist, who turned to the $30,000-a-year product-presentation writer . . . and they smiled. They smiled and they flushed with love and exuberance and excitement. They *did love* Craig Winn. They clapped and they clapped and they clapped some more. In between clapping they dreamed of their impending wealth.

Part Two

MONEY FOR NOTHING

CHAPTER FIVE

IPO: Instant Payoff Occasion

Sitting in the back of the DoubleTree ballroom watching Winn present, Value America's new vice president for public relations Michelle Morgan fluttered with excitement. Morgan — no relation to Tom — had been at Value America for only a week, having just finished up a stint as press secretary for the U.S. House Judiciary Committee during the Clinton impeachment trial. The Value America job just fell into her lap. A friend's recommendation led to an instant interview, which led to an instant job offer. Now, days later, she was prepping the company's go-public press blitz.

"David, it's the easiest job I've ever had," she bubbled over on the phone. "I pick up the phone, tell them I'm with an e-commerce company about to go public, and I don't even have to pitch . . . they are *dying* to talk to us!" Michelle, my friend of more than five years, sounded like an adrenalized hummingbird.

"And Value America," she chattered on, "Value America is *the hottest* thing around. Paul Allen and Fred Smith — he founded Federal Express — are backing it. It's going to go public and its stock is going to go through the roof and I'm part of it and I'm in on it and I'm so excited and I can't even explain it and it is so much fun!

"Oh, and Craig Winn, Value America's founder, is *so* brilliant and *so* dynamic and *so* amazing," she enthused.

I was really, truly, emphatically, genuinely happy for Michelle. After I'd spent more than ten years in politics and not-for-profit charitable ventures working with everyone from Ted Kennedy to Bill Bennett, Internet e-commerce companies held the same place in my imagination as Disneyland had when I was seven. These companies were magical places where dreams came true. The people who worked there made millions. They got rich while working on technology's cutting edge in an industry that was reshaping the world more rapidly and thoroughly than the industrial age had a hundred years before. And as someone who loved history, I hadn't missed the fact that leading intellectuals were saying that the concentration of great minds in Silicon Valley in the 1990s was *at least* equivalent to the gathering of great minds in the 1770s in Virginia that helped give birth to America. I wanted to be part of that world.

Instead, I was finalizing my departure from the charitable organization I'd launched and doing strategic communications consulting with some other high-tech companies. I wasn't at all *unhappy* doing what I was doing. But just like when I was seven, Disneyland was where I wanted to be.

While Michelle worked to ensure Value America would be properly introduced into the public consciousness, Craig Winn, Tom Morgan, Dean Johnson, and Rex Scatena settled into the tan leather seats of the spacious Challenger jet Robbie Stephens chartered for them and prepared to race west to California for their road show kickoff. It was March 22, and as they flew, Value America's top executives popped open a bottle of wine and raised their glasses in a toast to their impending IPO the first week of April.

Craig Winn, finally knowing his eighteen-month go-public quest was being realized, poured himself glass after glass of wine — offering not only louder and louder toasts but a mock run-through of his presentation for the gathered executives.

"*Value AMERICA!!!*" he hollered happily, "is the marketplace for a *new* MILLENNIUM!! NO! VALUE AMERICA is the marketplace for ALL millenniums . . . EVER!!!

"And DID I TELL YOU?" Winn blustered in mock seriousness. "Value America has *six* billion brands. They all ship instantly. Before the order is even placed!!

"Oh, oh, oh . . . and Value America is going to raise *billions* of dollars, and then we're going to have Value America blimps and Value America buses and Value America stadiums and Value America rocket ships and Value America space stations!"

Winn's traveling companions egged him on.

"Is that all?" "That all you got?"

Downing another glass of wine, Winn feigned seriousness again. "This *isn't* a joking matter. We . . . are . . . solving . . . America's retail crisis! It is the biggest problem in the world. If we do this correctly, we'll receive the Nobel Prize — actually, *I'll* get the Nobel Prize . . . but I'll mention you when I get it!!!" He dissolved into laughter. "Then we'll solve world hunger, poverty, disease, wars . . ." Someone started humming, "We are the world . . . we are the children . . ."

Hurtling across the sky at more than 500 m.p.h., Value America's executive leadership whooped it up loudly, far more drunk on their dreams than on the alcohol.

In more than fifty meetings over the next eight days, from San Francisco to Chicago to New York and Boston, *everyone* in *every* meeting wanted a piece of Value America. A successful IPO, it seemed, was a lot like a great soufflé — you had to mix it just right, cook it just right, take it out at just the right time — but at the end of the day, there was still an element of luck and timing to make it just perfect. Value America's timing was perfect.

In meeting after scripted meeting, bankers and investors needed bowls under their chins to catch the drool. The IPO timeline was so compressed that there were approximately two minutes for introductions, twenty-five minutes for the presentation, three minutes for questions, and then the Value America all-stars were out the door. In meeting after meeting, bankers in $1,000 shoes and $3,000 suits chased Winn and company to the elevators, trailing them, much as the lepers trailed Jesus.

"Please sir, can I have a million shares?" one Internet-Oliver after another asked.

"We can't make do with just ten thousand, Craig. We're _____ [fill in the blank of prestigious company], for God's sake. We need a million."

Though the demand for their stock made Winn and company *feel* good, there was little they could do to promise people shares. Exactly who got how many and at what price was Robbie Stephens's job, not theirs.

Winn and company decided there would be only 5 million shares released to the public. The other 40 million or so shares remained in the sticky hands of Value America's private owners. This initial stock allotment wasn't overly tiny, but the demand was such that Value America could have easily doubled the size of the IPO. But the small offering was an important part of Winn's business strategy — his sales strategy, that is. Scarcity creates desire. Competition for shares creates demand. That desire, in turn, not only drives demand for the stock during the IPO but also drives desire for what would happen after the IPO — the follow-on offering. It was Winn's intention to sell millions more shares of stock in a secondary offering that summer at an even higher valuation — probably somewhere north of $100 a share. *That* kind of an offering might raise Value America $300 or $400 million more — enough to last years and get Value America off the money-raising roller coaster.

For Value America to have a secondary offering, for its stock to climb into the stratosphere, Winn, Morgan, and the whole executive team knew they had to concentrate on driving *lots* of revenue. As such, their financial targets were highly aggressive. Value America just closed its first quarter in 1999, and preliminary estimates were for revenues close to $30 million. To keep riding the rocket Value America would need to show at least 40 percent to 50 percent growth quarter over quarter, closing 1999 with a holiday season in excess of $100 million in revenue — more than twice 1998's revenue in only three months. From there, Winn estimated the company would have to exceed $500 million in revenue for 2000 and $1 billion — at the very least — by 2001. Few companies in history had ever grown that quickly, but Winn and Morgan knew Wall Street was expecting that kind of growth from *every* e-commerce company. It was the only way to justify the day's lofty stock prices and market capitalizations.

The now almost-public Value America was a far cry from the small team Winn had shepherded across country into a Charlottesville attic. In addition to Morgan and Dorchak, an established corporate team ran things. Former Winn colleague Neal Harris left Costco to run Value America's operations. A former Target and CompUSA merchandiser, Paul Ewert, ran Value America's computer and electronics business. Jerry Goode was still overseeing technology. Michelle Morgan was there, too — to show Wall Street that Value America knew the importance of shaping public opinion.

The next to last night of the road show, March 31, Michelle called me from the St. Regis Hotel in New York, where a butler had just described how to use the bidet and a maid was fluffing her pillows.

"This is unreal," she said quietly with equal parts wonder and queasiness.

Michelle Morgan hadn't exactly grown up in squalor. Her father was a successful Miami lawyer. Her mother was the *Total Woman* author, who exhorted women everywhere to greet their husbands at the door wearing Saran Wrap. Their home on Biscayne Bay was a glass-on-ocean wonder. But that was old new money. She was blown away by the new new-money attitude she'd seen on the road show.

"They're talking about the planes they're going to buy. Rex is talking about his vineyards. Craig is going to build a better version of Camp David. Tom Morgan is going to buy a couple hundred acres and build an estate. Glenda is going to buy an airplane. They were all talking about airplanes like you and I talk about cars. This is nuts."

Her descriptions seduced me further. It was ever more clear to me e-commerce was the only world that mattered.

"I think we're going to get Tom Hanks to be our spokesman," Michelle added.

"Tom Hanks?" I marveled aloud.

"Yeah, might happen." Somehow I couldn't envision Tom Hanks hawking an e-commerce site — though admittedly, people were doing almost anything for stock options. Even the pricey L.A. call girls who served the stars had gone Internet: Swarms of them apparently relocated to Silicon Valley and no longer accepted cash or credit cards for their services — only stock options.

Dean Johnson was given the responsibility for apportioning the final hundred thousand or so friends-and-family stock to the appropriate people. During the weekend of April 2 and 3, he sat in his house with a long list of people and a calculator, trying to make sure the right people got the right number of shares. All of Charlottesville, half of the East Coast, and at least a quarter of the West Coast had heard about the IPO. It seemed to Johnson at least half of those people — the head of the local golf shop, Craig's pilot/gardener, etc. — had been promised shares by Winn at some point.

Some of Tim Driscoll's friends and family weren't on the list. Driscoll, who had mobilized every money-laden contact he had for Value America, couldn't believe it. He'd heard Winn promise Driscoll's uncle friends-and-family shares for his son. That was the kind of disloyalty he didn't forget.

Driscoll started calling Winn first thing on Monday morning and proceeded to call every ninety minutes that day. Winn never returned the calls.

April 4, 1999, dawned with an IPO certain that week — probably Wednesday or Thursday. Everyone pretended to be working hard while accomplishing little. It was a matter of waiting, BS-ing, waiting, BS-ing, and more waiting. Robbie Stephens called to say the stock was oversold. Translation: The road show had gone well and people wanted more shares than Value America actually had to offer. The oversold status included an overallotment Winn and Scatena arranged to come from *their* shares, not from the company's. All told, Winn offered 577,500 shares and Scatena 247,500. If the demand was there, Winn would walk away from the IPO with more than $11 million and Scatena with more than $4.5 million. Even after those sales, Winn would still own more than 14.5 million shares — or about 33 percent of the company — and Scatena would have 6.3 million shares, or about 14 percent.

When Value America filed its S-1, everyone expected the stock to trade somewhere around $17 or $18 a share. That would mean an almost-$90-million payday for the company. But a combination of the market's insatiable desire for e-commerce stocks and the company's successful road show presentations had driven that figure up. It was now likely they would clear at least $21 a share, which meant a payday in excess of $100 million. The pivotal question — how high would Value America trade after it went public — was a matter for rampant watercooler and e-mail speculation. Winn had been going around the company talking to friends, assuring them $100 was a sure bet and $200 was within the realm of the possible.

Not only did everyone in the company have stock options — ranging from a few hundred shares of stock for the lowest-level employees to thousands for middle managers to hundreds of thousands for top executives — but some employees owned actual stock as well. Those employees who "loaned" Value America money in the dark, failed IPO days had been offered to have their loans repaid with nominal interest or be given stock instead. Every single employee chose stock. And, while employees were technically "locked up" from selling Value America stock for six months, there were loopholes around that rule. If, for instance, a spouse or other family member owned the stock, the lockup didn't apply.

On Wednesday, April 7, the IPO became official. The SEC had given full, total, final, absolute approval, and Robbie Stephens was going to price the stock that night. Value America would start trading on Thursday morning, April 8, with the Nasdaq ticker symbol "VUSA."

Winn got the call, leaned back in his chair, closed his eyes, and watched the scene unfold. He'd actually seen it all in his mind for years — the skyrocketing stock, the free-flowing bubbly, the high fives, the hugs and slaps on the back. Payday.

That night, walking along Charlottesville's downtown mall — a brick-lined path of quaint shops — Steve Saltzman knew he'd never be happier than he was at that very moment. Two years before, he answered an advertisement in the local paper and trekked up to Value America's doorstep because they needed writers and he needed money. Winn took one look at his curly mop of brownish hair and almost marionettelike looseness of gait and hired him. Winn figured Steve was your typical southern, Jewish, gay, Ph.D. candidate who liked his dope. He was wrong on the gay part and the dope part. For his part, Steve looked around the State Farm Road attic, saw the cobbled-together servers, and thought, OK, maybe this place has the buzz.

Beside him, Michelle Morgan was lost in the options of her options. Fresh off some homemade PB&J's at Saltzman's pad, both were flush with the possibilities. How do you spend millions? What will it be like to wake up rich?

By morning Steve would be worth more than $3 million — and that was only if the stock didn't increase beyond its initial offering price. Michelle's stock options gave her a paper worth in the $1 million range as well — though they wouldn't begin vesting for almost a year.

Two years ago, Steve walked to his interview. Tonight, after bidding Michelle farewell, the man who headed up product-presentations wanted to walk the six miles from his apartment to his office to await the morning and the first public trades of VUSA.

He wasn't alone in the Commonwealth Drive building very long. April 8, 1999, was a day everyone at Value America wanted to be in the office early. Dozens of employees left local Charlottesville bars around 3:00 A.M. and stumbled straight into work. The rest of the crew ambled in around 7:00 A.M. or so. No one had slept much that night. This was the day Internet Santa would drop down the chimney.

Tom Morgan tried to stay focused. This was a business, after all, and you had to execute, execute, execute. He needed to talk to Jerry Goode about systems issues — he wanted to be sure the technology could handle a $100 million projected fourth quarter. Then Dean Johnson — he needed to figure out exactly how and when further options needed to be issued. Someone said a CEO of a big manufacturing company was coming in — with whom did he need to check on that? Oh, there was that party this evening at Keswick Hall Country Club. Gosh, he thought, has everyone been invited? It would be unacceptable if someone important were left off the list. Then, switching thoughts, he turned on his computer, adjusted the screen a quarter inch to the left so it aligned more perfectly with the speakers on either side of the credenza, and made sure his VUSA ticker window was active. It was important for him to stay informed about the day's happenings after all.

Hot news buzzed through the company at about 7:30 A.M. VUSA priced at $23 a share, and every last share of the allotment and the overallotment were sold. No matter what happened now, Value America would walk away from its IPO with more than $125 million in cash. The increased offering price also meant that Winn was now going to clear $13 million and Scatena $5.5 million.

Across Value America's six Charlottesville buildings, everyone was transfixed by the newly installed bubble stock ticker plopped in the middle of their computer monitors, displaying VUSA and a bunch of zeroes. The zeroes remained even after the market opened at 9:30 A.M. That meant only one thing — here the stock was in such demand it couldn't be traded yet. Too many people wanted to buy the stock . . . people like me, sitting on their beds in boxer shorts, praying to their laptop computers that the stock gods would smile and grant them shares cheap.

In a flurry of activity between Robbie Stephens's trading floor and the Nasdaq offices, traders were furiously trying to find a price where supply met the crazed demand. It was a laborious process. People with IPO shares were queried about where they would sell their shares. Others were queried about where they would buy.

By 9:45 A.M., fifteen minutes after the markets opened for trading, the frenzy in Value America's offices was reaching drug-altered levels. Even the people taking phone orders were delirious.

"Good morning, Value America, I'm rich, how may I help you?" one young lady answered.

Pocket calculators stood at the ready to determine net worth. Up and down the office corridors people looked at their computer screens, looked at each other, and called their friends. "Do you know how *rich* I am?" was the most common query. Winn's yellow Labrador retriever, Cristal, paced the halls as well, barking up a storm, presumably not knowing her owner was going to be a billionaire that morning but suspecting something intense was going on.

People roamed up and down the halls of the various buildings, passing on rumors: "Fifty dollars! . . . I heard fifty."

Minutes passed. 10:00 A.M., no news yet. 10:15, 10:30, the same — no news. Then suddenly at 11:00 A.M., the bubbles popped — VUSA . . . $69.19 . . . , VUSA . . . $71 . . . , VUSA $72 . . . , VUSA $72.14 . . . , VUSA $73.68. At first no one jumped up and down. They just stared at their computer screens with mouths agape. Their little company was trading over $70 a share on its first day! Then, as one, the company erupted.

Winn and Scatena were hopping and skipping through the halls, pouring champagne. Winn's remaining Value America stock was valued at $1.01 billion. He was a billionaire. He and Scatena cornered their buddy Ken Erickson, one of the business-development guys. They were tempted to spray champagne on each other's heads like sports stars after the World Series. They'd never done that before. Later, someone said Ken actually did go into the bathroom and secretly pour some on his face — just to see how it felt — only to realize the reason winning athletes and reporters squinted a lot after someone poured carbonated, fermented grape juice on their heads: It stung like hell. There was screaming, there was mirth, there was merriment.

Over in the technology department, Joe Page, chief technology officer, was giving everyone periodic updates on his net worth. "I'm worth forty-five million!" he shrieked when the first trades came across the wire. "Computers on me!" he yelled out loud to hearty cheers. Page's family was nearby. He'd flown them in to celebrate his first day as a really, really rich man. As the stock fluctuated throughout the day, Page would continue screaming updates to the technology team. Whenever it went down, he would pretend to be alarmed and shout, "Oh my God, I'm only worth forty million!"

Page, under the advice of counsel, had chosen to "exercise" his options at the IPO price. That meant he bought out his options at his "strike price" of only a few bucks per share. He had a six-month lockup when he couldn't sell, but knowing the stock would be in the hundreds by the time that six months came around made him feel pretty good about life. Plus, he'd have to pay taxes only on the difference between his option price and the $23 at which he exercised his options. If he waited until the stock was in the hundreds, the tax bill would be exponentially bigger. The only potential downside would come if the stock slipped below $23. At that point he'd still have to pay taxes on the $23 exercise price. But everyone knew *that* wasn't going to happen.

Back at one of the company's six buildings, a phantom voice echoed, "Welcome to Value America," in a voice meant to mimic Ricardo Montalban's white-tuxedo-wearing Mr. Roarke from *Fantasy Island.* This was *Fantasy Island,* only better. *Fantasy Island* didn't have IPOs.

Dean Johnson sat mute in his office and stared blank-eyed into the computer screen. We made it, we actually made it, he thought over and over and over again. They've all sipped the Kool-Aid now.

He'd seen many, many bad things in his last eighteen months. There were days after the failed IPO when he judged success by how many creditors' phone calls he avoided. The company had probably been bankrupt. Perhaps it was more accurate to say a non-dot.com company would have been bankrupt. Then there was the brands debate — and on and on.

Johnson slid his ever-present calculator in front of him, rapidly punched the buttons, and leaned back, absorbing the splendid figure. His share in Value America now exceeded $10 million. He could take a lot of bullshit for $10 million — he *had* taken a lot of bullshit for that money. Even if, he thought, we slide down over the next year, it'll still be worth a hell of a lot more money than I would be making anywhere else.

The stock jittered up and down throughout the day. It didn't hit $74 a share again but closed the day at $55, earning a market capitalization of nearly $2.5 billion. At that valuation, the company was worth twice that of Borders, which had revenues of $300 million and profits of more than $90 million.

That night, the Value America elite gathered at the lush Keswick Hall Country Club just east of Charlottesville. The club and inn, once owned by Lady Laura Ashley, looks like one of the majestic yellowstone estates that dot the English countryside. There are exquisite horses, frequent fox hunts, floral patterns galore, and an explosion of chintz. Inside, the virtual rich were comparing net worths.

"I'm thinking of becoming a gentleman farmer," giggled one woman.

"I think investing in artwork would be a grand way to diversify my holdings," said one twenty-seven-year-old merchandiser.

"Has anyone seen the Grey Poupon?" another asked.

Ken Power, one of VA's founding fathers, knew exactly where his $30 million was going. He wanted to open a big camp for foster kids. Business-development wunderkind Syd Kain, with a measly few million to his name, was appropriately more modest — a couple new BMWs and a long-term investment plan suited him just fine.

Just then, Winn and his entourage rolled up in a huge white stretch limousine to their colleagues' cheers. He hopped up the steps to greet his flock, leaving family and friends behind. The day had proven more splendid than his dreams, and he basked in it.

There were infinite toasts. There were heady inquiries into how much it would cost to buy Keswick and turn it into the private Value America country club. The celebration continued deep into the night.

Friday, April 9, dawned on Value America's first day as a *public* company. For more than two years, Winn and Value America had been fighting the revenue race in private. Now, as a public company, Craig Winn would get what he craved most — media coverage — and what many feared — intense public scrutiny. Now, every business decision, every statement, every announcement could be analyzed and scrutinized by Wall Street analysts, institutional investors, retail investors, the high-tech industry, the business press, the tech press, and dozens and dozens of others.

Winn welcomed the scrutiny. That Friday and all through the next week, Michelle Morgan and Craig Winn handled a flood of media requests from newspapers and TV news shows eager to get Value America's chairman on the record. Financial news channels like CNNfn sent camera crews to Charlottesville to interview Winn. Michelle had scheduled editorial board meetings with *USA Today* and the *Washington Post*. The immediate press coverage validated what Winn had long known: Value America was in the big leagues now.

Two weeks after the IPO, Winn and Michelle Morgan headed to D.C. for a *Washington Post* editorial board meeting. After a thirty-minute discussion on Value America, the conversation veered off into a long political discourse. As Morgan watched with not a small amount of horror her boss's discourse, Craig Winn told *Post* editors and reporters he anticipated a run for governor of Virginia in 2005 followed by a shot at the White House in 2008. Winn knew if he could be President, his life would have real, transcendent meaning. Merely serving one term, like Jimmy Carter or George Bush, wasn't good enough. They were losers, really. But two terms — like Reagan — *that* would be meaningful.

The *Post* decided against running the political discussion. It wasn't relevant to the dot.com angle they were pursuing. Besides, they knew that everyone in Washington, D.C., imagined themselves presidential material at one point or another.

Next up for Winn and Morgan was a date at Liberty University with Jerry Falwell and Henry Kissinger. It sounded like the beginning of a joke: "Jerry Falwell, Henry Kissinger, and an Internet billionaire are having dinner at a Holiday Inn in rural Virginia . . ." But Winn and Falwell had known each other since earlier in 1999, when they were introduced by mutual friends. Winn wanted Falwell's flock to be the cornerstone of Value America's custom store project. He saw the amply girthed preacher as the retail messiah for his fundamentalist flock. There would be, Winn believed, billions of dollars generated by a Falwell custom store. Falwell, meanwhile, saw Winn as a child of God and an Internet billionaire — therefore, someone who might assist in his ministry. It was a marriage of spiritual and temporal convenience.

Henry Kissinger had delivered a paid speech at Liberty earlier in the day and had agreed to a small dinner with Falwell and a few friends and donors afterward. Winn could scarcely believe it. There he was, seated next to Henry Kissinger, who held forth on foreign policy, domestic policy, wines, the Internet, the travails of being an immigrant playboy. Winn beamed. Henry Kissinger!

Together, Craig and Jerry turned the conversation to things eternal. Perhaps thinking the former "foreign-policy president" instead practiced ritual animal sacrifice, Falwell pressured him on his prayer life. "Diiiiiddd you praaaay," asked Falwell slowly, "as youuuuu connnnntemplated Vietnaaaaam, nuclear weapons, and mutuuuuuually assuuuuuured mass destruuuuuuuuuuction?"

Kissinger paused, looked Kissinger-like, and grumbled, "Of course. The case for the Almighty is quite convincing." Kabam! Enormous revelation! Headline: "Kissinger Does Not Slaughter Cats, Instead Prays to God." Subhead: "Former Secretary of State Believes God Exists." To Craig, Kissinger's statement was a tremendous affirmation of the intimate dinner they were sharing. After all, if such a reserved man as Kissinger would share his prayer life with this extraordinary group of people, what limits really existed to what they could discuss over glazed chicken?

In Kissinger Winn saw a potential political ally. Winn was unspeakably frustrated by what he perceived to be the overall lack of Republican electoral success and specific lack of marketing prowess. He figured with the billions he made on the Internet, he would set up nonprofit organizations to launch crusades on behalf of his policy initiatives. These policies, Winn was convinced, would be the foundation for reinvigorating the Republican Party. Their originality combined with his God-given marketing genius meant only one thing — a certain position of supreme importance in national politics. He'd welcome Henry Kissinger onto his team.

As the evening flickered out, Winn casually informed Kissinger "some people" had approached him about running for political office. Perhaps they could get together sometime in New York to discuss this? Kissinger obliged; he'd be "happy to discuss such political-type things" with the Value America chairman.

As the dinner broke up, Falwell returned to his church, Kissinger escaped from Lynchburg, and Winn roared back to Charlottesville with Michelle Morgan, the top down on his new convertible Jaguar. "Incredible," Winn bubbled. "Henry Kissinger wants to talk to me about my presidential campaign." Just as Winn had imagined that the boxes of returns stacking up in Value America's hallways didn't exist, he now imagined it was Kissinger who wanted Winn, not the other way around. Henry Kissinger had agreed to be an adviser to Craig Winn.

It was clear April 1999 would require a long chapter in Winn's presidential memoirs.

CHAPTER SIX

Ground Zero

Four weeks after my deft Value America stock-acquisition scheme, I still hadn't made a dollar on the VUSA shares I'd purchased for $72 on IPO day. Technically I'd lost a lot of money, since the stock was now trading at $34 a share. But that small financial deficit was of no concern to me now. I was about to leave the world of Value America investors and join the world of Value America *insiders*. On May 4, I had an audience with Craig Winn. The founder of the world's most perfect e-commerce company was going to interview *me* for a job. My life as a Value American was about to begin.

The job I was interviewing for was Michelle's. After weeks of internal anguish, she had decided to leave Value America. Just prior to starting at the company, she'd met the man of her dreams. After a month and a half of thirteen-hour days and seven-day work weeks one hundred miles away from that man, she'd decided that even the promise of Value America riches wasn't enough compensation for being away from her almost-fiancé. She was going to forfeit her stock options for love. It wasn't all bad. Her guy worked for Microsoft and had enough stock options for the both of them.

At 7:00 A.M. on May 4, I turned onto the six-laned Route 66 heading west from my Washington, D.C., home. My mind was popping with visions of what Value America would be like. I pictured a scaled-down version of the chic, lavish AOL complex where Kim, my almost-bride, worked. It would have high-tech security and cool offices and nifty perks. There would probably be a concierge to handle mundane chores like laundry, and there would be lunchtime runs and bike rides through the Shenandoah Mountains. Charlottesville itself, the home of Jefferson and the University of Virginia, would be quaint-cool. I imagined it as one huge Restoration Hardware–furnished country inn. There would be horses and farms and lots of Range Rovers. It was going to be Internet nirvana. In a decade or so, Charlottesville, Virginia, would be like Redmond, Washington, and Value America was going to be its Microsoft.

About thirty miles out of D.C., my path to Charlottesville dumped me onto Route 29. As I drove, Metro lines and buses and strip malls were quickly replaced by mobile-home lots and tractor dealerships. Old, mud-splashed pickup trucks replaced shiny new minivans. Starbucks yielded to gas stations with old Krispy Kreme doughnuts in boxes. Exit suburbia; enter Bumpkinville. Makeshift signs announced the local attractions: "Frish Sider 2 miles." More than a few Confederate flags adorned overgrown yards and chrome bumpers. Factories for things I never really considered people making — things like charcoal and mulch and Formica countertops — were strewn across the countryside.

The road to Charlottesville wound around and climbed and fell for another fifty miles until signs announced things like the Boar's Head Inn and Monticello Motel. Not too far from those signs, on the north edge of Charlottesville proper, was where my directions led me. I found a small spread of new, one-story brick office buildings that typically house doctors, dentists, chiropractors, and shrinks. These, apparently, were the modest brick buildings that housed much of Value America. The prefabricated brick structures looked like slightly updated army barracks. Value America must, I assumed, be saving its money and cutting corners. The only thing that distinguished these six buildings from the State Farm Insurance building across the street were the cars parked outside. No mud-splashed pickups in this parking lot. Some customized BMWs, a sleek convertible Jaguar, a shiny black Range Rover, a few convertible Mercedes. Clearly this was a parking lot for the Internet rich.

The interior matched the exterior — late-twentieth-century doctor's-office chic. The enclosed receptionists' area, the old magazines on a faded-veneer table, the industrial-grade carpet that could survive blood or barfing babies, the neutrally nonoffensive walls, the drop foam-board ceiling tiles, it was all of a kind. There was one big difference, however, between these offices and a typical professional complex — people. Everywhere people scampered about. As I peered down each hall, I saw people popping out of one office and into another. It was like Planet of the Prairie Dog People. They all seemed to carry jumbled papers and they all shared a common facial expression — exhausted panic. They were *tired* prairie dogs.

Unfortunately for me, as I stood in the frenetic receptionists' area, absolutely no one acknowledged my existence. That is not an easy oversight. I don't exactly blend in. Six-foot five-inch half Asians are not indigenous to rural Virginia. For a moment I thought I was having an out-of-body experience. Maybe on the drive down from D.C. I'd actually gotten squashed by one of those rapidly moving eighteen-wheelers that flew down the highway, and I was dead. Maybe I was like Bruce Willis in *The Sixth Sense*. That guy outside hadn't talked to me. No one here was talking to me. Oh no — I was not going to spend eternity in heaven after all, I was going to spend it in a converted medical complex in rural Virginia surrounded by a bunch of Internet kooks. Damn.

Then I heard a voice. "David!"

"Michelle!" I hugged her with particular gusto. I'm alive, I'm alive! She looked at me queerly and told me to follow her.

I followed her through the warren to her office. It was the smallest closet with walls and a door ever used as an office. It would have been impossible to lie down in that room. There are straitjackets larger than her office. Worse, it had two desks and two chairs.

She beamed. "Isn't it great?! I've even got a door to the outside." Indeed, there was a door leading outside. That explained the office . . . it was an entryway with walls. Then it dawned on me: This is where kids work to become millionaires. Cool!

There were stacks of paper everywhere. One in particular stood out. An exuberantly beaming man with blow-dried hair and manic-looking eyes adorned the cover of a magazine called *Chief Executive*. Next to the picture were the bold words, "The Prince of E-Commerce: Craig Winn thinks his model will defeat Amazon and dominate Internet Retailing." There were approximately five hundred copies of the magazine in her straitjacket . . . office.

Michelle and I strode down the bland hall past more tiny offices crowded with more frenetic people. Turning past yet another receptionist's cubicle, I saw a beautiful yellow lab with a red bandana around its neck. The pooch loped out to greet Michelle and take a sniff at me. As I bent down to make nice, I noticed a pair of feet crammed into a pair of expensive black loafers. Reaching down toward the dog, I glanced up, like a baseball catcher who decided it would be nice to glance at the stars. The star above me was Craig Winn. Fortunately, his eyes weren't fixed on me but on Michelle. I rose, she introduced us, and the three of us buzzed off to lunch.

I folded into Winn's convertible Jag, and, ignoring me, he began chattering to Michelle about a new idea. "You know those Tear Drop golf people?" he asked. "What if we put a computer link in all golf shops that custom design clubs, so people can order straight from us? It would save people money, enable the golf shops to avoid stocking inventory, get consumers to buy more, and we would book the revenue."

"Wow! Great idea!" she chirped. "You know, my dad works with —"

"We could expand our line of clubs from Tear Drop to include Ping, Callaway, all of them," he interrupted. It was a dialogue with himself that Michelle was allowed to be part of . . . occasionally.

Winn finally glanced at me as we took our seats at Amigo's, a strip-mall dive with faux plaster walls, cartoonish Mexican flags painted on them, and a bunch of dust-covered piñatas dangling from the ceiling. As he talked about the company, Winn's posture changed. His head cocked slightly. He started to glow. I looked for the socket he'd just plugged himself into. "Value America has the seven things consumers want most — quality, value, information, convenience, service, selection, and trust." He rattled through a series of slogans and sound bites. "You can shop in your bathrobe and bunny slippers." "We're down the hall, not down the street." "People don't shop stores, they shop for brands." As he spoke, his confidence and certainty bombarded me. The story he told wasn't just about him or his company. His story emphasized Value America was going to do something *great* for America. It wasn't just a store . . . it gave 1 percent of all revenues to charities. It worked with charities to give them e-commerce sites through custom stores so they could raise money. For me, this was too good to be true — a *for-profit* company with a not-for-profit heart. It was as if Winn knew me and knew what I was interested in, as if he knew I'd spent the past few years building an organization designed to get more funding for the best charities. It never dawned on me he probably did know all that from Michelle. I was smitten.

Had I been Paul Allen or Fred Smith, I probably would have pulled out a checkbook and written something with lots of zeroes. Instead, I was relegated to gazing across the table, infatuated by the vision and by the visionary. I managed to reference David Halberstam's classic work on the Kennedy Administration, *The Best and the Brightest,* and commented he needed to assemble people of serious substance for his company. I was grasping. I wanted him to like me, I wanted him to be impressed, I wanted him to hire me. I hoped it sounded good. It was a good thing Winn didn't know the Halberstam book — it was incredibly *critical* of the "best and the brightest" (a phrase Halberstam uses with bitter irony) in the Kennedy Administration.

Winn glanced at Michelle, squinted his eyes, rocked back and forth, and said, "Exactly, exactly." He looked at Michelle again and laughed. A decision had been reached. I didn't know whether I was headed for Winn-Heaven or Winn-Hell, but I knew that it wouldn't take long to discover.

"Your position is vitally important to me and to the company," he explained. It was, he emphasized, as vital a role as any in the company. My job would be to know *everything* about the company, *everything* about him. I needed to know it all, because I was the one who would be selling it to the media — selling *him* to the media. At times, he said, I'd have to *be* him . . . in writing and sometimes on the phone. For the company to work, he said, looking into my pupils and pausing, my job would have to be performed *perfectly*.

More than anything, I wanted to jump up and down and say, "I can do that! I can do that! I've done that before! I'm good at that! Really, seriously, I can do that." Instead I sat there impassively, looking at him, nodding, trying to look somehow executive-ish.

He paused again, still staring at me. His eyes narrowed. "One more thing. I want all my executives to be r-i-c-h. I don't mean comfortable, I don't mean financially worry-free. I mean *rich*. Everyone has taken a salary cut to come here, but we back it up with a generous stock-option plan. Because of your unique position to me and to the company, you would be eligible for eighty thousand shares over five years. In addition, I want to ensure that all my senior executives receive an additional incentive of five million per year after those five years to keep them in place. How does that sound to you?"

I thought about Bill Clinton's famous jaw-clenching and lip-pursing when he made a key point. I tried it. I clenched my jaw, pursed my lips, squinted, did a full body nod, and said, "That obviously sounds appealing." Inside I was wondering if I could afford a beach house in Nantucket and a ski chalet in Switzerland or whether I'd be forced to choose between the two. It was somehow tragic that my oversize body didn't fit well inside that nice little Jaguar convertible. Perhaps they could customize one to fit me?

We'd made a magical connection. I liked him. I was drawn to him. I wanted his blessing. He liked me. We shook hands. $125,000 a year, $40,000 in potential bonuses based on a standard we would mutually determine, 80,000 stock options vesting over five years. I was going to be a rich man. It felt very, very good.

One more thing he wanted me to know. Some people had been talking to him about running for governor of Virginia in a few years. He was considering it seriously and would love to have my input. He'd recently had dinner with Henry Kissinger. They hit it off. They really hit it off. Kissinger was now, he paused, his adviser. I wasn't sure what Kissinger knew about ending Virginia's personal-property tax or how to solve Beltway congestion, but it sure sounded impressive.

In fact, Winn was more dynamic, more persuasive, than any politician I'd ever met. There was absolutely no doubt in my mind he had political potential. The whole thing was too good to be true. I saw the next decade of my life in perfect perspective. I'd start working at Value America, help build it into the retail equivalent of Microsoft, be Craig Winn's right-hand man, help him get elected governor of Virginia and then maybe make a White House run. Why not?

Too quickly, we were back at the prefabricated office complex known as Hollymead. I was on the phone with Kim at the first possible moment. I chattered dreamily about Winn, about the vision, about the contract he offered me. She was blown away by the deal. We compared it to AOL. If I had had those same options at AOL a month after its IPO, they would now be worth in excess of $100,000,000. That was inconceivable. I was the son of a geophysics professor. We'd grown up comfortably by 1970s standards. We traveled a lot, met lots of interesting people. But money wasn't ever abundant. Kim and I quietly pondered these things. What *would* our life be like with that kind of money? The thought of it was somehow erotic.

I had more meetings to attend. In an ordinary job interview these would be important, but here they seemed to be formalities — even with the CEO. Tom Morgan's office was the antithesis of Craig's. Everything was in perfect order — the kind of perfect order that can't be faked. The kind of perfect order that extends to a top desk drawer meticulously arranged. Morgan was not the outwardly dynamic salesman. He was the consummately professional business executive. We sat down, and for the first time that day I received some questions. Standard interview fare: "Where are you from? Tell me about your past jobs. What have you liked most and least about working in those jobs?" The odd undercurrent we both realized, however, was that they were formalities. Craig kept popping into the office, telling Tom whom I should meet with next. "Have him see Dean and Neal." "See if Steve is around." "Is Rex in or out?" "Glenda is not that important, but see if Tom Starnes is around."

I noticed a strong religious undercurrent running through the company. I'd picked up on it a bit with Craig, had heard about it from Michelle, and soon heard about it from Tom Morgan. "I can't promise you anything about the future of the company," he told me. "Craig is the brightest man I've ever met. We are dependent upon God to make this thing prosper. It is out of our hands. We can only be faithful." I was a spiritually inclined person. I was intellectually overwhelmed by Jesus' teachings and love, but a divorce, work, and the passage of time had led me to a place where I believed in god but not necessarily in God. Something within me longed for God, longed for a great adventure with Him. But I didn't know if that was possible anymore. I knew Morgan and Winn talked about an intense faith commitment — not just about some generic spiritualism. There was something soothing about that — it was familiar. There was also something uncomfortable about it — it made me nervous. But I connected with these two guys. I trusted them. Perhaps they would help me rediscover God in Charlottesville.

Morgan asked me about the financial package Craig had proposed. He seemed relieved it wasn't too outlandish. I tried to buck him up a bit by assuring him it had been a reduction in pay. He paused a moment and contemplated whether he should give me the next piece of advice. "As you know, the stock priced at twenty-three dollars a share and closed trading the first day at fifty-five. The market has been in a downturn lately, and we've dropped a little ground — down to about thirty-three.

If you'd like, we can lock you in at today's price. Given all of the stuff going on here, we don't expect to see thirty-three again unless we split a couple of times."

The strike price is the price at which the company allows you to buy the stock. For early employees — like Joe Page — strike prices were pennies per share. But the later you arrived at a company, the higher the price went. Because I didn't get in prior to the IPO, I missed the pre-IPO strike price. But knowing the dynamic of the e-commerce market, the $33 strike price sounded just fine. Looking ahead a year, I assumed conservatively the stock would be worth $135 per share, not adjusted for any splits. That would mean a paper net worth of more than $8 million, of which 20 percent could be exercised immediately.

Tom Morgan bid me farewell with a signed agreement ensuring my excellent strike price and instructions to meet with Dean Johnson and Neal Harris. Passing still more closets crammed full of droopy-looking people, I headed toward my next set of interviews. I heard two voices in the office yucking it up and knocked on the partially closed door. *"Come!"* a voice boomed. Assuming that voice meant for me to enter, I poked my head hesitantly around the corner.

"Ah, Mr. Kuo, welcome," Johnson enunciated clearly. "I'm not sure why you're meeting with us, since the Master has already spoken, but have a seat."

The other man, like Johnson in his mid-forties, glanced bemusedly at him and said, "Hi, I'm Neal Harris, nice to meet you."

Johnson then grumbled, "Oh yeah, I'm Dean, nice to meet you. I have only one question for you, young man," he articulated crisply. "What are you going to do to get our stock price up?" Neal chuckled.

It was the beginning of an echoing company theme. People were addicted to the stock price. Damn revolutionizing retail. Corporate success wasn't dependent upon making quarters or meeting revenue targets or hitting profitability earlier than expected. It was about the undulating number next to the ticker symbol VUSA. It was beginning to create a morale problem throughout the company. I didn't have a clue what I was going to do to hike the corporate stock price, so I shot back at my new foils, "Hype."

They laughed. "Now I know why Craig likes you so much," Dean lobbed back. That concluded the interview.

It was an unsettling exchange. Why, I wondered, would two senior executives be so cynical about the man who founded Value America? I chalked it up to their lack of comfort with political-type personalities.

I dashed to Keswick Hall Country Club for dinner with another Winn recruit, Jamie Parsons, former *Time* magazine automobile dealer of the year. Winn's goal was to use the Value America model to dominate the auto industry as well. Parsons came highly recommended — he was a top fund-raiser for Jerry Falwell.

At dinner, a beaming Craig Winn introduced me. "As you all know, David Kuo has agreed to join Value America to work with me in communicating this company to the world." Polite applause. "He has worked with Bill Bennett, Jack Kemp, J.C. Watts, Bob Dole, and others. He recently turned down an opportunity to be George W. Bush's communications director. We're glad to have him here."

I smiled and looked at Craig curiously. Would that the latter claim were true. I had indeed been contracted with to write some campaign speeches for Governor Bush, but I'd never been offered a job as his communications director. In fact, my contract hadn't exactly been renewed. There wasn't any shame in that — Bush had gone through other speechwriters before me, and I was still working to raise money for his campaign — but all those details weren't something I wanted people to know. So instead of jumping up and down telling Craig he was wrong in front of the gathered team, confessing I had failed the governor in speechwriting and telling him the governor already had a brilliant and loyal communications director named Karen Hughes, I sat in my chair mute. For this night at least, I'd let him believe the story he was selling.

Two days after my interview, I was back in Charlottesville for an important meeting. Whirlpool had flown in a large part of its executive team for an all-day meeting with Value America's senior staff. Whirlpool was a major target for Value America. It was not only an upper-echelon manufacturer; it had limited its Internet presence to date and was looking for new avenues of distribution and new partners. Winn's agenda was first to get Whirlpool products in the store; second to get Whirlpool to pay for advertising; third to persuade Whirlpool to open a custom store for its employees; and fourth to convince Whirlpool to partner with Value America in a joint venture.

Winn opened the meeting by walking their executives through the

Value America vision. Then he proceeded to bring every senior executive and manager from all the company's divisions before the Whirlpool team to explain, briefly, what they did, where they came from, and how Value America was going to change the world. To someone almost as new to Value America as the Whirlpool executives, it was unambiguously impressive. The person in charge of customer service had been with AT&T when they won the Malcolm Baldridge Award for outstanding customer service. The woman in charge of phone sales had been with Dell at the start of that company. The merchandisers came from elite retail companies — CompUSA, Target, Costco. I was also impressed by my introduction. Like two nights before, it was dramatically embellished. I smiled and nodded and began to wonder about the resumes and credentials of everyone else Winn was introducing. Had they actually done the things he told everyone they'd done? Or was he exaggerating about them, too?

My only break from the meeting was to take a quick phone call from someone who had been recruiting me for a position at Goldman Sachs in New York. Was I, he wanted to know, prepared to fly to New York to meet with their senior executive team the next week? Much to his surprise, I told him I wasn't. He gasped when I told him about my stock options, salary, and bonuses. It wasn't anything Goldman could compete with. He did, however, want to know if he could help me recruit my staff for Value America — he said he'd work for stock options. We both laughed.

The Whirlpool meeting wore on and on. Winn sandwiched every executive presentation with opening and closing commentary of his own. It was as if he had to interpret what each manager said for the Whirlpool executives. When all was finally said and done, Winn wasn't yet said and done. On top of getting products in the store and getting a custom store and advertising monies, there was something else. There was something very, very important.

The important thing was Serve America. For Winn, Serve America was far bigger than Value America. It was also, conveniently, another way to cash in on the Internet craze. It was a whole different company that he alone owned and that he would parcel out very, very cautiously.

Serve America would be a company selling people a device to get online, a dedicated retail site to buy products with a single click, and a commitment to deliver their purchases to their doors the very next day. For Winn, it was even closer to his original grand vision than Value America was, because it was even more comprehensive. Serve America would have five partners — one would provide the Internet hookup; one would provide the device or the computer to access the Net; one would provide the shopping; one would supply the specialized credit card; and one would provide the shipping services. In his mind, Winn saw those partners as AT&T, IBM, Federal Express, FirstUSA, and Value America. Of course, just like the other partners, Value America would have to buy its way into the venture that Winn now exclusively owned.

That being said, he was open to other partners. That was why he brought it up with Whirlpool. Whirlpool should join Value America as part of Serve America.

I sat in the back of the room the whole day, listening, taking notes, trying to get inside Winn's head — to become him from a professional point of view. It was a thoroughly intimidating assignment. As he had been with me, he was in complete control of the Whirlpool meeting. He knew his agenda and made sure his agenda was the only agenda. The thing that staggered me most about the whole day was just how enormous Winn's Value America vision was. It wasn't limited to Value America or to retail. It seemed to encompass the whole Internet universe. If the Value America story sounded good to me secondhand, up close and personal it sounded like the Second Coming — actually better, because it was publicly traded.

Four days after the Whirlpool meeting, on May 10, Value America announced its first-quarter 1999 earnings. The annual growth was incomprehensible. From January through March 1999, the company had revenues of $28 million, a 1,173 percent increase over the $2.2 million from the same period in 1998. More proximately, the Q1 1999 results were nearly 50 percent higher than revenues in Q4 1998. But losses increased as well. While selling about $28 million worth of goods, the company lost nearly $35 million — though nearly $12 million of that loss was an accounting line item to cover the expenses and interest Value America incurred for its post-failed-IPO bridge loan. Because that debt was converted to stock, however, Value America offset the $12 million in expenses with no impact on its cash position.

The overwhelming leader in the loss column was the $17.8 million from sales, advertising, and marketing expenses, including nearly $14 million in ad spending alone. That ad spending, however, was just beginning. Value America made clear in its quarterly filing with the SEC that it would increase ad spending dramatically to grow the company. With its cash in hand, Value America was off to the revenue races.

The loss figure didn't concern anyone inside the company. As the press release read, "Value America intends to continue its emphasis on developing the world's finest e-commerce solutions, hiring the best management talent and driving revenues through its innovative advertising campaigns. The Company believes such expenditures, as well as continued growth in the breadth and depth of brand-name products sold in its online store . . . are critical to achieving scale and customer satisfaction."

Winn added, "Our focus is on building scale and satisfying our customers. We exceeded expectations in both areas." Amazingly, one month after we had gone public, a company press release boasted that Value America was now selling "more than 1,500 brands." Things were accelerating rapidly.

Wall Street and media response to Value America's numbers were muted. There wasn't any explicit criticism of Value America's performance. In a Dow Jones wire report, however, a throwaway sentence about Value America's losses exceeding its revenue suggested perhaps some on Wall Street were beginning to think it might not be *all* about revenue. No one inside Value America paid too much attention to that speculation.

They did, however, pay attention to Amazon.com's Q1 1999 earnings statement. After several quarters of greater-than-expected revenues and greater-than-expected losses, according to the whisper on the Street, Amazon was going to turn the corner with its first-quarter 1999 numbers. Instead of increasing losses, Amazon was expected to announce decreased losses and increasing revenues. It would be the ultimate proof that the "grab customers now, make profits later" strategy paid off.

In fact, the whispers were wrong. Amazon not only announced losses three times greater than a year before, but founder and Internet superhero Jeff Bezos announced losses would increase *indefinitely* as the company built out its distribution and technology infrastructure.

Quietly and suddenly, some investors, analysts, and bankers started discussing whether there were other ways of measuring the worth of Internet companies. Maybe monitoring revenue alone wasn't going to cut it.

A week after Value America's earnings announcement — and a week before I was to officially start at Value America — I was summoned to attend an important Washington, D.C., meeting.

Doug Holladay was a former partner at Goldman Sachs and a spiritual adviser to business executives like Value America's Tom Morgan. Thin, almost gaunt, with an angular face and thinning black hair, Holladay was tan and bubbling over with an athletic energy, like a prep school track star aged twenty-five years. Holladay was also a management consultant to a select cadre of influentials; essentially he was in business to introduce his contacts to his other contacts. To serve Value America's needs, he had arranged a meeting with former three-star general Claude M. (Mick) Kicklighter, former Reagan national security adviser Robert M. (Bud) McFarlane, top political reporter Fred Barnes, and Washington, D.C., attorney Robert Woody.

Everyone had an agenda. Kicklighter was ostensibly interviewing with Winn to become chief of staff, handling all aspects of Winn's life, from the political to the corporate to the philanthropic. A career military man and former commander in chief for the army forces in the Pacific, Kicklighter looked like a very distinguished version of Deputy Dawg, with big eyes, slightly droopy jowls, and a slow, steady style. Approaching sixty, he saw Value America as a potential financial windfall at a moment when he really wanted to help his family. His two grandsons had recently been diagnosed with diabetes. Health insurance wouldn't cover all the long-term costs, and the general wanted to help.

McFarlane, whose fame and infamy grew largely from his participation in the Iran-Contra scandal and a subsequent suicide attempt, needed Fund-raising 101 from Winn. The company he was now involved with had devised a way to convert spent nuclear waste into an inert and harmless gel-like substance. If Winn could raise more than $200 million to fund a virtual store, certainly he could help McFarlane raise a few million to help ease global nuclear-waste buildup.

Woody, tiring of his elite inside-the-Beltway attorney life, was potentially interested in becoming Value America's general counsel. The existing general counsel, Winn's co-founder, Rex Scatena, was not so quietly looking for a way ... any way ... to leave the company. He'd made some money before Value America, had a lot more money now, and wanted the freedom to spend it.

Fred Barnes wanted to see his friend Holladay and meet an almost-local Internet titan. Partners with former vice president Quayle's chief of staff, Bill Kristol, at Rupert Murdoch's political magazine *The Weekly Standard,* Barnes had covered politics at the highest levels for several decades. He was always up for new story ideas.

Looking around the room, Winn knew some divine power was at work. Who else could have orchestrated this stunning event? It wasn't a coincidence. It couldn't be. He smiled, looked deep into everyone's eyes, and mused as to what would most impress this inside-the-Beltway crowd. Connect, connect, connect, he thought. Then it hit him — Kissinger. He told the little group that he had met with Kissinger privately and was amazed by the statesman's reception. Kissinger wanted to work with Winn on some important projects. Together, they were going to start an important new political organization. Included in this organization would be William J. Bennett, former U.S. secretary of education and moral crusader.

Everyone's eyebrows raised and heads cocked curiously, including mine. Only a few days earlier I'd suggested setting up a meeting between Winn and Bennett to occur the last week in May. Bennett was my former boss and close friend. He would be enthusiastically pissed off to hear from Fred he was joining a political organization with some Internet guy he'd never met. Barnes interjected, "Tell me more about this new effort." What was it called? Where was it based? How much funding did it have? What would Bennett and Kissinger be doing for it? This was definitely a story.

Winn wasn't ready to reveal specifics. The important point here, *Fred,* was these great men *believed* in him. He'd brought these men together. They were famous men. Of course the organizational details were highly confidential, and it would jeopardize its success if word got out too soon. Everyone nodded their heads knowingly.

I was mystified by what, exactly, Craig could have been thinking to say something so obviously untrue. But I was also confident there had to be some explanation. Even if there wasn't, it was just a blip. It was like being out on a date with a supermodel and hearing her burp. I was completely infatuated by Winn and his vision. I unreeled another line of slack.

Winn then divulged to the day's confidants the *really big* secret. "I have something very important I want to share with each of you, but especially, Fred, with you." He surveyed the room. All eyes were fixed on him. That his friends might not actually be adoring him — that the stares might be the direct result of everyone's incredulity — didn't appear to dawn on him.

"You all might be familiar with LeClair Ryan. It is the largest and most politically connected Republican law firm in Richmond. Its principals have been responsible for the rise of George Allen, Jim Gilmore, and a host of Virginia's top elected officials. I've been approached by their most senior people about running for statewide office." Winn made a hard stop and a long pause. He needed someone else to ask the next question.

Everyone looked around awkwardly. Finally Barnes, the professional reporter and the one whose schedule was most encroaching on this meeting, bit. "For what office and when?" he asked, curious.

"I will run for governor of the Commonwealth of Virginia in 2005. Because the governor is limited to one term, I will run for the presidency in 2008, serve two terms, and retire. People will, of course, ask the question of why I would *want* to hold public office. They will attack me as a rich outsider. But for me it is all about public service. I mean, for me, moving to the Virginia governor's mansion or even to 1600 Pennsylvania Avenue means moving to a worse house in a worse neighborhood."

Winn marched on. "Value America is my platform. I am currently planning to devote tens of millions of dollars to a Lee Iacocca–style branding campaign that will make me a household name. My wife and I understand, of course, the tremendous loss in privacy this will require, but we are prepared for it. Value America's branding campaign will introduce me to the American people and help pave the way for my political success."

There was silence. Barnes wasn't surprised. Everyone in Washington thought they should be President — why not a billionaire from Charlottesville? Kicklighter was even impressed. He was drawn to Craig as military leaders are drawn to the strong political leaders whose orders they must execute. Attorney Bob Woody, who also spent a lifetime around politics, was speechless. Doug Holladay did what he always did. He smiled, nodded with his whole body, clapped his hands, and said, "Well, that's great."

I thought Winn's timing was a bit odd, but I was thoroughly impressed that Virginia politicos had shown interest in him. Things were getting better and better. The Value America world I was trying to learn was merging with the political world I knew, and the net effect was a dizzyingly exciting ride.

The meeting continued for another hour as Craig expounded on his policy ideas. As the meeting broke up, Winn cornered Kicklighter and strolled off with him and Holladay. Fred Barnes ambled over to me. "David, are you sure about this guy?" I looked at him, raised one eyebrow, and nodded heartily. Duh.

CHAPTER SEVEN

Evangelizing

Value America's board had evolved from a hodgepodge of Winn's friends at the founding to a collection of heavyweights. Fred Smith joined it. Paul Allen appointed Bill Savoy to represent his interests. Other friends had introduced executive search firm Heidrick & Struggles chairman Gerry Roche to the team. Mike Steed represented the union money, and another friend of his, Tom Casey, vice chairman of the hugely successful telecommunications giant Global Crossing, was on as well. To each of these new board members, the chance to serve on a hot dot.com board was their chance to be part of the new Big Thing.

The grown-up theme played well with investors. Because Value America had a former *Fortune* 500 CEO at the helm and a seasoned entrepreneur as its founder, it could be trusted. Value America wasn't going to spend recklessly — it was going to pursue grown-up business strategies and do so with a high-profile board overseeing things.

Bill Bennett fit this image perfectly.

Bill Bennett had been my boss for more than two years and my friend for nearly five more. Next to my father, he was the man I most admired. And Value America was my gift to him — an Internet company where he could make a ton of money and serve alongside some of America's business titans.

I picked up Winn and Jamie Parsons, the new head of Value America's automotive division, from the private air terminal at Reagan National Airport on May 20. The two men had jetted up for the meeting from Charlottesville. *Jetting* was actually not the appropriate word. They had puttered their way to D.C. in Craig's plane.

Winn loved to fly and had become quite good at it. His aircraft of choice, a Cessna single-engine, was a fine, safe, exciting plane. But it lacked certain things — a second engine for instance. It also lacked pressurization, individual seats, air-conditioning, heat, jets, mass, and peanuts. Sitting inside the plane was rather like sitting inside a carnival ride — cramped and musty with a hint of danger. It made the little commercial puddle jumpers most people try to avoid look rather like the *Spruce Goose*. Michelle had told me about the plane and her perceived near-misses with death. I was determined to avoid flying in it at all costs.

To Craig, however, the plane was more akin to either a 747 or an F-14, depending upon his mood. He talked about the bird like it could cross the Himalayas. He'd installed tens of thousands of dollars' worth of the latest equipment to make it safer and more fun to fly. To novice single-engine flyers, however, it looked more like someone had strapped a lawnmower engine to the front of a carnival ride. Of course, now that Value America had navigated its way through an IPO, the little Cessna wasn't an appropriate company plane. Executives of hot public companies needed something much more significant — something with jets and professional pilots. That would come sometime in June, probably. Maybe sooner. If it meant avoiding the single-engine plane, I hoped for sooner.

The two men survived the trip intact and were excited about the meeting, as we made our way to Bennett's offices overlooking the White House and Old Executive Office Building. Seating Winn and Parsons in the reception area, I rushed in to prep Bennett for the meeting. "I've never made a business introduction for you before," I reminded him. "These guys are first-rate. Winn is a bit of a salesman, but the business plan is genius, and he's got great people like Fred Smith around him." I thought I sounded like I was on speed. He smiled and nodded his head. I found myself using the names Fred Smith and Paul Allen like pronouns — they populated every reference to Value America and every description of the company. I was just nervous; this convergence of friends and business colleagues was maybe a bit too intimate.

As Bennett lumbered toward the conference room, I headed to collect Winn and Parsons from the lobby. "Remember, free and easy," I implored, smiling at them both. Winn, game face on, reached down for his laptop.

Bennett, shy by nature, and Winn, shy by nature and gregarious by will, exchanged stilted hellos. Parsons, genuinely gregarious, piped in, "I understand your wife, Elayne, is an NC girl."

"A Tri-Delt," Bennett said proudly, referring to his wife's UNC sorority pedigree. Tri-Delt was the pinnacle of UNC sororities, and Elayne, beautiful, smart, and professionally accomplished, was the top Tri-Delt — and now the head of Best Friends, one of the nation's leading teen-empowerment programs.

Parsons grinned admiringly. "That's a good thing."

"You bet," Bennett volleyed right back.

Winn watched the exchange with the awkwardness of a new kid on the block. He kept fiddling with his laptop, eager to open it up and get things moving.

Parsons and Bennett, meanwhile, were chatting about mountain climbing — a passion for both men. Bennett was animatedly talking about the apparent discovery of the remains of famed Everest climbers Mallory and Irvine. Parsons was recounting his own thoughts on their famous, doomed expedition. From the other side of the table, Winn piped in, "I once went climbing with Tenzing Norgay," the famous Sherpa who led Sir Edmund Hillary up Everest for the first successful summit. The conversation ceased, and all heads whipped around toward Winn. Tenzing Norgay was a big deal, especially to Bennett. He looked expectantly at Winn. Craig had nothing more to add. But, like the correct answerer of a *Jeopardy!* question, he was now in control of the board, and up came the laptop.

The Value America logo with the swirling globe filled the screen as Winn set himself to selling Bennett on his company. The screen faded into text proclaiming "the marketplace for a new millennium." Now I was forlorn as I glanced at Parsons, who just raised an eyebrow in bewilderment. Bennett, meanwhile, was looking alternately at the computer screen and at me with dumbstruck wonder. As his former staffer I knew Bill didn't like sitting through packaged presentations. He wanted facts, dialogue, exchange. He looked at me in a way I'd seen many times before. It said, "Kuo, what, exactly, have you gotten me into?" Winn by now was chattering through the fourth screen.

"Great, great, yeah, got it, uh-huh, next," Bennett said, as Winn started talking faster and faster. He never changed his script, just the pace at which he delivered it. When, as now, things didn't seem to be going quite as well as planned, the volume would increase, as did the grand descriptions of the company. Value America wasn't simply "a leader." It became a "world-class leader." Its technology wasn't just "leading," it was "world-class and proprietary." Its potential wasn't just "great," it had the "power to transform the world."

Winn was up to his disclosure of Fred Smith's generous praise of the company. "I called Fred the other day," Bennett blurbed. "Haven't heard back yet."

Winn struck. Pulling out his wallet, he removed a bit of paper, much like a kid revealing the secrets of the magic decoder ring he got in this morning's cereal. "Do you have Fred Smith's *private* line?"

"No," Bennett replied.

"Here, let me give it to you."

"Don't want it."

"His secretary will answer and patch you right through. Otherwise, you'll never get through."

"I don't want it."

"Here, do you have a pen?"

"*I don't want the number.* If Fred Smith wants to call me back, he will. If he doesn't, he won't," Bennett thundered.

Hearing Bill for the first time, Craig sheepishly placed the magic number back in his wallet. Silence abounded.

I watched the whole exchange with wide-eyed horror. This meeting was supposed to be a gift to my friend and make me look like someone who could deliver significant connections for Value America. I sat back — way back — in my chair, wanting to say anything that would be — take your pick — witty, funny, helpful, diversionary, interesting, racy. My mind was thoroughly blank.

Parsons saved the day. "Say, Dr. Bennett," he inquired happily, "what's your favorite fourteener in the lower forty-eight?"

Back now on the firm ground of mountain climbing and relationship building, the conversation found its way to some semblance of comfort. Bennett left, saying he'd think it over, consult with his lawyer and brother Bob Bennett, President Clinton's counsel, and get back to Winn. He shook Winn's and Parsons's hands, arched his eyebrow at me, and smiled. We gathered our stuff and left.

Bennett was actually already sold. Value America made sense to him. It did well — it donated money to charities, and it had a world-class board. Plus, it was in the e-commerce space. That could mean some significant dollars. What could possibly go wrong? His only real hesitation was the lack of connection he felt with the chairman, but he chalked that up to first-go-round jitters and didn't give it much thought. After all, if he prejudged someone in D.C. for spouting crap, he'd never be able to do business with *anyone.*

Chugging back to Charlottesville in his windup airplane, Winn was confident that he had landed Bennett. He was also intent on getting Jamie Parsons to develop the automotive side of the company as soon as possible. People hated the car-buying process even more than they hated going to the dentist. Value America's inventoryless model was tailor-made for selling cars — and eventually trucks and maybe even airplanes. He told Parsons to take $20 million and just get it done. It's not important if you lose that $20 million, he added. What's important is getting the business built *fast.*

Parsons balked. He didn't want that much money. He didn't need that much money. He wanted to grow the business slowly — develop a plan, set benchmarks, grow regionally, make money from day one.

Winn respected Parsons's sincere intentions. He would, however, have to educate his new friend in the ways of the Internet world.

Four days later, I walked into Value America's offices around 7:00 A.M. for my first official day of work, hoping for an office other than Michelle's former one. In fact, I immediately saw two people crammed into her old space. Uh-oh. Now I began to wonder if I even *had* someplace to sit. Every office looked occupied except for one nice-size one three doors down from Winn. Poking my head in, I saw two notes on the desk. One simply said, "Kuo." The other asked that I pen a press release announcing Value America's new automotive division. My first official assignment. I was officially a dot.commer. Even better, I was a dot.commer with a door to send my work out of. I was stylin'.

My office, I was informed some minutes later, had been personally selected by the chairman for its proximity to his office. And my new title had been selected by Winn as well: *senior vice president* of communications. I wasn't just a VP of PR. That felt *good.*

That morning, scores of people dropped by to say hi, congratulate me on my new position, and ask me, as casually as they could manage, how I was going to get the company's stock back up. I was surprised to learn I was Value America's Viagra. That morning, the company dropped below $20 a share for the first time. The drop didn't have any impact on how the company operated on a day-to-day basis; with its $130 million–plus IPO take in the bank, Value America wasn't exactly hurting for cash — even though it was burning through about $12 million a month. But for company morale, it wasn't a great thing.

I didn't care. Stock went up, stock went down. No big thing. My mind was set a year or two down the road. I didn't have any doubt Value America was going to succeed. My biggest concern was whether I could still readjust my stock option strike price. It was sweet of Tom Morgan to price it at $35 a share when we'd met a few weeks earlier, but it was now $19 a share. If Morgan could adjust my strike price to the day's $19 share price, I'd be golden. By the time it hit $100 a share — which was sure to happen — my options would be worth that much more.

Value America was hardly alone in its stock downturn. In late May 1999, nearly every other e-tailer was being hit hard as well. Amazon had declined 20 percent, and many other companies that had gone public with Value America were similarly down. Cyberian Outpost, a big online computer retailer, was down more than 40 percent, Beyond.com, a software company, 35 percent. IVillage 55 percent.

But the list of deal possibilities was lengthy — the AFL-CIO, American Heart Association, and American Cancer Society just in the custom store area. Whirlpool would certainly come through soon. Intel was considering launching a branded Intel computer in partnership with Value America, and there were rumors about partnerships with Apple and Compaq. There were possibilities for the Serve America launch, and there were literally scores of other deals I'd heard rumblings about. The stock might be down, but every bit of logic pointed to an inescapable conclusion: Value America would be back. Value America always came back.

Not only did Value America have computer-sales traction, it was committed to building the best e-commerce engine in the world. An important part of that building process was the implementation of an "enterprise resource protocol" made by a German company, SAP. SAP was an amazingly complex software system originally designed to help big manufacturers manage their supply chain. Because SAP tracked and integrated every gruesome detail of the manufacturing process, the company could manage an entire production chain simultaneously. Value

America's interest in SAP was borne of a desperate need to manage its inventoryless system. Because there were so many moving parts and because all those parts needed to be flawlessly coordinated, Value America operated as much like a manufacturer as it did a conventional retailer. Fulfilling orders required coordinating numerous warehouses and shipping companies simultaneously. The interest in SAP was also borne of the reportable condition from the failed 1998 IPO.

Typically it took a year or more to install SAP and get it running — best-case scenario. Value America would be the first e-commerce company to implement SAP, and we boasted we would fully employ the system in less than six months from start to finish — a new record.

Moments into my first day, Tom Morgan strolled into my office wearing all black; the combination of all Armani black in the hickish setting of Charlottesville was almost jarring. One of the divisions of his former company, US Office Products, was close to a deal with Value America, he informed me. Mail Boxes Etc. would accept deliveries to city apartments at local Mail Boxes Etc. locations. In addition, there would be a small Value America kiosk in every Mail Boxes Etc. store. This was just added to the list of deal possibilities.

"Oh," he said, "and I think we need to have an announcement today on our deal with MIM Pharmaceuticals." MIM Corporation — which was, among other things, a prescription mail-order service — would enable Value America to branch out into the online drugstore business, expanding health and beauty offerings as well as offering prescription drugs. Now Value America shoppers could get Prozac and Prell. It seemed to be a nice, if not altogether sexy, deal.

Unless I was missing something, there was no news here. From what I could tell, Value America had simply agreed with this company to sell products. It was akin to Macy's announcing that it had decided to sell Teva sandals. Nice, interesting, hope you sell a lot, but that ain't real news.

Bill Hunt was a merchandiser in charge of, among other things, health and beauty aids. "Quick question," I asked him, skipping formalities. "Is there anything more to this MIM deal than the fact that we're now able to sell some prescription drugs and health and beauty aids?"

"Well, you see, actually, this is mostly Craig's deal. A couple weeks ago we met with Jerry Falwell, and Falwell mentioned this company in

New York he had a relationship with and thought it would be a good fit for us. So we did it."

I hadn't realized Jerry Falwell was one of our business rainmakers. To me, he was still the guy who believed one of the Teletubbies was leading our youth down the road to Sodom and Gomorrah. I understood the business potential he had for Value America. But I also knew that in the information age, perception was more real than reality. Value America couldn't be labeled as some right-wing wacko crusade. That, I knew, wouldn't sell.

"Got a second?" I asked, poking my head into Winn's office. Winn responded with a Cheshire grin. I came to understand the Cheshire grin was not the result of any particular accomplishment or guilt, it was simply the default. When in doubt, grin . . . big. "Two quick questions. First, what is your one-sentence description of Value America? Second, what is the real value to the MIM thing?"

No more Cheshire grin. Winn looked rather disquieted. "First, I don't believe in sound-bite descriptions. There is no way to relate the revolutionary story of Value America in just one sentence." All my internal voices sang in harmony, "Run away!" It was a virtual symphony of fear.

I pressed on. "*But,* if Amazon is the world's-biggest store, and if AOL is the Internet-based worldwide media company, and if Sony is the global electronics and computer giant, what, exactly, are we?"

"We . . . are . . . Value America . . . the *marketplace for a new millennium.* I *thought* you understood that."

"I do understand that, I do, I really do, but what do we actually do that no one else does? What differentiates us from the e-commerce masses? Are we just a general online retailer? Are we Amazon in drag? What, exactly, are we? That's all I was asking."

Clearly frustrated that his star hire had turned village idiot in only a morning, he sputtered, "You tell me. How do you communicate that we give one percent of revenues to charity, that we don't have any inventory, that we have more products than anyone else, that we give consumers the seven things they want and businesses the four things they need, and that we are the next retail revolution? — in a single sentence."

I punted and moved on to the need of the moment. What, I asked, is the news with MIM?

"We have entered into a revolutionary new phase in the company where we are expanding exponentially into new areas. No one else is selling this vast array of stunning products on the Internet. Value America is the first — *that* is a big story."

He had a point. Value America was now selling products in more than twenty-five categories — far more than anyone else on the Internet. Winn saw the MIM relationship as the next step in that progression.

I asked him what quote he wanted in the release. He asked me if my pen and paper were ready. "The pharmaceutical industry benefits from Value America's unique multimedia presentations, which allow drug manufacturers to effectively communicate both benefits and usage information for their products. This serves both consumers and manufacturers. In addition, Value America's unique ability to efficiently unite producers and consumers will make health care more affordable."

I stared blankly at Winn. In my mind I tried to visualize a multimedia product demonstration for Band-Aids. First, fall down and scrape your knee. Next, stand up, cry, and ask for your mommy. Cut to Mommy opening up this wonderful, colorful, and revolutionary "wound protection device" to help you feel better. I just didn't see it. I also didn't see how our store was going to unite producers and consumers to make health care more affordable. Health-care costs were, after all, an issue only slightly more vexing than online retail. I tried to put my raging ignorance in perspective by reminding myself it was just my first day. I'd learn more quickly.

My press release was greeted by collective media silence.

Despite the rhetoric of Value America's product comprehensiveness, it seemed clear to me Value America was a one-stop shop modeled not after Harrods or even after a local Wal-Mart, where everything could be found under one roof. Instead, it was based on the Price Club/Costco/ SAM'S Club model.

Almost all of Winn's top people came from Price Club/Costco, and they knew there was absolutely nothing objectively wrong with the Price Club/Costco approach. It worked very well for that company. But what Price Club couldn't promise was the world's greatest selection of the world's greatest products. At any given point in time at any given Price Club store, customers would find a vast array of different products. For instance, Price Club's merchandisers might come across ten thousand red and blue Polo shirts. Polo might have made too many, some store might not have needed what they'd originally ordered, Ralph Lauren might have simply consulted the stars one morning and been informed he needed to increase the level of red and blue in his personal aura — whatever. Price Club would buy them for a song, double the price — a somewhat low margin for a big retailer — and peddle them in as many stores as possible.

Shoppers, meanwhile, who'd come to the store that day to pick up bulk groceries — perhaps twenty-five pounds of peanut butter and one hundred rolls of Charmin — would stroll by the well-placed allotment of red and blue Polo shirts and say, "Golly gee, Stan, would ya look at that? — genuine Polo shirts for only $29.95! We gotta get us some of those." The Polo shirts disappeared, Price Club made a pile of money, and consumers delighted in the Price Club shopping adventure. When shoppers returned for their next spree, they wouldn't find any Polos, but they might find some great Nike sneakers or perhaps a hot digital camera or a collector's edition of Disney's *Pocahontas*.

This adventure-shopping mentality, combined with limited membership, created a certain air of happy exclusivity. Never mind that basically anyone could become a member — show a bowling card or a library card and you'd probably qualify. The point was that people paid for the privilege of the rousing shopping experience. Did they really need ten-pound canisters of beef jerky or bundles of toilet paper as large as a desk? Sure they did — as much as they needed those Polo shirts.

For an e-shopper browsing Value America's store in mid-1999, a vast array of product categories was displayed, suggesting vast comprehensiveness of products. One could reasonably assume Value America was the opposite of Price Club: Here was, well, *everything*. Such an assumption would prove grossly mistaken. Often, within those categories there were only one or two items. Yes, Value America carried New Balance sneakers, but of the eighty-plus styles, VA offered only one. There were books, but only about forty best sellers. Amana had only about three stoves in the store. In short, Value America promised to be a one-stop shop, but to many it looked more like a closeout basement.

By the time I arrived, this situation was the source of some internal tension. Winn, Harris, and the merchandisers all believed there weren't any real problems with this approach. It worked for Price Club, it worked for SAM'S Club, it worked for Costco, it would work for Value America. They believed consumers liked coming to the store and finding one or two great products at great prices. More products would come in time, and consumers would come back. Another camp, however, included Dean Johnson and Glenda Dorchak, who were greatly concerned by the dearth of selections. From a marketing and advertising perspective, Value America was promising to be a vast warehouse of products and was instead an online garage sale. In the midst of this disagreement, Tom Morgan tried to see both sides and understand how to rectify the situation.

The product-placement issue highlighted an odd dynamic that was developing inside Value America. Winn was growing insulated from the daily criticisms and concerns that go with managing day-to-day operations. Every executive and manager found it easier to approach the easygoing Morgan than to be confronted by the hard-charging Winn. Morgan tried to apprise Winn of these criticisms and concerns, but he found what others before him found — Winn always had a persuasive answer for why any given criticism or concern wasn't really a concern if you properly understood the situation.

Case in point: the products. Winn told Morgan it would certainly be dandy to have everything under the sun available at Value America. There should ideally be fifty kinds of Nikes and Adidas and Asics. The goal was to reach the point where that was reality. But in the meantime, it was important to have *some* of those products on sale in the store for consumers who wanted to purchase them. Lacking a retail background and the confidence to confront Winn on the spot, Morgan agreed, the matter was shelved, and the dissenters just talked quietly among themselves.

A little more than a week later, I was sitting at my desk, digging through piles of unopened mail and unread magazines, when I came across a mid-May Goldman Sachs report on the key metrics for predicting e-commerce success. Evaluating all the companies selling goods online, Goldman settled on a best case and worst case for success. The best bets for success were companies with the highest gross margins. Simply put, gross margin is the difference between what a company pays for a product and how much it charges for the product. The greater the difference, the greater the gross margin. The rationale was that gross margin reflected a company's eventual ability to reach profitability. Goldman recognized companies had to spend tens of millions of dollars building their brand. But once the advertising spend curtailed, it was the gross margin that would eventually become the net margin. In other words, unless a company had high enough gross margins to offset its standard non-brand-growth expenses, it would never hit profitability. As Goldman surveyed the landscape, it concluded Amazon was the best bet for success. Because most of Amazon's business was in high-margin categories like books, CDs, and videos, it could count on standard gross margins of more than 35 percent. Once Amazon curtailed its hefty advertising and building expenses, it would, according to Goldman, demonstrate nice, tidy profits. It might, perhaps, even justify its lofty $30 billion valuation.

Goldman also found a worst bet for success. Value America.

Value America's gross margins, the report pointed out, were closer to 1 percent. Value America was driving sales by charging, on average, 1 percent more for merchandise than it cost the company. If a printer cost us $200, for example, we charged $202 and kept the difference. Goldman calculated Value America would need to increase its revenues more than 150-fold to make a profit. Put another way, Value America would need billions in revenue to ever approach profitability. Alternatively, according to Goldman, Value America would have to raise its gross margins (to about 20 percent) or cut expenses down to .1 percent of revenue — not likely this side of retail nirvana.

So over Diet Coke and Krispy Kremes, I discovered the wonderful news as to why our stock was falling faster than a dead star. The most influential investment bank in the world had issued a report four weeks earlier damning our business. I processed. There were two ways to look at it. One, every institution that might have considered buying the stock now wouldn't. Every day trader who was trying to work the stock up was now passionately shorting it. The other way to look at it, however, was to see it as I saw it — a challenge we would overcome. Metrics, it seemed, came and went like menopausal hot flashes. We would persevere. We would definitely win this race. Every company, from Microsoft to Apple Computers to AOL, suffered through periods of criticism and skepticism. Apple was pronounced dead and ready for the grave in 1997. By late 1998, it had the iMac and a lot of momentum. Microsoft was considered a relic of the computing past when Apple came out with the Macintosh's icon-based operating system in 1984. By 1999, it was arguably the most valuable company on earth. AOL saw its stock fall off a cliff during the so-called access crisis in 1995, when it was overwhelmed with subscribers. By 1999, AOL was rivaling Microsoft for global dominance. The new economy may be ruthless in its judgment, but it also makes Phoenix-like rebirths possible. And Value America hadn't even crashed. We were just on a moderately bumpy stretch.

Running the report by Dean Johnson seemed an appropriate first step. *"Come!"* he again bellowed as I knocked on the door. I gave him the lowdown, shifting from "the sky is falling" to "boy, aren't the people at Goldman Sachs complete idiots?" to "you know, this is exciting, we know where to focus now."

"Yeah, I know," he said. "Anything else?" No, that was all. I ambled out, feeling like the dunce in a kindergarten class. Why wouldn't the CFO of our public company be obsessed with a report by the most influential investment bank in the world? Especially when they kicked our teeth out? I clearly needed to learn a lot more about this business thing.

Johnson, however, had partially checked out. With Morgan's arrival, Johnson was a level removed from Winn, and he felt increasingly incapable of influencing events. He knew this was trouble and would talk about it with Morgan later, but he wasn't about to engage me in a long discussion. It wasn't really his problem anymore. It was quite literally above his pay grade.

Tom Morgan was next on my list. Matter-of-factly telling him about the report seemed to deliver a more satisfying impact than my interaction with Dean. Morgan was miffed; not only hadn't he seen the report for a month, he didn't know what to do about it. Value America was into the final month of 1999's second quarter, in which it aimed to achieve $35 million in revenue. We couldn't suddenly boost prices. Of course higher prices would improve the gross-margin picture, but it would also depress sales. We couldn't miss the quarter's sales figures — that *would* be death. There were probably ways to squeeze a couple points of margin out of the quarter, but that would require some detailed accounting work and still wouldn't address the bigger problem Goldman had pointed out. Value America *did* have low margins. It was *designed* that way.

As originally conceived, Value America, like Price Club, was going to charge membership fees. Each $20 annual fee was going to translate into almost $20 of pure profit for the company. Winn extrapolated from industry data that Value America would likely have more than two hundred thousand paying members, each spending $20 for the privilege of getting the low Value America prices. That would mean $4 million in pure profit to a company that anticipated total revenues of about $150 million in 1999. In business terms, that would have significantly enhanced gross margin. Unfortunately, however, Value America had long ago tossed the membership idea, because no one, save pornographers, was successfully charging membership fees on the Web.

Morgan and I walked in to see Craig. If Morgan was miffed, Winn was mad . . . literally. He turned blue. Craig Winn *hated* stupid people, and the idiots who wrote this report were clearly *very* stupid people. "These people just don't *get* it," he said with attempted, but ultimately futile, restraint. He fumed that these Internet analysts knew nothing about how retail worked. He fumed that they pulled all the strings.

After Morgan left, Winn pulled me aside. He leaned against his desk, folded his arms, and sighed softly. Retail was a formulaic beast, he explained. Price was what caused customers to abandon their loyalty to one store and shop at another. That was just a fact of retail life. It's why new stores have grand-opening sales. Since it was necessary to acquire customers via price, offering lower prices initially despite lower gross margins was a necessary part of the business equation. That was, he told me, why gross margin wasn't a leading indicator of eventual business success. It was variable. Price gets customers. You have to have low gross margins to start with. You raise them later. It is retail's axiom: Get customers on price, keep them on service. Nordstrom overstaffs and overtrains its sales team because it knows if it serves its customers better than anyone else does, then higher prices won't matter. People will come back for the service. Price gets customers and service keeps customers. It was retail's greatest truism. But none of these basic retail realities were in any way reflected in the Goldman report. One way or another, Winn was determined to change this. It was Wall Street versus Craig A. Winn. It wasn't that big a challenge. Really, it was just a sales job.

Winn looked me in the eye like he was telling me an intimate secret. Value America *could* and *would* make money, he said passionately, measuring each word. Together, he reminded me, we were going to tell that to the world.

First, he said, he was working on a membership plan that might work. Instead of a flat membership fee for everyone, people could buy into different membership plans. A gold plan that cost $50 a year might enable consumers to get 15 percent off every product. A silver plan at $30 a year would translate into a 10 percent discount. There could be multiple plans, all of which would reward Value America with pure profit. Second, and more important, he pointed out that even without the membership fees, Value America would still make money. The key, he reminded me, was in the inventoryless model — something Goldman probably didn't, indeed *couldn't,* take into account because it was so revolutionary. Without having to pay for overhead, Value America could charge low prices and still make money.

And just like that, my worries vanished. Winn had entrusted me with his innermost thoughts and concerns. And you know what? I was going to kill for this guy. I was going to *make* the press coverage come through. It didn't matter if it was a MIM release or a leveraged buyout of AT&T. I was going to deliver for Winn. I was also going to recruit as many of my friends as possible into what I knew was the future not only of the Internet but of retail . . . Value America.

CHAPTER EIGHT

Wrenching

My timing had once been uncanny. I could make it from my Arlington home to Capitol Hill in twenty-two minutes. It didn't seem to matter how many lights I hit, how fast I went, or how much traffic there seemed to be. But I hadn't made the trek in several years, so I gave myself thirty minutes to get from my house to the meeting with Craig Winn and U.S. senator John McCain. Thirty-five minutes into the trip, running at breakneck — for me — speed toward the Russell Senate Office Building, I cursed overpopulation, suburban sprawl, and the greenhouse effect. How could it have taken me that long?

It was the first week in June, and I was sure my boss was going to have my head on a platter. How could I be late for such an important meeting?

Winn had already been down to Austin, Texas, in March with Jerry Falwell to meet Gov. George W. Bush. Bush, Winn thought, was likable enough, but he didn't strike Winn as being very Reaganesque. Plus, his advisers didn't seem all that sharp. So Winn figured he'd shop around and meet the competition. He'd seen Congressman John Kasich and liked him a lot but thought he was a bit too young. He knew the Forbes family and didn't see brother Steve as presidential timber. That really left only McCain, a true American hero and someone Winn felt deserved to be President of the United States.

Winn regularly told people he had already had breakfast once with the senator. It was in New York during the spring road show, when the team was at the St. Regis Hotel. The hole in Winn's story was that although they ate breakfast together, they didn't *have* breakfast together. McCain was sitting at his table conducting his meeting, and Winn was at his table conducting his meeting. Now they were really going to meet — without me.

I walked quickly through Russell's great, echoing marble halls and was reminded that this old building where I used to work was a perfect Hollywood picture of what Capitol Hill should look like. Rounding the last corner before McCain's office, I saw Winn. Expecting the worst, I began my traffic soliloquy. Winn just looked at me with a growing smile and said, "Don't worry about it. People get late. It's OK. No need to worry." He opened the door to McCain's office for me and waved his arm for me to enter. I just *loved* this guy.

I was so enamored with my boss that I almost smacked into the senator. Senator McCain stood there ready for us with his trademark crooked smile. He put his arm around Winn and guided him slowly into his office. Value America's media consultant, Greg Stevens, and I followed them in. The senator launched into his vision for America. It was his stump pitch, something he had repeated so many times he could say it backward. It was exactly like Winn's Value America pitch in that way. Winn interjected from time to time with his own sales pitch about Value America. The two men stumped away at each other with their pitches.

Winn was impressed. McCain was real. He wasn't afraid to fight. He wasn't afraid to lose. Sure, Winn knew McCain was an underdog, but so what? McCain was the guy he wanted to support for President. He told McCain that right then and there. McCain wanted just one thing from Winn — money. If McCain's campaign was going to make it against the money-raising juggernaut from Austin, he was going to need money. Winn promised he'd host a Charlottesville fund-raiser and get McCain at least $100,000.

Winn was so excited by his proximity to power that I didn't know quite how to tell him he was being used. It wasn't that McCain *didn't* like him. It was just that McCain, at that point in a presidential race, was incapable of *not* liking him. If someone — especially someone with money — shows interest, the candidate will like him. Winn may have understood that, but the dizzy-in-love look in his eyes suggested otherwise.

Winn floated out of the meeting, and I followed along, trying to hold his tether. I dropped him off at the airport and promised I'd see him back in Charlottesville in three hours. I was avoiding the little Cessna as long as I could. Winn didn't seem to mind. I really did love the guy.

Walking back into the office that afternoon, I saw that another Winn hire, General Kicklighter, was moving into his new office. Kicklighter had accepted Winn's offer to be his chief of staff. It wasn't clear to anyone what exactly a chief of staff did for an Internet company, but it was clear General Mick was the man for the job. His assignment was to introduce order and discipline to everything from Winn's schedule to the promises he made in meetings. Nothing was going to fall through the cracks. Kicklighter was also going to help run Winn's new charitable foundation and his political action committee. Winn planned to endow each with $5 million.

The shift out of the military was a genuine shock for the general. The very recently retired three-star had just vacated a five-office suite in the Pentagon. He was now sitting in an 8 x 10 cell overlooking a small parking lot. Surrounding him were boxes some nice lieutenant had packed for him. Actually, for most of the past decade some nice lieutenant or major or colonel had done everything for him.

I poked my head in to say hi. Turning his chair toward me, he stood up, stiffened his back, looked me over with soft eyes, and said, "Good afternoon, David. How are you?" It was the general's way. He taught us all to stand when someone entered the room.

At various points in his career, he had had everything from a top-of-the-line Gulfstream jet to a chauffeured car and a butler at his disposal. Now he was trying to figure out how exactly one opens cardboard boxes with twenty-five layers of tape. He also looked at the boxes and tried to figure out which was which. It was clear he was going to have to choose — no way all those pictures would fit in his new digs. He wanted to find that signed Mother Teresa picture. *That* was a woman of God. It would be fun to put the Stephen Spielberg picture right next to it. Opening the boxes, he instead found the picture his troops gave him when he retired from commanding the army forces in the Pacific.

Sans secretaries and assistants, he looked a bit lost amid the pile of boxes and stacks of magazines. He picked up one, *Yahoo! Internet Life,* looked at it quizzically, and asked if I wanted it. I took it and the whole pile of Internet-related magazines. He didn't object.

Meanwhile, Craig Winn had been working on a secret weapon: the store was going to sell a magic wrench. Some guy and his son had invented the gadget and were looking for ways to sell it. Winn looked at it, played with it, and knew *everyone* needed a wrench like this. Instead of fumbling with a bunch of different-size wrenches while trying to tackle a project, a handyman could use this single wrench with its patented features that made it automatically adjust to the appropriate-size nut. Winn tested it on each of his digits. In addition, the wrench tightened nuts in close quarters. It was truly an ingenious design. This wrench was going to be the first item sold on Value America's new infomercials. While it couldn't cut through aluminum cans and slice tomatoes neatly, it was still pretty awesome. Winn figured he could sell a million.

Infomercials are ridiculously easy to make. All they require is a soundstage, a script, a cheesy host, some local TV airtime, and a bunch of people at a call center waiting for the orders to come rolling in. The basic calculus is that if you put a product out there, talk about it appealingly, make it sound important, and make it easy to afford, people will buy it. As if to prove that point, most infomercials ran around 2:00 A.M. in cities from Los Angeles to Rome, Georgia. There, in the middle of the night, insomniacs would flip past the tenth airing of SportsCenter, stop at an infomercial, tune in, and find happiness because they finally discovered that gadget they'd always wanted.

Winn tasked the company's advertising team with crafting a script and pricing production costs. He, meanwhile, would negotiate the deal with the wrench men so both parties would be winners in what was sure to be a very profitable venture.

A few days later, Bill Bennett called Winn to ask if he was still wanted for the Value America board. He wasn't sure he could add much on the business side, but he'd love to do what he could. Winn enthusiastically embraced the newest and most valued American. In addition to the magic wrench and Bill Bennett, Value America was slowly but surely recovering some of its lost stock momentum. After Value America hit a $16 low, Winn and I orchestrated our public-relations blitz to turn that around. It worked. It started on June 2, when the hyperinfluential business weekly *Barron's* published a devastating story detailing how Amazon was destined to fail. Amazon, the article argued, had lost its "virtualness." The company now had about 2.7 million square feet in warehouse space that cost them nearly $50 million in 1999 alone — about 5 percent of revenues, a figure in line with the costs of traditional retailers. On top of that, Amazon.com was losing market share to companies like barnesandnoble.com, borders.com, and buybooks.com. At the same time, *Barron's* argued that Amazon was late getting into other industries, like technology and computers. Their business strategy of acquiring (or investing in) a lot of smaller companies — an auction house, online drugstore, online pet store, and online groceries — was similarly criticized, because Amazon faced stiff competition in these industries that hadn't proven profitable either.

Winn and I decided to do an old-fashioned pile-on. This was a big no-no in business. In business, companies are simply supposed to focus on their core strategy, regardless of what the competition is doing. But Winn appreciated my argument that the Internet world wasn't as much about traditional business as it was about grassroots politics. We drafted a release. Every point of concern *Barron's* voiced about Amazon emphasized an area of Value America's strength.

Our release pounded the points home: "Amazon currently sells books, music, and videos — and operates an auction house. Value America operates in 25 different categories/industries. And while some of those categories are still growing, we are establishing the first online presence in many of them." We also noted, "Amazon grew based on its status as a 'virtual store.' Today there is nothing virtual about it as it builds its inventory capacity. Value America is 100 percent inventory-free and factory-direct. There are no warehouse or storefront lease commitments. None." We tried to emphasize our strengths as well: "Value America provides top-flight customer service in the most difficult areas — computers and electronics — so there are no barriers to our growth and expansion into other categories/industries. Amazon's customer service to date has focused solely on books and videos — it is a lot harder for them to ramp that service up to other industries like computers or televisions or refrigerators." Finally, we tried to play up our greatest perceived competitive advantage — custom stores: "Amazon's customer acquisition costs are extraordinary — they are spending $1.10 for every $1 in revenues. In our last quarter our ratio was about $1.50 in revenue for *every $1 in advertising and sales*. In addition, our Custom Stores with corporations, schools, charities, and community organizations mean millions of extra customers at almost no expense."

What we didn't say was that Amazon's sales figures were ten times ours, that their Web site was far more responsive to customers, or that they had ten times the number of customers we had at that moment.

We circulated the draft to senior management for their input. The corporate guys were none too pleased. Glenda Dorchak was incensed. You can't, she said, put something like this out. It was too inflammatory. Dean Johnson and Tom Morgan agreed with her. Much to my displeasure, Winn relented, and we ended up issuing a release comparing Value America's model to "Brand X's" model. While everyone receiving the release probably knew we were comparing ourselves to Amazon, it lacked the pop the original release had.

When no one picked up on that release, we churned out others. The company announced my hiring on June 4. On Monday, June 7, we announced the complete board of directors — the stock went up more than 10 percent. We kept stressing Value America was a serious company run by serious people who believed in the company and were going to make it work. It worked: by June 9, the stock was above the $23 IPO price again, up nearly 50 percent in just a week.

The clear lesson for me and for the company was that we had to feed the media tiger regularly. As long as we showed good news and good progress, we would be well received. The only real danger would be going silent or overpromising and underdelivering.

No sooner had we gotten the stock back up than Winn popped into my office, waved his hand, and said, "Aloha, Kuo." With that, Winn, Scatena, and their families headed to Hawaii for a ten-day vacation.

With Winn gone, not only was the office calmer, but I finally had the chance to meet some of my fellow employees. One of those employees was a great mystery to me. He sat in the office next to mine and rarely opened his door. In fact, during the first few weeks of my tenure, I never officially met him. On occasion I'd see him wander out of his office late at night, clearly deep in thought, bustle out of the building, hop into his gold Lexus, and drive off. Invariably, he'd be in the office before I was the next morning. As the slower pace of work allowed it, I began to wonder who he was and what he was doing. One day out of the blue, I just knocked on his door, walked in, extended my hand, and introduced myself. "David Kuo," I said. He looked up at me, still deep in thought about something, and said, "Oh, hi, Tom Starnes."

Starnes, it turned out, worked with Tom Morgan at US Office Products and was part of the original USOP team that explored a potential business alliance with Value America. He'd been so impressed with

Winn's presentation and business model, he was half tempted to see if the company might hire him. Then, out of the blue, Morgan joined Value America and Starnes was left behind. Since Morgan had a non-solicitation agreement, he couldn't ethically talk to Starnes about a job at Value America so long as Starnes worked at USOP. So one morning Starnes handed in his letter of resignation and called Morgan in the afternoon. He was hired as executive vice president of business development, replacing Rex Scatena, days later.

The son of a German immigrant turned FBI agent, Starnes was a big, tall man in his late thirties, with salt-and-pepper hair, a Harvard MBA, and a penchant for argyle sweater vests. With two special-needs kids, he was also a motivated man. His son, Mack, required twenty-four-hour nursing care. Tom needed Value America to grow big enough to cover his son's medical needs when his USOP health coverage ran out in a year. With this in mind, Tom worked night and day to develop a plan for Value America to make a lot of money quickly. It didn't involve selling wrenches — even magic ones — on TV. During the previous month, Starnes had discovered a small northern Virginia company called eFed that had developed an electronic-purchasing-software suite for federal and state governments. The little company had already integrated the software into several federal government agencies. That was important, because they alone were filling a Federal Office of Management and Budget requirement that all federal-government commodities purchasing be done online by the end of 2001. In 1998, according to Starnes's figures, that amounted to at least $200 billion and perhaps as much as $300 billion. With its proprietary software that allowed federal purchasing agents to comparison-shop based on price for whatever they needed to buy, eFed was the early leader in the electronic government-purchasing arena.

When Starnes cross-checked what the federal government was buying with what Value America was selling, he was pleased to learn Value America currently sold at least 60 percent of those goods. On almost every one of those items, Value America's prices were lower — often significantly lower — than the competition's. He also discovered one other important thing — the government preferred to purchase off contract for at least 80 percent of the commodities they purchased. *On contract* meant the government was obliged to purchase a certain number of items at a certain price by a certain time. *Off contract* gave them more flexibility.

He started extrapolating the numbers. If the federal commodities market was $200 billion, the potential off-contract market was $160 billion. That, combined with a similar state-government purchasing market of $200 billion, meant the total government commodities-purchasing market in the United States was at least $360 billion. Assuming all government purchasers bought the 60 percent of goods that Value America sold, our company would have a chance of selling up to $196 *billion* worth of goods annually. Knowing that would obviously never happen and wanting to be conservative, Starnes estimated Value America might get only 1 percent of those sales to start with. If those figures were true, Value America stood to earn nearly $2 billion in revenue from the government market alone. Even better was that eFed desperately wanted to partner with Value America, and Starnes thought it *might* be possible to buy the company.

The best part of his discovery, however, was that unlike the custom store model, whereby Value America gave away 5 percent of revenue to affiliated charities operating a Value America–operated online store, Value America wouldn't have to give any money away in the government realm. Governments don't typically give a hoot about donating to charities. In addition, advertising to the government market would be extremely limited, enabling Value America to minimize marketing and advertising costs. And because it was the government, prices didn't exactly have to be rock-bottom to be acceptable.

The more he explained to me, the more convinced I became that it was the perfect addition to the perfect business model. It was something I'd never even heard Winn talk about. I immediately forgave Starnes's aloofness and told him to quit talking to me and get back to making the company billions. I offered to bring breakfast, lunch, and dinner to his desk for as long as he needed.

June was a closing month. In short, that meant Value America's quarter was going to close at the end of the month and certain targets had to be met. Chief among those targets was a $35 million revenue figure we *had* to meet — one we actually had to *beat*.

On Monday, June 21, the weekly executive meeting got under way. Tom Morgan was going through his standard list of questions for the team.

"What's going on with SAP?"

From the technology side of the table: "Fine, on course."

"Where do we stand with the new building?"

From operations: "Great, working that out. Looks like we'll have a construction coordinator hired anytime."

"Anything happening on the investor or press front?"

From me: "Release out, releases in queue."

"What's up with the quarter?"

From the sales side: Silence.

"Glenda, what's up with the quarter?" Tom asked again.

"Well, we are not quite there yet — we think."

Morgan glanced up from the piece of paper he was happily ticking through and gave one of those peering-over-the-eyeglasses looks that grandfathers with pipes often give. Except in this case Tom didn't have a pipe or eyeglasses. He was just *intrigued* by the answer. "Excuse me?"

Dorchak, who had a habit of handing out many pieces of paper and going through them with great gusto, looked about, hoping that maybe she had missed a piece of paper somewhere. None to be found. Damn.

"Well, Tom, I've got Melissa [Monk, head of the call center] and Zimm [Zimmerman, head of reporting] looking it up, but we aren't quite on target yet. Of course, we don't know the exact numbers."

With all the technological changes Value America was undergoing, the sales team couldn't determine just how much had been sold, how many orders were in queue, who had been buying the items, and what had been returned. With the quarter's end only ten days away, that was cause for some concern.

"OK, well, anybody have anything else? No? OK, meeting adjourned." Morgan showed absolutely no sign of stress, worry, or annoyance. It was business as usual.

As the group jostled to the door, Morgan piped up nonchalantly, "Glenda, do you have a second?"

Before he had a chance to say anything, she assured him. "Tom, we're on this. There isn't any need to worry, I haven't missed a quarter yet."

Morgan agreed but thought to himself, she hasn't made a quarter yet either. This was Value America's first complete quarter as a public company, and therefore there hadn't been any expectations to meet before this one. It was rather like Glenda telling him she was going out for the

LPGA tour because she had never made a bogey. That was true. But she'd never made a birdie or a par either.

Value America had several ways of making a sale. Dorchak was in charge of most of them. Most important, there was the Web site. The Web site was the preferred way to make any sale, because it was the cheapest way. On the Web site there was absolutely no one around to answer questions about the products — that was why Winn had developed the product presentations — which meant no paid employees were needed. There weren't any 800 phone-line charges to accrue either. Servicing a customer on the Web cost a fraction of what it did by any other means.

Unfortunately, Value America didn't sell much over the Internet. The most product sales by far came in over the telephone. Of Value America's $28 million in first-quarter 1999 sales, about 70 percent were sales taken over the telephone.

Of course, there was a perfectly logical reason for this un–e-commerce fact. Customers came to Value America primarily through its offline advertising, and Value America's advertising prominently featured an 800 number. Most e-commerce companies were driving sales via online ads. Interested parties just clicked directly on an ad and were taken to the appropriate Web site. But Winn still didn't believe in these ads and hadn't seen Value America's experiments with them pay off.

Value America was experiencing a little-known reality. In mid-1999, people didn't read their newspapers with their computers handy, they read them with their phones nearby. So if they saw something they wanted, they picked up the phone and dialed.

The conversation generally went something like this.

"Hello, Value America, the marketplace for a *new* millennium. How may I help you?" a friendly salesperson would say.

"Uh, hello. Yeah, I want to order one of them Apple computers."

"Great. Would you like to do that over the phone or online at our convenient Web site?"

"Uh, on the phone."

"Great! Now, would you like me to take that order, or would you like me to show you how to do it online at www.valueamerica.com?"

"Uh, well, since we're on the phone now and since I don't actually have a computer yet — you see, I'm trying to order one — let's stick to the phone."

"Terrific! Well, now, would you like to learn how to use the Web?"

"NO, DAMN IT, I JUST WANT A DAMN COMPUTER."

"Great! MasterCard or Visa?"

Dean Johnson knew the general skew toward telephone sales but didn't really want to know how badly things were going. Glenda Dorchak knew almost exactly what was going on but didn't want to share the numbers because they reflected poorly on our attempts to gain customer interest in the online store. Perhaps most important, Craig Winn didn't really care what the figures were. He just wanted people buying products. Instead of answering the telephone and telling customers that the company couldn't take their orders over the phone — and risk losing those customers — Winn just wanted to fill their orders and make them comfortable using a dot.com online retailer. Next time they shopped, he figured, there was a higher likelihood they would purchase from Value America and purchase online. Good things both.

This approach made sense to me. It made sense to Winn. It made sense to Tom Morgan. But as I talked to Kim on the phone, I could hear the great sucking sound of incredulity on the other end of the phone. Maybe it was just her AOL arrogance.

"Hey, love, how are sales?" she asked.

"Great, so far as we know. Hey, did you know that we sell a lot of stuff over the phone?"

"Really? Why?"

"Well, so people can buy the things that are in the newspaper."

"Great. Why don't they go online to do it?"

"Well, a lot of them don't have computers yet," I said proudly. I was learning my lines.

"OK, but you are an *e*-commerce company. That means you do things electronically . . . like over the computer, for instance."

"Yeah, but telephones are electronic, and besides, our salespeople use computers."

"You have salespeople?"

"Yeah, lots."

"Just how much of your revenue do you take in over the phone?" she asked with some wonder.

"Um, I don't know."

She pulled up the latest Web traffic figures and couldn't find Value America anywhere on the top one hundred sites. That wasn't good. Media Metrix, the firm that monitored how much traffic various Web sites received, was consistently reporting that Value America had a fraction of Amazon's traffic and barely more traffic than sites that had very little revenue at all. People other than Kim were noticing.

One of them was David Trossman, a top analyst at the global financial services company Legg Mason in Baltimore. Days after Value America's IPO, he issued a report that recommended that purchasers stay away from two newly minted dot.coms — Priceline, the place where you could bid on airline tickets, and Value America. His rationale was simple: For Value America, the cost of acquiring customers was too high, the market was too competitive, and its gross margins were too low. The business, in that environment, couldn't work.

Now, with a week left in the quarter, Trossman called to ask some key questions. "I've got the new Media Metrix numbers in front of me, and Value America is way down at the bottom of the pack. Can you explain that?"

Before I had a chance to respond, he suggested a possible answer.

"The only thing that makes sense is that you guys are driving your revenue from the phones. A phone-order business doesn't justify dot.com valuations."

I'm in a room, it is getting dark, it is getting cold, it is getting darker, I'm starting to lose feeling in my limbs, I'm falling, I'm falling . . . "David," I said, "we absolutely drive a certain amount of revenue from the phones — how much I don't know — but if you think about it, it makes sense. We want to acclimate people to e-commerce. We want the customers who aren't yet a hundred percent comfortable with giving their credit-card numbers online to get comfortable, to have a great experience, to make Value America their home."

He was silent. Finally he muttered, "Right."

Glenda Dorchak was holed up in her office. With only about ten days to go in the quarter, we were about $6 million short of what six analysts following the company were predicting and about $10 million short of the minimal amount Value America needed to keep its growth momentum. Dorchak said her only choice seemed to be buying lots of advertising and praying that people called en masse to place orders. All she had to do was get the orders in the door. From there, Value America could process the credit cards and immediately count the revenue. She was frantic as she pulled her team into a crisis meeting.

She turned to Paul Ewert, head of computer merchandising. Ewert, short, chubby-faced, and a bit older than most in the company at fifty, scurried about like an inquisitive ferret. His appearance and flitty demeanor belied the enormous credibility that Ewert had gained during a distinguished retailing career. He had worked at Target and Dayton Hudson and eventually helped CompUSA grow into a computer powerhouse. He also knew all the big computer players on a first-name basis. People trusted Paul, and Paul was now working for Value America.

Ewert was also an innovator. He was one of the first, if not the first, to start offering consumers computer bundles that included a computer and monitor, printer, disks, and tables. It was a great way to make big sales and also maximize gross margin. He and Dorchak sat together crunching the numbers as I looked on.

To save money Value America generally bought leftover space. This is how it works: Newspapers sell ad space to companies and strike deals about where the ads will appear and offer packages to encourage more than one off purchasing. Two or three days before the paper closes, however, it is possible to pick up remaining space for a dramatically reduced cost. In general, this approach is just smart business. Instead of paying top dollar for an ad to appear above the fold on page A6, a company spends half as much for the ad to appear on the bottom of A7 or C16 or wherever a vacancy can be found.

Now that the quarter was in jeopardy, however, Dorchak wanted space — lots and lots of ad space. She couldn't afford to wait for the unused corners; Value America needed to pay whatever it took and dominate the page.

Ken Power, the angelic copywriter, and Phil Ramsey, the former preacher turned ad guy, knew they had to be at their snappiest to produce the best possible copy. "An Apple a Day" was the headline for the new Apple iMac offering. "The Grill Is Mine" got a round of applause for a Weber grill spot.

Outside, we all heard the roar of an unmuffled engine and the screech of really big tires. Melissa Monk had arrived a bit late for the meeting. A Rosie O'Donnell lookalike with a fun biker-like edge, Monk had been at Dell when it was getting started. Her customized license plate read CLOZER — a testament to her skill at closing a sale and also an advertisement for the Clozer Dome, the call center where inbound sales calls were handled.

As much as anything in life, Monk loved a good white board. It didn't matter what topic was being discussed — sales figures or favorite contraceptive devices — she needed a white board. Unfortunately, at this moment the white board was monopolized by Dorchak, who furiously scribbled figures and numbers. Monk looked around with a big smile but was forced to quietly grab a seat in the back.

Monk was vital to the "Save the Quarter" plan, because it was her call center that was going to field the calls to sell the products. The group discussed exactly how to motivate the salespeople. It would be a combination of sales commissions and intangible incentives. The commissions would be increased a bit to encourage the phone team to sell just a little bit harder. It would certainly cost more, but it wasn't about *how* Value America drove revenues, it was about *driving* the revenues. Period.

The intangible benefits were a little more unique. If Value America made the quarter, it promised to rent a dunking booth for the sales team. On the dunking platform would be the company's chief executives — Craig Winn, Tom Morgan, Glenda Dorchak, and Dean Johnson. "Dunk the Exec" signs started popping up around the call center.

Less than a month into the job, my head was spinning on a daily basis. I was trying to learn corporate communications, retail, e-commerce, and the Internet simultaneously. I was concerned about our lack of product depth and our lack of competitive differentiation.

But experience taught me to keep my head down and focus on the things I could focus on. Working in a setting full of people who knew a hell of a lot more than I did about basically everything corporate, I decided to just shut up.

CHAPTER NINE

Hear Me Roar

A mysterious set of offices lurked in the building next to mine, with huge signs attached to the door that said ENTER AT OWN RISK. PORNOGRAPHY. NECESSARY DUE TO THE NATURE OF OUR WORK. I had seen this my second day on the job but hadn't yet mustered the courage to investigate.

Finally, a month into the job, I stood up from my desk in Hollymead E building, marched across the dirt swath to Hollymead D building, and headed with mounting resolve to the porn corner. I paused, knocked on the door, and went in. There, seated at two computers, were two innocuous-looking women.

"Hello," said one.

"Uh, hi . . . ," said I.

"Can we help you?" the same one asked, a slightly puzzled look on her face.

"Um, well, I'm David Kuo. I'm new here and just wanted to . . . well, see what was behind these doors."

They both rolled their eyes, sighing deeply. Clearly, I wasn't the first guy to come strolling oh so casually into their office.

Their job was to browse the Internet for highly trafficked sites to create so-called affiliate programs. Value America buttons — a small logo or ad — would be placed on those sites so that visitors could click on them to transfer them to Value America's store. If visitors did this, the host site would get a small percentage of any revenue generated from sales. To find these sites, however, meant surfing through a lot of porn on display — both because the women ran across some of it accidentally in their search for popular sites and also because there might be a few "tasteful adult-oriented" sites that they deemed appropriate for having a Value America button. I began to wonder what someone from a tasteful porn site would want from Value America. Would they suddenly get the urge for a new toaster oven while browsing Pamela Anderson in 69 postures? Fancy lingerie from the clothing section, perhaps? Whipped cream from gourmet foods? Honey?

Abutting Building D was Building C, Value America's technological center. I had envisioned all the computers that ran Value America's virtual store being housed in a sophisticated control room full of flashing lights and specially cooled and filtered air. But walking through, I saw a whole lot of computers packed into what looked like a converted conference room with a rent-a-cop to one side. All someone would have to do would be tiptoe past the guard with a water bucket, slosh quickly, and *kapow!*, Value America would be no more.

These were just a few of the things I got to see during Winn's ten-day absence. With him gone, a predictable morning routine developed. Whoever got to the office first would walk to the fax machine, gather the pages of Winn's straight-from-Hawaii handwritten ad copy (he insisted he would do a better job than anyone else), and then make copies for the other executives. Deciphering Winn's messages was arduous work. Scrawled on notepad paper, they were generally illegible. Winn had written about a dozen scripts in all, with no apparent theme to tie them all together. One was a seemingly tongue-in-cheek look at how Value America's researchers screen products for multimedia online demonstrations — Winn had them barbecuing by a pool for the Weber grills, channel surfing on a television, and playing games on a laptop. Another was a commercial that began with a close-up of Monticello and a Jefferson bust and then cut to Value America's store, where the narrator would announce that "another great revolution" was being launched.

While Value America may have been the first dot.com to advertise in newspapers, by mid-1999, Value America may have been the only dot.com not to have been hitting the airwaves with branding commercials. Yahoo! had their Eskimos in Igloos, Amazon was airing two guys in perpetual pursuit of a place big enough to house their millions of books, and dozens of lesser-known companies were advertising everything from job hunting over the Web to buying pet food. The ads were sort of similar — quirky, cutting-edge, and trying very hard to be memorable. Mostly, they all just bled together into a great and completely undefined dot.com consciousness.

For Value America, Winn's ads didn't only raise tempers over what the company was supposed to represent, they also highlighted the corporate/entrepreneurial fault line inside Value America.

On one side were the corporate types led by Glenda Dorchak. Creating branding ads, they argued, would take six to nine months. First, you had to hire a branding agency to determine what exactly the company stood for. What were the company's fundamental attributes? What feeling did it want to leave with the audience? Second, when that was done, you had to hire another agency to produce the ads. That agency needed time to brainstorm, develop storyboards, write scripts, hold meetings, and on and on and on. There might be two or three rotating spots that came out of that long process. The whole process would cost a few million bucks, not including the cost of actually putting the ads on the air.

The other side of the company had a slightly different approach. For Ken Power and some of the others who'd been around Value America for a while, ads should be trial and error. First, write the scripts. Second, debate the scripts. Third, film the ads. Four, pick good ads. Fifth, run the ads. It wouldn't cost very much — not including air time. After the ads ran, regroup and do a better job next time.

I didn't much like the ad scripts, but I found the multimillion-dollar approach absurd. My ad experience had all come from political campaigns and nonprofit organizations, where ads could be written, filmed, and slapped on the air in hours. I knew of course that low-budget ads with cheesy sets, elevator music, a bunch of flags, and a voice-over weren't what an aspiring Internet titan should be putting out there, but I also figured if we didn't know what our glorious brand stood for by now, we had bigger problems than settling on the right adjectives with which to describe Value America. I was fairly sure we did know who we were. We just needed to all get on the same page.

Tom Morgan's office was the epicenter of dissatisfied executives ranting about the ad scripts. The consensus was that they were amateurish and that Value America couldn't afford that. But the scripts were also just part of what folks were upset about: Executive dissatisfaction with Winn extended beyond the advertising process.

On the merchandising side, Morgan learned, Winn was ordering the merchandisers to bring in certain products, ignore others, and make particular deals. He wanted, for instance, a much greater gourmet foods presence, whether the merchandisers thought it made sense or not.

Jerry Goode, CIO, complained that Winn treated the technologists like they reported directly to him. For example, he had them working on custom store designs for Falwell, the American Heart Association, and others. Winn also sometimes dropped by for no apparent reason and told the tech guys to tweak particular parts of the store. Worse, Goode lamented, the increased workload of Winn's extracurricular projects was starting to threaten SAP and Oracle implementations.

Another executive was nervous about Winn's intense involvement in the new Value America corporate campus. They spent days together going over every nook and cranny of the pre-architectural drawings. Wasn't Winn supposed to be doing other things?

The complaints and concerns of the other executives about Winn's management style went on and on. Just about everyone agreed that less of Winn was more. Morgan believed he was surrounded by executives who knew how to run the corporate divisions and who were empowered by his trust. With Winn in Hawaii, for the first time since his arrival, Morgan found his team was executing — not flawlessly, but manageably. Winn's meddling threatened that.

Of course, the differences between Winn and Morgan couldn't have been more profound. The two men had fundamentally opposite business styles. For Craig, building a business was like playing with Legos. You dumped them on the ground and built whatever you saw in your mind as big and fast as possible. The only limitations were gravity and imagination. And after it was built, you sold it to people. But for Tom Morgan, building a business was like playing with Lincoln Logs; for whatever you wanted to build, there was a proper order and pace. The logs had to fit together precisely — tongue and groove — as the building went up. If you put them together fast, haphazardly, they wouldn't be strong, and they wouldn't look right.

What became clear in Winn's absence was that Morgan was beginning to believe that his Value America task was a radical assignment: to build a permanent structure with Lincoln Logs while jumping up and down on a trampoline during an earthquake with the company's founder tackling him. It was at a minimum, and in his dignified manner of expressing things, challenging. To Morgan, challenges didn't have to be discouraging; they just needed to be faced and identified. What, therefore, was the fix?

For Morgan, the fix was to focus. Seven days into Winn's absence,

Tom Morgan and I headed to the Outback Steakhouse for some late-night after-work eats. Morgan drank a glass or two of wine and rambled about various things — his family, the new Range Rover he'd just bought, the new 150-acre spread he'd just bought. Then he blurted out, "Geez, you know, we've got to focus. We've *got* to focus. We've got all these plans and these ideas and these goals, but we don't have any focus."

Morgan was the rock. He didn't waver and didn't show emotion. His pronouncements tended to surprise. It was obvious the company was scattered. But this business, I told him, felt just like a political campaign. Chaos was to be expected. We were all in a race to grow, grow, grow.

"But this *isn't* politics, David," Morgan politely disagreed. "We've got to build a business. We've got to make money. We've got to have priorities."

The first priority was familiar: to drive revenues. That was the foundational log. Second, Value America needed to exceed customer expectations. If the customers weren't happy, there wouldn't be any business. Third, top-notch systems were key to surviving. Fourth, costs *had* to be controlled. It didn't matter if a business was on the Internet fast track or the brick-making slow track — costs had to be controlled. He kept mulling and kept chattering. This, he said, was his focus list. Everything Value America did — everything — had to be vetted against his list. Unless it helped to achieve these goals, it wasn't something Value America was going to do.

Morgan's list meant focus, something horribly lacking not only across the company in general but in the custom stores program in particular. Winn's brainchild had made progress. More than two dozen charitable organizations had signed up to have Value America create online stores for them. If all worked according to plan, these stores would provide both the charities and our company with revenue.

But Tom Starnes just couldn't get his arms around the custom stores program. The people managing Value America had haphazardly signed up charities without any contracts, official agreements, or expectations. In late June 1999, however, many of the organizations that had signed up with the company still didn't have a functioning store, even though their names had been used by Value America as examples of successful custom store partners. Complaints from these organizations plopped down on Starnes's desk.

While there was little question that custom stores had the potential to drive enormous revenue for Value America, that potential wasn't playing out. The largest functioning custom store was Attorneys Online, which, as its name suggested, was an online destination for lawyers. That store had generated only a few thousand dollars in revenue. A convincing argument could be made that the reason the stores weren't doing better was that no money had been spent promoting them. Yet even the Falwell store, which Jerry Falwell had promoted on his television program, had yet to break $50,000 in total revenue. No one was making much off this program — not the charities and not Value America.

This lack of traction was causing Tom Starnes great concern. Our gross margins were well below 5 percent. Value America was promising that 5 percent of all custom store revenues would go to the charities. Since the difference between how much we paid for something and how much we charged for it was *less* than 5 percent, this setup was, to Starnes, a recipe for infinite losses — once revenues started flowing, that is.

The custom stores also stood in stark contrast to the gold mine Starnes saw in eFed. On June 24, Starnes and Morgan headed to eFed's headquarters in Reston, Virginia, to negotiate a purchase. Sixty minutes of meetings later, they had a deal, $15 million in cash and stock — mostly stock. EFed's team loved the idea of affiliating with Value America because our company was an e-commerce player and because our stock was low, which meant more potential upside for them. They were also attracted to Value America because they knew that Tom Starnes and Tom Morgan were both men of deep faith. It was a faith the eFed team shared.

Despite my initial questions about and discomfort with Value America's religious orientation, my affection for Morgan, Starnes, and Winn was slowly convincing me these guys weren't religious zealots. They were men who wanted to build an integrity-filled business that would, in its way, honor God. Like a lot of Generation Xers, I wanted a purpose — I wanted to make a difference. In Value America I had found a company on technology's cutting edge that was working with charities and was committed to making America better. It was definitely an idealistic/utopian/pie-in-the-sky feeling, but it was a highly motivating idealistic/utopian/pie-in-the-sky feeling. The fact that I could get rich in the process certainly *did not suck*. After all, as a kid I'd promised my dad a Porsche by the time I was thirty.

We gathered early Monday morning, June 28, for an executive retreat in one of the chintz-and-stone rooms of the Keswick Club. Morgan and Starnes had a big announcement. A few days earlier they'd told everyone about the eFed acquisition. Now they said they both believed Value America should consider leaving the consumer retail space altogether and focus strictly on business-to-business and business-to-government commerce. Starnes presented the government and the business models while simultaneously critiquing the consumer model. The latter, he said, was actually flawed. The custom store program was too expensive to be profitable, and the consumer arena itself was getting too crowded with too many players all wanting the same piece of the pie. The business-to-business and business-to-government fields, however, were relatively wide open. Value America, he argued, could become a significant player in them very, very quickly.

While still enthusiastic about the sheer possibility of the eFed deal, we also recognized that Starnes's plan just made sense. It meant not only huge revenue potential but real profit possibility as well. Under this plan, the fundamentals of the business remained intact. We were still an inventoryless business and still had manufacturers shipping products. But instead of simply trying to attract fickle consumers, we were going after guys who didn't care about things like gift cards, coupons, gift wrap, or other little frills. They just wanted their products at a good price delivered quickly. We knew we could do that.

Also, by diminishing the importance of the consumer space, we could reduce our $13-million-a-month cash burn, $7 million of which went for newspaper advertising alone. That amount made Value America not only one of the dot.com world's top advertisers — second at that point only to E*trade — but also one of the top advertisers period in papers like the *Washington Post, New York Times,* and *USA Today.* A business and government focus would allow us to shift ads to trade and government publications. Even Dorchak, who controlled the ad spending and therefore possessed significant power inside Value America, was supportive.

Giving up on the consumer market was obviously a huge step. Winn had created the company as a consumer dot.com, and that was what the investors had signed up for. At the same time, I saw exactly what Starnes was talking about, since our weaknesses and the competition in the consumer market were clear. More than anything, though, I was psyched, because this was finally a *big* piece of news. While I'd hoped for lots of impending deals when I arrived at Value America, I was staring into July and August without much to announce. The June news — the board, the Amazon comparison, the automotive division — had all helped our stock and our company. But news of the eFed purchase would be gigantic.

As we sat brainstorming about how exactly the new Value America focus would work, Morgan's cell phone rang. His secretary was calling to tell him Winn had arrived back from Hawaii earlier than expected and was not happy. He was roaming the offices looking for the executives, and no one was around. He wanted to know what was happening with his commercials, and no one seemed to have an answer. Winn, she warned Morgan, looked a bit rabid.

Glenda Dorchak and I were dispatched to talk to him about the commercials. Racing back to the offices in our separate cars, we chattered back and forth on cell phones about what to say. We both decided to just lay it on the line and tell Winn what we really thought. I had a lot of respect for Dorchak's attitude. She was tough enough to step up to the plate. We agreed that I would start first and then she would drive the point home.

We walked into Winn's office smiling as confidently as possible. He didn't return our smiles. We tried to ask him how the trip was, to which he muttered, "Long and tiring." He quickly asked, "Where are we with the commercials?"

I told him studio space had been rented, but the entire executive team was unanimous in believing the scripts needed a lot of work because they weren't entirely effective.

His face starting to flush, he looked at me and said dismissively, "And you know how much about making commercials?"

I stammered that I watched a lot of them and that I'd worked on political ads in the past, but he wasn't listening. Instead, his eyes were boring in on Dorchak, as he waited for her response.

"Well, Craig," she mumbled, "I think David is overstating people's concern. We think the commercials are obviously great and with some tweaking will be just fine."

Winn was pleased to hear it. I was confused. What were those words coming from her mouth? What alien had possessed her between the corridor and now? Was I imagining things, or was that a nice serrated knife I felt jutting out from between my shoulder blades?

I knew it wasn't personal. Dorchak had endured a lot from Winn. Almost from the moment she started at Value America, the two had been at odds. She had a defined corporate way of operating. Like Tom Morgan, she believed there were rules and steps and procedures to be followed. You couldn't just make it up as you went along. She had stood up to Winn, told him what she thought, and been beaten down in the process. Perhaps this is what came of long-term Winn exposure. Maybe, after a while, everyone just curled up fetal.

Slowly the rest of the executive team trickled in, and Winn picked off a few of them for a crisis meeting to discuss his ads. Neal Harris, Winn's old friend, was selected, Tom Starnes was told his presence wasn't needed. All Winn's old California buddies were summoned as well — Ken Power, Joe Page, and Rex Scatena. Under direct examination by Winn, all the executives more or less supported Dorchak's contention that while the ads were early drafts, they could certainly be polished off nicely. Joe Page, the technology guru, went even further, declaring that he *really* liked the ads. Ken Power agreed. Even Dorchak smiled a lot and told Winn that she had rarely seen such great first drafts of ads before.

If this exercise in ass kissing was the same thing people called corporate diplomacy, I was ready to become a corporate anarchist. The ads sucked. They were embarrassing. There wasn't a single common thread to tie them together. The idea of Winn narrating every one of them with a substantial amount of face time on the camera would have given them the feel of second-rate *political* ads — the kind that schoolboard members or animal-control-board chairmen run. They were pathetic.

OK, I was overreacting. I do that when I get pissed. But the sentiment was true. These weren't ready for primetime — hell, they weren't ready for a 2:00 A.M. running on the bass-fishing network. That could be dealt with though. What was pissing me off most were these colleagues who seemed to be competing to see who could land a bigger pucker on Winn's butt.

Morgan was the lone dissenter. He said he had heard a lot of concern from various parties about the scripts.

No one was going to mistake Tom Morgan for the Terminator. It simply wasn't his style to whack someone upside the head — no matter how I might wish it were so. But for Morgan to disagree with Winn in a public setting was a first. I sincerely hoped Winn and the others noticed that Morgan didn't much like the 180-degree turn he, too, had just seen from his management team.

Winn dismissed Morgan calmly by reminding him he had once told Winn he'd never had any experience in advertising. Morgan looked around the room, smiled, and said nothing.

Besides, Winn informed the dozen-person crowd, he *knew* where a lot of their concerns had come from. Someone within the company was working to subvert him — to undermine his creative output. That person, he said, was Phil Ramsey. Ramsey, who was not in the meeting, exuded a middle-aged Gomer Pyle persona — a bit spacey but ultimately good and very well meaning. He had been with the company for more than a year and had become one of the chief advertising guys because he wrote copy Winn liked so much. He had produced and helped write all of Value America's limited TV and radio ads the previous year, and one of them had even won an honorable-mention award from the ad industry. About Winn's scripts, however, Ramsey was nervous. Like the other voices of concern, he felt they lacked the professional polish and messaging Value America required. They were, he felt, damaging. Ramsey had put his concerns in an e-mail to Glenda Dorchak, Tom Morgan, and General Kicklighter: "What everyone appears afraid to say is what we all know to be true. With these ads, it is clear that the emperor has no clothes." That e-mail had been a mistake; Kicklighter had forwarded it to Winn, arguing that such insubordination must be squashed immediately.

After the meeting, as Winn, Morgan, and I gathered, Winn ordered Morgan to fire Ramsey. Morgan said no. He told Winn that he would investigate the situation, examine Ramsey's evaluations, and talk to him personally. But he was not, under any circumstances, going to fire Ramsey on the spot.

Continuing, Winn declared the commercials would be finalized and filmed sometime during the first week of July. Instead of using local studios, he had arranged to use Jerry Falwell's soundstage in Lynchburg. There was, he had heard, a nice backdrop of rich oak bookshelves and a faux fireplace. It sounded, he said, extremely presidential.

I loved Value America, loved Winn, loved Morgan, and hated what had just happened. It was my first disillusioning Value America moment. What I wanted to do was go outside, hop in my car, drop the top, blast the stereo, and cruise around a bit. No such luck. I had twenty phone calls to return and two hundred e-mails in my in box. We'd been out of the office all morning. There was much work to do.

Later that afternoon, Morgan and Starnes sat in Morgan's office facing a perplexing decision — how, given Winn's mood, to present the eFed deal? Even more pressing was how to present their conviction that Value America needed to move away from the consumer market to the government market. Morgan, they both decided, would sit down with Winn the next morning.

Seven o'clock the next morning, Morgan did exactly that. He walked Winn through the government market, told him about eFed's solution, and then told Winn about the $15 million letter of intent. Morgan decided not to broach the strategic realignment.

Winn sat impassively looking as Morgan presented the information. When he was done, Winn looked at him and said, "Tom, I respect you very much. But in my opinion it isn't in Value America's interest to buy eFed. I vote against it."

Winn's challenge was clear: Tom, do you really want to take an issue to the board that you are opposing me on? Winn knew he couldn't technically tell Morgan what to do, since Morgan was CEO and Winn had no official executive role as chairman of the board. But Morgan knew what Winn was saying. He didn't want to take this one to the board, since he didn't want to show the board there was a rift between him and Winn. eFed would be dropped, the realignment temporarily dashed.

Several hours later, Winn grabbed the general and me for lunch at Amigo's. Sitting down, he commented quietly that the eFed deal was arguably the most stupid and overvalued deal he'd ever heard of. Why spend $15 million on a company with no profits and hardly any revenue? Only a fool, he said, would do something like that. He'd be willing to entertain purchasing them but only for a fraction of the cost. Besides, he said, Value America didn't have to spend a dime to take advantage of their e-commerce suite — we could just partner with eFed and have the same impact.

Without suggesting that if that same logic had been applied to Value America, no one would have invested in us, I tried to argue with him about the terms of the deal and the potential of the market, but he'd already decided: eFed was dead. Besides, he said, he had already tried to penetrate the government market and it hadn't worked. Obviously, this deal was a sham. If there were real government sales potential, he, Craig Winn, would have found it already.

Morgan and Starnes tried talking to Winn again that afternoon. He should, they argued, listen to eFed present its vision and its company. Fine, Winn said, but it won't change my mind.

Within a few days, Ramsey's decreed firing, Winn's ad obsession, and the eFed deal killing all sent an unambiguous message to the executive team: Value America was Craig Winn's company. The episodes also suggested Winn was incapable of supporting any deal that hadn't originated with him. If a deal came to pass without his initiative, it was somehow a second-tier deal.

Early that evening, Winn came by my office, shut the door, and plopped down in the chair next to my desk. Most government purchasing, he said, was done on GSA contract — it was an arduous task to get through all the bureaucracy to have the chance to sell anything. It was also, he said, an obscenely competitive market. The biggest problem, he continued, with Starnes's eFed purchase proposal was that the numbers didn't add up. There was no way, he said, that Value America had 60 percent of what the federal government bought in commodities purchasing. Plus, a lot of that purchasing — or at least a lot of the expenditure — wasn't just for Post-its and computers. It was for things like gas generators and steam engines and items that cost tens of millions of dollars. The idea that we had a shot at that much revenue was ludicrous. He didn't, he admitted, have the heart to tell Starnes that in front of Morgan or others.

On the ad front, he didn't want to spend the tens of millions required for a frou-frou New York ad agency to do its shtick. He'd talked with J. Walter Thompson and contemplated using them but was worried it would take too long and cost too much. We could, he said, think about using his ads in local markets and then go down the national road with J. Walter Thompson for a bigger splash.

Winn's eFed thoughts made sense, but to me Tom Starnes's arguments seemed just as sound. I didn't have a firm foundation from which to argue. On the ad front, however, I was grateful that the Craig Winn I knew appeared to be back. The local/national approach made sense. While I didn't know much about J. Walter Thompson, I told Winn it would be very cool to work through that process with him.

He looked at me, smiled his big, toothy grin, and said, "Great idea. You make contact with J. Walter Thompson and make sure this happens."

A renewed sense of love for Winn washed over me. He was a great man. The love was perhaps even enough to obscure the fact that eFed would soon sell to someone else for $30 million with potentially millions more if the company met certain financial targets. Bank of America had even come in at the last minute with an offer of $65 million — $50 million more than what we could have bought it for. Bank of America was too late. In any case, I didn't have time to think about what might have been. Now all I had to do was figure out whether J. Walter Thompson was in fact a person or a firm or both.

CHAPTER TEN

Purloined Sirloins

After the initial turmoil of Winn's return, things settled back into a nice, normal manic hum. I learned that J. Walter Thompson was actually a huge ad agency, not some geeky overachiever, after visiting its Web site, which cited such clients as Ford, Kraft, and Nike. Contacting them went on my twelve-page to-do list.

Web surfing gave me another idea: ordering from Value America. Ordering, I'd heard, was especially sweet for employees. Winn had arranged for Value America employees to buy things from the store *at cost*. That meant we paid exactly what Value America paid, which meant, presumably, great savings. Eagerly I popped open the front page with its checkerboard of little pictures representing the different product categories. For fun, I decided to shop by brands. Giddily I clicked the little brands button. The brands logos splashed in front of me. It was a bit too much — and I didn't know a lot of the brands anyway — Replogle? Ampad? BALT? Galoob Toys? I quickly switched to product categories and settled on a new *Stars Wars: Phantom Menace* computer game, a collection of Bobby Kennedy's speeches, and a superdeluxe Weber grill that someone was apparently going to bring to my D.C. house and set up for me. I couldn't wait. My employee discount saved me $300 on the grill alone! The whole experience was a blast. I spent more than an hour clicking on this category and that category. We may have only been an inch deep with selection, but we were several miles wide.

Value America closed its second quarter and appeared to have not only salvaged things, but actually exceeded the Street's $28.8 million expectations. Morgan, Winn, Dorchak, and Johnson headed to the call center for their ritual dunkings.

While the eFed purchase was dead, Starnes was still working hard to get Value America's products into its government comparison-shopping engine. We might not own eFed and the government purchasing engine, but we could still hope to capture a large chunk of the marketplace.

Frustrated by Winn's summary dismissal of eFed, Morgan decided to play a waiting game. Value America was still primarily aimed at the consumer market. But Starnes and Morgan were rabidly committed to pursuing the plan Starnes laid out at the June 28 management retreat. It would be a major strategic shift, and Morgan was biding his time, waiting for a moment when Winn might be more receptive.

With the quarter in hand, the stock somewhat recovered, and his executives reminded of who was really boss, Winn was ready to celebrate. He invited all six hundred employees out to a Fourth of July celebration at his home, Winndom. During the preceding months, he had stockpiled a small warehouse full of rockets and Roman candles and various and sundry exploding objects. As the sun went down, Winn set up row after row of fireworks, with his dog Cristal nipping at his heels and his two boys running around with books of matches threatening to light random fuses. Then, one by one he lit the rockets. Up each one went — *pop! bang! pop! bang!* It wasn't exactly a coordinated fireworks show — more like a little bang and flash every few seconds. There was no food, no free bar — just the quirky light show. After about thirty minutes, people at the fringes of the crowd slowly and stealthily sneaked to their cars to escape. More than an hour of random fireworks later, Winn turned around to find only a fraction of his employees still remaining.

My fiancée, Kim, and I weren't in Charlottesville. We'd trekked to the place of her birth — Sterling, Kansas — for the Fourth of July weekend. It was her tenth high school reunion. I'd never been to Kansas, and I was eager to check out her idyllic-sounding corn-fed roots prior to our nuptials. (Actually, she corrected me, it was a *wheat*-fed upbringing — most of the corn was in Iowa.) It was a wonder we actually found the town. It is one square mile bordered by endless miles of wheat and sunflowers, like a Hollywood movie set — a midwestern, weather-beaten version of *The Truman Show.*

This was the first time I'd had any time away from Value America since I began six weeks ago and the first concentrated time I'd had with my bride-to-be. Kim and I were both Internet addicts. Kim, AOL's director of communications, had become one of AOL's prime media spokespersons. She was handling media for AOL Anywhere, new store design, new product initiatives, and a dozen other things. Her company was the king of the Internet, and she couldn't have been happier.

My company was somewhere between a court jester and a lottery winner — but the whole world seemed ours. We could see the revenue growing, the brands signing up, the inventoryless model working. Value America, I knew, was on the verge of greatness. That the stock was still in the teens was irrelevant. It was, actually, a huge bonus, because when we took off, we were gonna be like a rocket.

Even in Sterling, Kansas, population 1,500, the locals knew that people who worked for the Internet were very cool. When Kim told the hometowners where she was working, there were audible gasps. When I mentioned Value America, there were fewer gasps — but that there were *any* gasps was a morale booster. We'd penetrated the heartland.

Kim's sister, Heather, and brother-in-law, Scott, listened to our breathless recounting of what it was like to work in the Internet world and felt a bit of the buzz themselves. Heather audited for the U.S. Olympic Committee, and Scott worked in business development for Junior Achievement. As Kim and I talked about our jobs, we glimpsed in their eyes the same glow of wonder that had probably been in ours when the Internet became real to us. We'd both, inadvertently, become Internet evangelists.

Over Sunday brunch, as I enthused about Value America's custom stores and how they were a yet-to-be-developed revenue source for our company, I looked at Heather and Scott and was hit with the idea of a lifetime. "Scott, Heather, you should come work for Value America! You should! I'm serious! It would be awesome." My breathless monologue continued: "You guys could both work with the custom stores! They need to be improved! They need structure and discipline! You guys would be perfect! Perfect! You could get Internet experience! You'd be working with great people! It could be awesome, we could *all* work together at Value America! And Charlottesville — Charlottesville is gorgeous, right there in the Shenandoah Valley, kind of like Colorado . . . sort of . . . kind of . . . different . . . but there are mountains!"

Heather, Scott, and Kim just looked at me. I was buzzing. Kim's first reaction was, "Hey! You can't all work together without me."

"Come on along!" Heather replied, giving her a big hug.

Heather and Scott were blown away — completely unprepared.

They were also surprising themselves by how seriously appealing they found the idea.

I turned on the overdrive. I hadn't even mentioned the potential monetary upside yet. "The stock is low. With the stock low, it is only going to go up. It'll go way up. It'll, it'll be . . . like being at AOL when they went public. It'll be huge."

I don't think I stopped for the next thirty minutes. I told them everything about Value America — the way it served customers, the way it served brands, how it was leading the new retail revolution. It never dawned on me that I sounded almost exactly like Craig Winn.

Even if I did sound like Winn, that didn't matter. I was just telling the truth. At least truth as I knew it in my heart. Value America was going to succeed. It *was* revolutionary. It *was* going to change the world. Any other outcome was inconceivable. If it took me a lot of words and not too many breaths to explain that to people, so be it. We all departed, mulling new Internet dreams.

As the holiday weekend passed, Winn became fixated on another idea that he was sure would help Value America. With the company's market cap hovering around a billion dollars, it seemed to Winn that buying another company would dramatically increase revenues. The climate was ripe for such deals. Every day, it seemed, the wires and airwaves were atwitter with the latest merger, acquisition, or investment by one Internet company or another. Amazon had taken a large position in the luxe-goods dealer Ashford.com. EToys had snapped up Kids.com. The buzz was great for the companies being acquired, and even better for those that were acquiring. The idea of purchasing, investing, and aligning had been run up the Wall Street flagpoles, and the great oracles had decreed it sound. Everyone knew that at the early stages of Internet development, there were going to be clear winners and clear losers. Consolidation, repositioning, and the like were natural byproducts of a maturing industry. Those that were buying were thought to be the victors. Translation: BUY!

Tom Morgan wasn't against buying a company. He'd bought a ton of them while at US Office Products. USOP was a rollup of other companies. And he'd been in favor of the eFed acquisition. But eFed had been the exception. Morgan knew how hard it was to merge multiple companies. What Value America needed, he knew, was to execute on the inventoryless model, build the business and government markets, and grow organically.

Internet acquisitions weren't always quite on the up-and-up. The whole Internet financing world was actually a bit too incestuous to make anyone comfortable. Take Goldman, for instance. Goldman Sachs had taken eToys public earlier in the year. From that deal they made several million dollars in fees, not counting any stock options they might have also obtained in the deal. Meanwhile, as eToys began trading, the powerful Goldman analyst team came out with report after report lauding eToys as an e-commerce pioneer that was going to make a huge and lasting retail impact. This helped the company's stock price climb, so any shares Goldman owned were even more valuable. And a hot eToys meant even more potential moneymaking deals for Goldman.

Lo and behold, just when Winn had decided it was time to buy, Goldman came calling. Perhaps Goldman and the eToys team felt an acquisition would be best for eToys's long-term success. Perhaps they wanted to cash in while they could. Regardless, Goldman was making it clear that eToys was "exploring its options," and that Value America might be the ideal partner.

Of course from Value America's perspective, an alliance backed by Goldman Sachs could be a great thing. The big investment banks were much like the old-time precinct bosses when political machines controlled the polls: If they blessed you, you were virtually guaranteed a measure of success. Value America — more precisely, our stock price — could use that kind of an endorsement.

Going through the sketchy data he collected from his direct reports and quizzing them on how they thought our past quarter went, Morgan looked ahead. It looked like we had come in somewhere around $25 million in computer sales and $3 million in peripherals (printers, monitors, etc.). Total consumer-goods revenue was around $3 or $4 million. Based on his assessment, Morgan calculated Value America could realistically grow by more than 50 percent. More and more people knew about us. We were going to increase business-to-business sales that had thus far been anemic. We had a better and better sense of what items sold best in our ads. If things ran as they should, Value America could clear $56 million from July to September on losses of less than $35 million. It wasn't anywhere close to profitability, but it would be good news on all fronts.

Getting there, however, would be done with a rickety technological infrastructure. Value America's cobbled-together network of computers and the Value America attic crew's initial technology creations weren't keeping up with the demand. It wasn't that there was anything intrinsically wrong with the technology software — it had performed admirably. It was just too complicated for the other Value America programmers. No one but the few men who had built it really knew how to alter it, advance it, perfect it. This complexity was one of the reasons that Value America was moving forward with the SAP implementation and upgrading to Oracle and a slew of new high-powered IBM servers. The net effect of all these changes was that Value America was precariously perched on the edge of a crevasse. Below was destruction. Behind, utter chaos. Across this crevasse, however, beckoned e-retail nirvana.

Morgan needed everyone in technology to be focused and the rest of the company to respect and assist with that focus. Mergers, acquisitions, wholesale changes, in fact, from his point of view, threatened the company.

Winn listened politely as Morgan expressed his concerns. Then he brushed them aside. Value America was going to pursue acquisitions anyway. It wasn't a personal thing; Winn just disagreed with Morgan on the subject. He'd seen how Value America got built. Precariousness was simply a characteristic of this Internet age. It had to be dealt with. If Value America didn't drive revenue, it didn't matter how nice the systems were.

Every CEO engages in some head butting, not only with the chairman but with the rest of the board, too. But Morgan was beginning to feel like he was a ceremonial figure — he looked nice, talked nice, and was patted on the head and told he was steering the ship. But he wondered whether his wheel was actually attached to the ship's rudder.

Winn didn't know anything about the eToys possibility — Goldman had gone to Morgan directly — but he'd had his eyes on two other targets. First, publisher Thomas Nelson. Thomas Nelson was the country's largest Christian book publisher, and its founders were looking to cash in. Not surprisingly, Jerry Falwell had brought Thomas Nelson to Winn's attention. Winn liked their $75 million in annual revenue and their established business.

Word of Winn's pursuit of Nelson reached Fred Smith. Smith called Winn and asked him why he was pursuing a company that held inventory. Winn said he was just looking. The Thomas Nelson purchase died soon after.

Then there was Shop At Home. Shop At Home was a distant third to QVC and the Home Shopping Network in the TV home-shopping race. Shop At Home had never really taken off and didn't seem to be going anywhere. Winn's plan was to take control of the company and brand it as the only home-shopping channel that sold name-brand goods as opposed to just cheap stuff that appealed to overweight suburban housewives with twenty-five credit cards and a Chia-pet collection.

Morgan and others on the executive management staff wanted to veto the Shop At Home deal. Not only would it divert focus away from Value America's core Internet retail business, but, at less than $20 a share, Value America's stock was too undervalued to make a deal. Winn agreed on the latter but not on the former. The Web was an evolutionary business, he explained. The business plan wasn't a thing you stuck to like a color-by-number picture; it was just a document that showed investors you were smart enough to make a business run. Once you had the money, your job was to just figure it out as you went along. Buying Shop At Home was one of those things that would be good. He decided to put Shop At Home on ice till the stock recovered.

As Winn contemplated mergers in the first couple weeks of July, Value America made its NASCAR debut. It wasn't *exactly* the NASCAR that racing fans think about. In the NASCAR major leagues, companies like DuPont and McDonald's ante up several million dollars each year for the privilege of slapping their logos on a racecar hood. Value America, on the other hand, was starting out by sponsoring some of the minor-league stock car races to boost the company's name recognition with the NASCAR demographic. The deal cost a few hundred thousand bucks. Perhaps we should have seen it as a sign when the car hit the wall on lap 50 and ended up crinkled and smoking in the pits.

Thirty-six hours after the crash, I arrived at the office to find people congregated outside Rex's office, pointing, chuckling, laughing. Everyone slapped one another on the back. There in the middle of the pack was Ken Erickson, wearing a smiling Buddha air of contentment. I maneuvered my way into a sight line. There, leaning up against Rex's wall was the partially disfigured engine hood of a stock car with the Value America logo emblazoned in the middle in big letters and pictures. In the upper left-hand corner was a fitting autograph that appeared to read: "To Value America, from Dusty Rusty . . . balls to the wall!!!"

In the midst of all the craziness, Winn got his jet. Winn argued that it made sense. One of the advantages of locating the company in Virginia's rural horse country was that it saved a ton of money. Salaries could be 50 percent of what another dot.com would have to pay in Silicon Valley or in New York. General administrative costs — insurance, office space, etc. — were likewise a fraction of the cost in a big city. The only real downside was transportation. Charlottesville, despite its recent airport overhaul, which increased gate capacity by 50 percent, wasn't exactly a regional hub. It had only four gates and you could only get to New York, Charlotte, Pittsburgh, and Washington, D.C., non-stop.

Morgan didn't disagree with Winn's points. He just didn't think that Value America needed to *own* its own jet. At $4,000 per flight hour, a jet would eat up a lot of money. In fact, one trip to D.C. on the jet cost more than ten round-trip tickets on one of the little puddle jumpers that flew the ninety-mile hop to Dulles International Airport. Morgan wanted to buy into NetJets or another airplane-lease company for those occasions when the company did need a plane. It would save money and still give Value America the mobility it needed.

But Winn's sense was that the Internet demanded it. Internet executives couldn't afford to be flying little prop planes back and forth to meetings. The jet could save *hours* every trip. In the course of a single day, he could fly to New York for a breakfast meeting, Memphis for a lunch meeting, Chicago for a mid-afternoon meeting, and be home in Charlottesville by dinner. That such a trip would probably cost about $32,000 wasn't all that important when you had just raised more than $130,000,000 in your initial public offering.

Winn relented a bit. He and Scatena decided *they* would buy the jet and then lease it to Value America for business purposes. They talked to a bunch of salesmen and finally found the jet they wanted — a Raytheon Hawker 800. Problem was, the interior was maroon. To Winn, maroon was a blah color. It couldn't make up its mind between red and purple. It lacked definition and purpose. But the Hawker 800 was a Craig kind of jet. It could fly from coast to coast and comfortably fit six — eight in a squeeze. Heck, it could even sleep three people lying down no problem at all.

The Raytheon salesman had a compromise. The deal was, Winn later told me, he and Rex would buy the Hawker 800 — with the maroon interior — for about $14 million. They would keep it for about a year. At that point, Raytheon would buy back the Hawker 800 for the price they paid and upgrade Craig and Rex to the new Hawker 800XP for just a bit more. In another year they would buy back the Hawker 800XP for the same price and sell them a brand-new Hawker 1000 for about $18 million, clean and simple. It was so easy.

The jet didn't fly itself, but Winn and Scatena didn't want to pay for everything, so they worked out a deal with Morgan by which Value America would pay for the pilots. Except at Value America, they weren't pilots anymore; they had become customer-service executives. When they weren't flying for the company, they would earn their $85,000 paychecks helping us out in customer service.

We were all excited about the plane and couldn't wait to ride in it. We were also worried that no one would distinguish between Value America buying a jet and Value America's chairman/founder buying a jet. We were right to be concerned. Hours after Winn and Scatena closed the deal, a message popped on the Yahoo! Value America message board that we had bought a $20 million jet.

Message boards were another Internet phenomenon. Someone sets up a common place where everyone with an interest in a particular subject can post messages about said topic. There are probably ten thousand Britney Spears message boards and at least as many for *NSync and the Backstreet Boys. There was also one for Value America. This board gave management fits. Sometimes a hundred or more messages a day, most of them distinctly unflattering to the company, showed up there. A lot of them sounded like they were coming from company insiders. Problem was, there wasn't any way to track who was posting. Yahoo! protected user anonymity, and while it was hypothetically possible to figure out who was posting inside Value America, our technology systems were too taxed as it was. So people inside the company posted with relative confidence that they'd never be found out.

By July 12, Value America's systems were getting so slow and unreliable that orders were getting lost, customers were abandoning their shopping because it took so long to place an order, and our financial reporting was so slow that we still didn't know exactly how much merchandise we had sold in June.

How slow was the store? Somewhere someone was typing in www.valueamerica.com and thinking to himself about that great new Panasonic DVD player he would be getting.

"Wow, can't wait to see those crystal-clear images. I'm so excited about the perfect sound." He waited for the page to load.

"I wonder what movies I'm going to order."

"Oh, I LOVE *Close Encounters!*"

The page was still loading.

"I wonder what that funky music at the end of the movie was supposed to represent?

"Maybe there was a deeper meaning! Maybe the movie was made by aliens and that music holds the key!" The page was still loading.

"Boy, aliens are cool, and so was *Alien*. . . . I'm going to order that, too." The page was still loading.

"Boy, Sigourney Weaver is hot, hot, hot. I wonder if there are any pictures of her on the Web? Maybe they could be downloaded. Boy, I love Sigourney Weaver."

Somewhere the Value America page was still being loaded, but the customer was off at Amazon.com or Buy.com or any of a hundred other stores actually buying his DVD. This matter led many people in the Value America technology department to ask a very important existential question: "If someone visits your Web page but leaves before he sees your Web page, has he seen your Web page?"

The slowness was an inconvenience. The lost orders were a genuine problem. Complaints about them started trickling in like the first ants discovering an open jelly jar at the annual company picnic.

"Um, hi, I ordered a Weber grill from you ten weeks ago, and it hasn't arrived yet."

"Excuse me, I hate to bother you, but I ordered a computer from you five weeks ago, and I've had my card billed but I haven't gotten my machine yet."

"Where the *hell is my stuff?*"

The latter people were the fire ants. The former ones were simply stomped on in hopes that they would magically disappear. Linda Harmon, the administrative assistant to both Winn and Morgan, would pipe up, "I got another one." Or sometimes we could hear her side of a conversation that we just knew was with an unhappy customer:

"Yes sir, I understand." . . . "Yes, we are horrible." . . . "Yes, that is horrible." . . . "Well, could you give me your order number?" . . . "I'm sorry, sir."

Some of the ants were bold. Instead of just calling for a customer-service manager, they decided that the informality of the information economy meant that they could call the chairman or CEO and get their problem taken care of. They used the Internet to find Winn's and Morgan's direct-dial numbers.

Very quickly, however, the ants overran the place. We *all* started getting e-mails and phone calls from irate customers who wanted, incredibly enough, their products. We got calls from people who wanted their caviar and their computers; sneakers and Sonys; refrigerators and RAM modules. I waited anxiously for my favorite item — I wanted someone to call and complain about the Good Humor ice cream they ordered online.

Nothing spoke quite as loudly to me about the potential problems we faced as Good Humor. Flipping through the store, clicking on specialty foods, clicking on brands, and clicking on Good Humor led you to a screen that showed you a multipack of Good Humor ice cream. It was all the stuff I loved as a kid. They had those waxy chocolate éclairs, ice-cream sandwiches, little cone sundaes, the whole thing. The package cost about $18 for fifty items — a great deal. Actually, for regular customers it was $25. Unfortunately, it cost another $15 to ship it. So, for nearly $40 you could get Good Humor delivered to your doorstep. So, one day I ordered. I couldn't wait to find out (a) how long it was going to take and (b) in what condition it would arrive.

In the meanwhile, we had these customer-service issues to deal with. One day I got a call on my voice mail from one of Peter Jennings's producers at *World News Tonight*. This was exciting. I'd been hoping ABC would do a story about what a great company Value America was. They were going to send a crew down to Charlottesville. They'd tape Winn, tape Morgan, and discover the hidden genius of this company.

It was with a measure of insane excitement, therefore, that I called the producer back. Even better — he had left his home number. I was going to reclaim my position as Value America's savior.

"Hello, Mr. Jones, please. This is David Kuo from Value America returning his call."

"This is Mr. Jones. David, I don't mean to use my position with ABC to get special treatment, but I didn't know where else to turn."

Uh-oh. Something was going on, and it wasn't going to win me accolades from the bosses.

"I ordered a computer for my son's birthday several weeks ago. I've been billed, but I haven't gotten anything yet. I'm ... getting ... annoyed."

Well, I thought, ABC might well run a story, but it sure won't be one for mom and dad to tape for the highlights reel.

Naturally I did what every other Value America executive did when faced with a customer-service problem. I tried to order someone to fix the problem. I fired off an e-mail to our seemingly anonymous head of customer service and demanded immediate action. To customer service's credit, those people personally passed off to them by executives did get their problems resolved. But as for everyone else . . .

I would have been terrified by this seeming explosion of problems, but Value America's experienced retail hands reassured me that customer complaints weren't anything to get too vexed about. When the topic came up at the weekly executive meetings, they would collectively roll their eyes and chuckle a bit.

In fact, the retail guys were right — to a point. Customer-service issues are common at every store, no matter how well or how poorly it is run. In fact, the best stores use customer-service complaints as a chance to win new customer loyalty. Nothing can turn a ticked-off purchaser into a store evangelist faster than great service. Got a bad toaster? No problem, we'll get you a new one, and an upgraded model to boot. That pair of pants not quite what you expected? No problem, we'll take them back no matter how many times you've worn them. I hoped like heck that was what we were doing.

Of course, it didn't help that the brands we were carrying weren't shipping the products fast enough. A few were — IBM's distributor, for instance, was sending its stuff out right away. Of course, IBM accounted for nearly 50 percent of Value America's business in 1998 and only slightly less so far in 1999, so they were motivated to ship. Everyone else, however, had only a few orders trickling in. There were, for instance, only five hundred #2 pencils ordered during the previous quarter. In another month, there were two Tear Drop golf putters. Panasonic's distributor was told to ship out twelve DVD players. These quantities weren't compelling enough for the brands to ship as quickly as we needed them to in order to keep our customers happy. This added up to real problems.

As Tom Morgan sat at his desk discussing the shipping problems with me, Craig opened the door and walked in.

Oh Lord, what *now?* Morgan wondered to himself. He buzzed through a list of possibilities before Craig even opened his mouth. It had actually turned into a little game for Morgan.

He was up to about twelve when Craig sheepishly said, "Hi. Kathy hasn't gotten her steaks. Could someone look into it, please?"

That was one that Tom never saw coming.

Morgan picked up the phone to call the head of customer service. Merchandisers were on the phone with the Omaha Steaks company. The operations people tracked the missing items. It was like the hunt for John F. Kennedy Jr.'s airplane. I half expected men in SWAT outfits to storm the building in search of the purloined sirloins.

My subsidized Weber grill was AWOL, my computer game was somewhere else, and my book wasn't anywhere to be found either. Even worse, my Good Humor ice cream was lost somewhere in cyber limbo. Who was looking out for my needs? Who was going to help me find *my* ice-cream sandwich?

CHAPTER ELEVEN

Hog-Tied

Although my orders still hadn't turned up, the sirloins were recovered in time for my inaugural dinner at the Winn house. I'd heard stories about Winndom but figured people were just pulling the new guy's leg. After all, who would build five buildings on one lot of land?

Craig Winn. Winndom was, he animatedly told me over tasty Omaha steaks, a Georgian-style revival, and a "carefully planned combination" of Mount Vernon (Washington's home on the Potomac) and Monticello (Jefferson's home in Charlottesville). He'd sketched out the plans one evening with a compass and a book of America's great homes. There was a main house, a "Greek garden" of marble and reflecting pool, a seven-acre man-made lake, a cedar-lined carriage house, and a custom-designed log cabin. It cost, Winn told me gently, "about two hundred and fifty grand a month" for him to get things just the way they needed to be. Winn built and razed, rebuilt and modified, and revised and changed most parts of the estate regularly in order to achieve perfection. Right now, he had decided Winndom really, truly, needed *seven miles* of stone fence–lined roads throughout the 125-acre estate. So he contracted with all available — and some technically unavailable — stonemasons to build the walls.

The decorative walls were partly for protection, ensuring that when Craig strapped on his helmet, pulled on his driving gloves, and plopped down inside the cage of one of his overpowered go-carts, he wouldn't go careening off into a tree. He wanted to show me how that worked.

We strapped on helmets and climbed into big go-carts encased in tubular steel skeletons. Craig just yelled, "Let's go!" and we were off. I'd been in go-carts before, the little kind that puttered around tracks powered by lawnmower engines. These were different. These little buggers moved. And soon enough I was winging through Winndom's miles of unmarked, semi-wall-lined roads, never knowing if at some moment, very soon, Chairman Winn, cheeks flapping in the breeze like a basset hound, might come zooming around the corner, crash into me, and kill me dead. For most people this thought was inhibiting enough to provide easy victory to the host. For me it was inhibiting enough to try and stay as close as possible to him to ensure he couldn't crash into me. Worst-case scenario I'd run over him. My excuse? Everyone knows Asians are bad drivers.

I survived and loved every minute of it. I loved Winndom, I loved the go-carts, I loved hanging out with Craig on his estate. The winding, paved roads would be a perfect spot for Kim's marathon-length runs. I asked him if it would be OK to have her jog them when she was in town. "Of course!" he said, smiling mightily. "Maybe you could even convince her to move down and work with us." The thought was at the front of my mind.

Kim and I had been talking about working together more and more since the Kansas Fourth of July weekend. She loved AOL, but with me and potentially her sister and brother-in-law in Charlottesville, the family seemed more attractive than the stock possibilities. Everything was on ice, however, until Heather and Scott came to interview with the company in early August.

The day after the Winndom experience, July 13, I was jetting up to D.C. with the pilots/Value America customer-service representatives. It was hard not to feel cool walking through the private air terminal, waving to John Grisham as he sipped an espresso, and walking out to my . . . our jet. Of course I was merely an escort. I was taking the thirteen-minute flight to meet Keith Benjamin, head Internet analyst for BancBoston Robertson Stephens. My assignment, conveyed from Winn via Kicklighter, was to hype the company and gain any intelligence I could about what Benjamin was thinking about Value America.

Hanging out at Winndom was a blast; going in to work, increasingly less so. I'd arrive at the office before 7:30 A.M. with a set of objectives: finalize upcoming press releases, figure out what other deals/projects/ partnerships were in the pipeline, follow up on press inquiries, work on executive speeches, pursue the J. Walter Thompson relationship, manage our public relations firm. Invariably by about 9:00 A.M. I'd be drawn into some meeting or brainstorming session by either Winn or Morgan.

I didn't have any complaints. It was fun to sit around and strategize about various plans or problem-solve issues. I loved the unstructured nature of it. The only real problem was I still needed to get my assigned job done. That task regularly kept me in the office till 10:00 P.M. Without Kim around, it was easier to dig into work.

I'd already talked to Morgan and Winn about hiring a couple other people in the communications shop to handle the load that was more than one person could bear over the long haul. Someone needed to be making outreach calls to the press every day. Someone else needed to figure out what stories members of the media were working on and angle ways for Value America to appear in them. We needed a finalized press kit that captured our store in a compelling way for journalists. Someone needed to get a hold on internal communications, so all our employees felt like they were part of a single, successful company. The more I thought about my list of potential to-dos, the more freaked out I got that they weren't getting done. As I sat on the plane, I recognized the only flaw in my hiring plan: Somehow I'd have to find time to locate, interview, and hire these people. Drat.

The plane landed, and I set out to find Keith. I pegged him right away, with his thinning hair, casually chic chunky shoes, a fashionably baggy suit, and a floppy briefcase. It was hard for me to believe this guy was important enough to warrant the jet treatment. He was. Keith's commentaries and analyses were watched religiously by big and small investors alike. If he was really hot on a company and said so publicly, that company's stock would rise significantly and immediately. The converse was also true. He was part of that elite crop of Internet analysts who were the Silicon Samurai. Like their counterparts in feudal Japan, they weren't the grand rulers but they did control life and death for the commoners — in this case the up-and-coming Internet companies.

What made Keith even more important was that he was *our* analyst. His bank had taken us public and made millions off it. From our perspective, it was his job to simultaneously convince all of the Robbie Stephens buyers and brokers to buy our stock while also convincing the investment community to buy our stock. Every morning he needed to be telling his people at Robbie about all the great things happening at Value America — the deals, the great management, the potential. To hit the day-trading community as well as the broader investor market, Keith needed to be publishing reports telling the world that we were better than AOL and Microsoft had ever been. He should have been lauding us in articles and on CNBC and CNNfn and in the bathroom. That was the way this world was supposed to work.

But Keith wasn't pimping our stock. He was silent. Sure, he put out a couple of reports and recommended Value America, but he wasn't *psyched* about it. When Robbie finally came out with its initial recommendation on Value America, we warranted only a "buy" rating. Its top rating was a "strong buy," which it had given to Amazon, AOL, and a handful of other favorites — and by all accounts it should have given it to us as well. The fact that Value America was not on the same level as those companies sent an unambiguous message. The next twenty-four hours — from the jet to D.C. to the evening party to the morning meetings — were designed to get Keith to add "strong" in front of "buy" to our rating.

Keith was aggressively unimpressed by our jet. He looked around casually and tried but failed to recline his seat as he commented that while Hawkers were nice, he really thought Challenger made a far superior plane. He was also disappointed that the chilled gulf shrimp in his appetizer weren't more "plump."

"So, you're my escort?" he mumbled.

"I'm the senior vice president for communications and investor relations," I proudly informed him.

"Yeah, great," he mumbled, barely able to contain his apathy at my grand title.

"Ah, David," one of the pilots/customer-service representatives announced from the cockpit, "Tom Morgan on the phone."

Morgan and his family were taking a long weekend vacation to Bermuda. He needed some distance from Value America and Craig, and he needed some time with his family. He'd been working like a dog and living away from his family, who remained in northern Virginia during the week.

Morgan sounded relaxed. "I'm thinking about quitting," he announced. "I'm tired of the battles. Craig is off doing all these crazy things, I'm never consulted, I can't run a business like that. I know how to run a business — I've done it for years. This isn't how to run a business. I may just come back and pack it all in."

I looked at Keith Benjamin, smiled confidently, nodded, and attempted to keep my composure. "Great, Tom, great, that'll be huge news. *Huge.* We've got to keep it quiet, but seriously, this will help the stock break through. Wow, hey, I'll call you later, I'm not in a secure place."

For the rest of the flight, I alternately stared at the map that showed our little animated plane creeping toward Charlottesville and tried to entertain and impress Keith Benjamin as he fondled and inspected the in-flight food. Tom Morgan in Bermuda, more relaxed than a yoga master, hovered in the back of my mind, telling me how peaceful he was feeling about quitting. Ack! The customer-service pilots dropped us into Charlottesville after the blessedly short fourteen-minute, $4,000 flight from Dulles.

I was to take Keith to Value America's Tear Drop Tour party. What, you might ask, is the Tear Drop Tour? Until they create a separate tour solely for Tiger Woods, there are three main professional golfing tours. First, there is the PGA. That's the major leagues. It's the land of *Fortune* 500 sponsorships, the Masters, the U.S. Open, the PGA, and the British Open. It rakes in millions of bucks. Players on this tour who have never even won a tournament are still millionaires. Significantly below that is the former Nike Tour, now the Buy.com Tour. It is best known for being the tour where Casey Martin first petitioned to ride in a golf cart rather than walk the course. It is filled with people you don't know, people you'll likely never know. A few of them will graduate to the PGA Tour. They just aren't *great* golfers. Those two tours most golf enthusiasts know. There is a third tour, however, that few have ever heard of. It is called the Tear Drop Tour. It is sponsored by Tear Drop Golf, a company that makes things like Tear Drop putters and Cobra-brand golf products.

The more exposure, the better — this was an Internet dogma. Sponsorship of a Tear Drop Tour event was going to cost Value America upward of $1 million. The first annual Value America Classic was going to be broadcast on the Golf Channel!

One million dollars can buy a lot of ads that can reach more people than just golf addicts. Several weeks before the tournament we realized this, as the staggering cost of the event was made known. We made frantic efforts to get other companies to help sponsor the tournament, hang out with the Value America crowd, and play golf. There weren't any takers. Despite the fact that we were spending millions in advertising in major newspapers like the *Washington Post* and the *New York Times* and in major periodicals, none of them wanted to put up $10,000 to be a "Monticello Partner" or $5,000 to be a "Jeffersonian Member" of the Value America Classic. (This despite the fact that the packages would have meant free golf, free tickets, and free meals.) In desperation, the company invited all of its brand-manufacturing partners to come down for the tournament as a way to thank them for their faith in Value America.

As Keith and I drove up to the Keswick Hall Country Club, we saw what seemed to be UFOs in the distance landing on the lawn. They were whitish and translucent. They glowed. We approached slowly and circled curiously. Finally, Keith's face lit up. "Ahh, tear drops!" Yes, three-story tall, inflatable tear drops — the calling card of the Tear Drop Tour. Obviously the result of a highly paid consultant's marketing genius — and for a cool $1 million, we were associated with them.

Inside the Keswick clubhouse, the party was going strong. There must have been at least a hundred people — all of whom I recognized . . . from Value America. For most of them it was probably their first million-dollar party. People around the buffet happily poked each other. "Hey, try those fajitas." "Hey, get a load of that flank steak." For a million bucks, Tear Drop should have been cutting their food, wiping their mouths, and giving them golf lessons.

Craig Winn was having a blast at the first-ever Value America Classic tournament party. What wasn't to love? A throng of adoring employees surrounded him, Value America's name was going to be on television screens everywhere when the tournament aired, and tonight he was going to convince Keith Benjamin that Value America was the hottest and most revolutionary company in the world.

Of course, tentacles of doubt sometimes threatened Winn in his moments of bravado. The gut-level grumbling and rumbling would occasionally take his biceps down a peg and make him want to stand back and step down. But to Winn, those were mere ghosts, to be crushed and destroyed — mastered.

Probably the only one not having fun was Keith Benjamin. He knew Value America was important to his company. The Robbie Stephens powers that were had looked at their charts and figured out the burn rates — the amount of cash required to keep the company afloat — and knew that within six months or so, Value America was going to need more money. Since the stock price was down in the dumps, a secondary offering wasn't in the cards. But there were lots of other options. A convertible stock deal, for instance, offered the benefits of stock for the purchasers if the stock went up and the safety of bonds with a fixed return if the stock failed to perform. For Robbie Stephens it could mean another payday. For Keith Benjamin it meant another day of meetings.

Over dinner Winn talked about the Value America Classic tournament glowingly. Yes, it had cost a bit of money, but this tournament gave Value America a prestige boost. It was just like Cadillac's sponsorship of the Masters every spring. Of course, the Masters was shown on network TV and internationally, but . . .

Then, as dinner concluded, Winn herded Benjamin and twenty Value America employees to a private room where everyone could have a nice casual discussion about Value America. There was an overview of the company's operations. The custom store opportunities were next. Through it all, Benjamin yawned a lot and squirmed, trying to get comfortable in his seat. After another hour, he sighed loudly, put on a pathetic grin, and said, "Listen, I've enjoyed our discussion, but yesterday I ran a marathon and today I'm zapped. I think we have meetings scheduled tomorrow, so we'll pick right back up then. OK? Good night." With that he stood up, grimaced, and hobbled out the door.

Winn was peeved. He hadn't seen Benjamin *get it*. He gave the guy a country club party. He flew him down on his private jet. He let his executive team discuss the intimate details of the company. And still Winn got nothing.

Winn chased after the Robbie Stephens analyst. Reaching him near the stairs, Winn patted him on the shoulder and said, "Impressive, isn't it? Revolutionary! We are changing the face of retail. We are launching the next great revolution. We are changing the world."

Benjamin froze. He smiled bravely and said, "Craig, I love Value America. Really, I do. But it is an online store. That's it. You're an online store. I'll see you in the morning."

I caught Winn on the rebound.

"Craig, just a thought. You know, I think when Tom gets back tomorrow, it would be really good for you to welcome him back enthusiastically. You know, tell him he was missed. Tell him that the place runs better with him. Let him know you actually do appreciate him being around."

Winn was surprised. Appreciate Tom? Of course he appreciated Tom. Why would he have gone to the trouble of recruiting him and paying him $700,000 a year if he didn't appreciate him? He needed Tom to run the business — he was *counting* on Tom to run the business. But he understood what I was saying, and he knew what he needed to do.

Winn was in the office the next morning at 7:00 A.M., Morgan's usual arrival time. His speech was prepared.

"Tom," Winn said sincerely, "we really missed you here these past few days. I really missed you. This company just isn't right without you around."

Fully prepared to announce his intention to leave, Morgan was a bit surprised by Winn's effusive greeting. But he was also determined to resolve the issues that were bothering him. He told Winn he couldn't operate the way things had been going. It was too frustrating for him to have only partial control of the company. Dividing things up so that Winn had a certain amount of control and he had a certain amount of control only contributed to the fundamental problem the company was having — no clear direction and no clear areas of accountability.

To his surprise, Winn agreed. Winn told him that he'd been thinking the same thing and that frankly, there were other things in the world he wanted to be doing. Politics, he told Morgan, was important to him, and he might spend more time doing that. He wasn't, however, prepared to give up deal making. That, Winn was certain, required his day-to-day involvement.

For Morgan it was precisely what he wanted to hear. More precisely, it was what he *needed* to hear to stay. Tom desperately wanted to keep running Value America. More correctly, he wanted the chance to actually run Value America. God was answering his prayers.

That morning, at Value America's offices, Keith Benjamin was greeted by a smiling and effusive Craig Winn, who introduced his "partner and the man running Value America," Tom Morgan.

Together, the three men dug down into Value America's business. Benjamin wanted to know specifics: How was Value America going to drive consumers? How was the company going to reduce costs? How was the company going to brand itself? How was the company going to improve gross margins? How were the custom stores really going to work? What was the company's cash situation?

Winn and Morgan explained it all. Value America's customer-acquisition strategy — Winn didn't even cringe at the phrase — was to leverage its unique business relationships to drive customers. Slowly, they explained, they would begin to move away from the kind of massive advertising spending that had defined their early days and toward more direct marketing, empowered by the custom store solution.

Morgan explained that Value America was exploring both the business-to-business and business-to-government markets in earnest. The potential for those markets, he explained to Benjamin, was very impressive, and Value America's model was uniquely suited to taking advantage of those markets. They were not, he assured him, undergoing any radical change in business focus but were recognizing that their business needed to evolve.

Sitting next to Morgan, Winn smiled and nodded and gave his wholehearted endorsement to the idea.

Keith Benjamin walked away impressed. The company might, he believed, have found a measure of balance. He particularly liked that Winn felt comfortable utilizing an accomplished corporate executive like Morgan to put things on the straight and narrow. As I escorted him back to Dulles on the company Hawker, he was much more chatty — and he seemed to enjoy the sandwiches and cookies arranged nicely on a platter.

With Keith Benjamin gone, the company turned its focus to the next important meeting. On Friday, July 15, Value America's powerful board would convene for the first time at Keswick. Winn's plan was for the entire company to appear before the board and give short presentations describing what each functioning division in the company was trying to accomplish. That plan had paralyzed the company for three full days. Every manager of every little section of the company had to present what his or her division did, who worked there, what their goals were, and why they loved Value America.

The night before the board meeting, I was thrilled to be invited to a dinner honoring the board. All the members were going to be there — Fred Smith, Gerry Roche, Tom Casey. It was a who's who of American business. We gathered in one of the Keswick Hall dining rooms over-looking the golf course and rolling Charlottesville hills.

As dinner wrapped up, Winn got up to give a short speech. He thanked Gary LeClair for helping save the company from death in September 1998. He thanked Fred and Gerry and the other board members. Turning to the meeting the next day, he outlined what they would be seeing, including a special guest who would be sitting in on the board meeting — Ken Lerer, PR svengali and head of Robinson Lerer Montgomery. RLM was one of the top public relations and investor-relations companies in the new economy. It had a single, spectacular, claim to fame. For all intents and purposes, RLM ran AOL's communications division. Frankly, RLM didn't even need other clients. AOL wasn't just the gravy train; it was the whole railroad.

But the wise folks at RLM knew the prestige of AOL meant others would pay big bucks for their advice and input. So they made themselves available to a select group of elite clients. They agreed to take on Value America because we had a good story, I was soon to be related to the AOL-employed Kim, and because we assured them that next to AOL, we wanted to be their biggest client.

To help me understand how it might work, Kim told me confidentially that RLM billed AOL upward of $1 million a month and provided the entire basis for AOL's communications strategy and tactics. With her approval I confidentially passed that information on to Winn for him to consider as we worked with them.

"And while AOL pays them a million a month and has them run their whole PR operation, we're going to get them for only twenty-five thousand a month!" Winn announced to the board.

I wished I had my hands on a Turkish dagger to hurl into Winn at that moment. I couldn't believe that he would betray my confidence and potentially harm my almost-wife as well. He wasn't speaking to a bunch of Nanooks from the North; he was talking to business leaders who also talked a lot.

After the meeting, I cornered Winn. "What the hell were you thinking?"

He looked at me with wide eyes and a stunned face. "About what?"

"About RLM."

"What did I say?"

Ten feet away, Tom Morgan and Tom Starnes cast cautious eyes our way. Morgan knew what Winn had done and also knew I was none too pleased.

"You told everyone about RLM's and AOL's deal."

"No, I didn't," Winn said with wide eyes.

"You sure as hell did."

Winn paused and thought. He couldn't for the life of him remember what he'd just said about RLM and AOL, other than that they were coming. "David, if I said something — and I don't recall it — that would have been wrong. But really, I don't recall."

"I just can't believe it." I shook my head sadly and walked off.

Morgan fell in beside me. "You did the right thing."

There weren't too many people in the company who did anything even remotely resembling standing up to Craig Winn. It wasn't easy to confront the man who founded, ran, and largely owned the company.

I was shaking. Morgan and I headed out for ice cream — it was our solace. "Listen, if you get fired, I'll find you a job for double the salary."

I didn't want another job. I didn't want to get fired. I wanted Value America. I just didn't want Winn to break confidences and blather on about stuff he wasn't supposed to talk about.

Back in one of my everchanging hotel rooms (I'd never had a free moment to get an apartment and therefore spent my nights in a rotation of nondescript hotel chains), I lay back on my bed in my suit and stared at the water-stained ceiling. I was too tired to call Kim, too frustrated to go to sleep, and still too excited about what we were trying to build.

Board Meeting Day dawned. Winn had sent a chartered jet up to New York early that morning to pick up Lerer, Lauren Hurvitz, his deputy, and Eric Fanning, a hotshot young PR gun. (Our *other* jet was shuttling in a weather-delayed Bill Bennett.) I went to greet them.

To the RLM folks, sending a jet was a bit of an odd move. Newly minted e-commerce companies, they thought, should be spending money wisely, not haphazardly. Not even AOL sent company jets for Lerer — he just hopped on the Delta shuttle. Landing in Charlottesville, they peered out the plane window and saw a long white limousine crawling across the tarmac toward their plane. It was, no doubt, a bit surreal.

We arrived in time for me to hear Craig reading the speech I had written for him the day before. He seemed careful to read every single word exactly as I'd written it. I listened to him and just smiled. It was the only real way he knew to say he was really sorry. He grabbed me during the first break to tell me how very much he appreciated my work. We both knew what he was saying: We were a happy family again.

As Winn played host throughout the day, providing commentary before, after, and during every presentation, he made reference after reference to how RLM was responsible for AOL's resurrection and would be instrumental in Value America's growth as a multinational company.

Ken Lerer pulled me aside as the meetings concluded. "I am . . . *concerned* . . . about Craig," he said. He paused, sighed, and stuck his hands in the pockets of his olive Armani-looking suit pants. "He doesn't seem . . . quite right. It is like he's hiding something. I get this weird feeling about him. I don't know. I don't know. I've got to think about this."

I didn't think there was anything hidden about Winn, no great secrets. I was concerned, however, that RLM's head guy was implying that we might not be able to sell Winn publicly. I assumed that was what he meant.

Except for Lerer, by the end of the day everyone was abuzz. The board was excited by all the amazing projects, partnerships, and potential. RLM believed they might have found a project of great prestige and — for them — revenue. For Value America's employees, it was a chance to see that the company really had grown out of its infancy and into maturity. Even Bill Bennett looked happy chatting away with the other board luminaries.

As the employee presentations concluded, the board met in a closed session to discuss key business items. The biggest question on most of the members' minds was who was running the company. Fresh off his meeting with Tom Morgan, Winn answered their query emphatically. Tom Morgan, he told them passionately, is the *only* man who could and should run Value America. They had worked together for nearly six months, and Winn said that he had never known another executive with the kind of character, integrity, and business acumen that Morgan had. Tom Morgan, Winn said, looking around the room, was the chief executive officer of Value America. This was *his* company to run. Winn knew that he'd done most of the talking during the day's meeting, but that was because of his pride in the people he'd assembled. It was also because he wanted to guide the board through the company person by person. From now on, it was Morgan's show to run.

The board nodded as one, like kids in a kindergarten class. That was, Smith said, the only way to run a business. The CEO needed to have control, authority, and accountability. They applauded Winn's insight and his relationship with Morgan.

The board also disposed of other business. They quashed any ideas Winn had about mergers or acquisitions and expressed a measure of concern about whether the automobile division was too much of a diversion. Apart from those caution flags, it gave a wholehearted endorsement to all the projects Value America had going.

Late that afternoon, before adjourning for the weekend, Winn, Morgan, Starnes, and I were hanging out in Morgan's office, deep in male bonding. We pulled out a golf club from behind Morgan's desk and started a putting contest. We chattered about cars and boats and planes. We kibitzed about all the amazing business that lay ahead. All past sins were long ago forgiven.

Winn, in particular, was excited about potential partnerships with Saks Incorporated and Citibank. If executed properly, each of those deals could be worth billions and billions.

In Saks's case, Value America was vying to become their exclusive e-commerce partner. The relationship would enable Value America to carry the full line of Saks merchandise in its store while simultaneously giving Saks access to lines of goods — like technology and computers — it had never carried before.

The potential Citibank relationship was in its earliest stages. But minimally, Value America would become Citibank's e-commerce partner for their twenty million cardholders. Winn would drive both deals in the ensuing weeks.

At one point, Starnes announced he was willing to bet that his government initiative would reach a billion dollars faster than either of Winn's potential big deals.

Winn loved the bet, and as Morgan and I watched, he instantly negotiated the terms. If Starnes was right and the government sector had a billion-annualized-run rate before either of Winn's projects, he would be judged the winner. In that case, Winn would personally buy him and his wife *any* production car made in the world. It didn't matter if it was a Ford Focus or a Ferrari Testarossa, all Starnes had to do was tell Winn which color and where he wanted it delivered. In addition, he would pay for a one-week vacation anywhere in the continental United States or Caribbean and fly Starnes and his wife there on the Hawker.

If Winn was right, however, Starnes would have to pay up as well. Winn paused and considered an offer. He couldn't have the bet recipro- cated, because Starnes didn't have that kind of money. But he wanted the wager to be real for Starnes as well. Winn therefore proposed that if he won, Starnes and his wife would have to take Craig and Kathy out for dinner at any restaurant in the United States and let them order whatever food or wine they wanted.

Starnes took the terms of the bet, and the two men shook hands en- thusiastically. For Morgan and me, the mere race warmed our hearts — we knew that if the company hit a billion in revenue from either one of the projects, we'd all be in very good shape indeed.

All Value America employees were still subject to the six-month lockup, when no one could sell any stock. It wouldn't end till early No- vember. If Winn or Starnes or both could come through with their deals, life would be just fine by the time the lockup ended.

Following the board meeting, Winn's focus returned to his commer- cials. He had arranged for the advertising team to fly down to Lynch- burg to Falwell's studios for the shoots. The setting was perfect. Falwell did have some very presidential-looking backdrops — bookcases, fire- places, even a little country-room setting. The idea was to shoot Winn standing in front of these backdrops narrating the scripts. In the finished product, the commercial would cut back and forth between Winn and segments illustrating the products.

The ad team had secretly concluded that the only real hope of pre- venting the commercials from airing was to delay the whole process as much as possible. By not moving at lightning speed through all the background filming and general editing necessary to make the commer- cials even moderately acceptable, they'd have at least a month, maybe two, before there would be anything anyone could actually put on the air.

Winn was having a blast. He'd never filmed commercials before and loved every little bit of it — aside from the need to keep his rambling within a strict time limit. He especially liked the set. Between takes, looking seriously at the cameras, he would intone, "My fellow Americans . . ." He could just picture himself sitting or standing in front of the cameras giving a national address. It was, he was certain, just a matter of time.

The next day Winn brought the rough videotapes into my office for viewing. He slid one into the VCR and stood back, half watching my reaction and half admiring his performance. I was underwhelmed. Ad after ad with Winn in a dark suit and alternating blue shirts and ties standing in front of faux bookcases didn't seem very exciting, progressive, or memorable. Even for political ads they were stiff. Compared to the other dot.com commercials that had begun appearing, they were appalling. There just wasn't any soul. Winn knew I wasn't impressed, so he ripped out the tape and bolted from my office.

The commercials were temporarily shelved as Winn moved on to his next project. Saks Incorporated was one of the country's premier retail conglomerates, with a total of 362 stores in thirty-nine states, more than $6 billion in annual revenues, and nearly sixty thousand associates. The prize of the lot were the sixty-two Saks Fifth Avenue stores. In addition, Saks, Inc. owned and operated another three hundred national and regional department stores and outlet stores, including Parisian, Proffitt's, and Carson Pirie Scott. Saks also owned Saks Direct, which included the Folio and Bullock & Jones catalogs.

The Saks relationship had sparked about a month earlier, when Doug Holladay introduced Morgan and Winn to Bill Haslam, a personal friend of his and a consultant to Saks. Saks's problem was the same problem faced by a lot of other bricks-and-mortar retailers: how, exactly, to capitalize on the e-commerce phenomenon. There was a fundamental difference of opinion within Saks. One camp believed they needed to create their own branded e-commerce site to leverage the prestige of the Saks name. Not surprisingly, that camp was led by the Saks Internet team. The other camp, led by the CEO, believed it would be best for Saks to create some kind of partnership with an existing e-tailer. That approach would serve two ends. First, it would defray Saks's cost and their risk. Second, it would allow Saks to get online much faster than if they built a site on their own.

No one in the entire world — not even Internet analysts — annoyed Winn more than retailers. As a group, he had always found them irredeemably stupid and obtuse. He remained a retailer only because he wanted to show them how a professional really worked. Winn met with Haslam in Charlottesville, listened to Saks's conundrum, and promptly pronounced that anyone at Saks who thought they could build something themselves was an idiot and should be instantly fired. Haslam told Winn he himself was actually leaning toward recommending Saks do it alone. If the shoe fits, wear it, Winn replied. If Haslam could be persuaded to change his stunningly stupid position, however, Winn would help Saks do what it needed to do. Haslam returned to Saks headquarters and told Saks chairman and CEO Brad Martin there wasn't anything worth pursuing with Value America.

Winn was not ready to give up, however. He called Fred Smith, who happened to be good friends with Martin. Winn described for Fred exactly what he wanted to do with Saks — namely, provide an integrated e-commerce solution that would capitalize on the Saks Fifth Avenue brand for high-end consumers but also be able to leverage the more mainstream Parisian and Bullock brands. Smith agreed, called Martin, and brokered a telephone relationship between Martin and Winn.

Martin liked Winn's big thinking. The foundation of the relationship, Winn proclaimed, would be the saks.com custom store. This high-end site would be custom tailored for the very wealthy. There would be a personal shopper available for online assistance or for assistance via the telephone if that was easier. This personal shopping assistant would also effectively serve as a concierge for all of life's needs for the wealthy. They would be able to book travel, vacations, hotels, restaurant reservations, and tickets to concerts and sporting events, and even order fresh flowers. But, Winn told Martin, it didn't end there. By partnering with Value America, saks.com would also be able to offer high-end personal computers, home-computer networks, high-end stereos, TVs, and other electronics accessories. Value America and Saks could even arrange to place a Saks-branded computer in the home of its most valued customers. Nothing like it existed on the Web, and Saks was uniquely positioned to make it happen. The other potential competitors, Winn told Martin, weren't anywhere near ready to challenge anything like this. Neiman Marcus was taking a niche sales approach with their high-end items, and Nordstrom was simply focusing on providing a massive selection of shoes.

It was, Winn told Martin, the *perfect* plan. From Saks's perspective, the Value America relationship would enable them to get online faster and more aggressively than anything else that they could do. For Value America it made a lot of sense, too. In return for creating a custom store for Saks, Value America would instantly become the biggest clothing department store on the Web. By leveraging the products from Saks's other stores, it wouldn't be offering just high-end merchandise but also brands that middle-class consumers appreciated as well. It was quintessential Winn; he knew what Value America needed and what the other guys needed and was now driving toward that win-win goal line that had served him his whole life.

Winn and Martin scheduled a morning meeting for July 22 in New York to discuss the opportunity. Buoyed by his success with the Whirlpool meeting in late May and the recent board meeting, Winn decided to bring as many Value America leaders as possible along with him. Persuaded by Morgan not to rent a larger jet to accommodate more people, the Value America entourage that morning numbered eighteen, ten of whom had flown commercial. Saks countered with eight of their own people: Brad Martin, his top adviser, Bill Haslam, the two top people from their Internet team, as well as four people from the New York office who were along for the ride.

Winn began the meeting by handing out his thirty-one-point memo on the potential relationship as well as his financial projections. According to his calculations, if the two companies executed on the relationship only moderately well, they would probably see more than $400 million in revenue in their first year. If, however, they did everything that Winn envisioned and they hit it out of the park, that number would be *at least* $1 billion that first year.

The Saks underlings looked at Winn's sheets of paper and snickered.

"What's wrong?" he asked, noticing their sideways glances. "Don't they teach you to read where you come from?" Winn barely held it together.

From the other end of the table, one of the Saks execs shot back, "Yeah, they teach us to read, but they also teach us to add. What's your excuse?"

At the Saks end, Brad Martin reached over to his left and patted the man on the back. "Let's just discuss the possibilities for this terrific idea," he reminded his team.

"Let's do that," Winn said. "Let me be clear," he continued, "unless

Saks adopts this strategy, it will have absolutely no hope for an Internet presence before Christmas 2000. The idea that you can build something from scratch is as absurd as if I told you I was going to belly dance naked in the Saks Fifth Avenue windows down the block. Am I making myself clear?"

For the next two hours, Winn and the Saks team went back and forth about his contention that their Internet approach was asinine and their contention that his numbers and his plan were absurd.

I didn't know whether to shrink off into the corner or try to hog-tie our chairman with the nearest lasso. With every exchange and every caustic comment, we all saw the Saks deal blow away.

No one else from the Value America team said a word. We left without a signed deal.

After the meeting, Craig gathered our shaken team together on the street in front of the Saks corporate building. I want everyone to know, he began, that everything that happened up there today was intentional. I needed to send a message to these people. There is no more arrogant group of people in the world than retailers. These guys might be the worst of the bunch. I don't know if we'll end up with a deal or not. I suspect that we probably will. But I don't want anyone to be concerned with what happened. It is just part of business, he reminded us.

At that, the other Value America executives, with combined business experience of more than 250 years, looked at each other, shrugged their shoulders, and hoped their guru was right.

CHAPTER TWELVE

Counting Sheep

Within minutes of Saks's death, Winn and a smaller group of executives headed out of Manhattan, over the East River and into Queens for a meeting with Citibank. Citibank had a big problem. Like a lot of other mammoth corporations, they had seen the growth of the Internet and said, "OK, we need to be there, too." So they formed an e-commerce group, devoted hundreds of millions of dollars to establishing a Web presence, and waited for the cash to roll in. And waited. And waited. Like Linus waiting for the Great Pumpkin, they waited. Unlike Linus, though, when the Great Pumpkin didn't show up, they spent buckets of money hiring consultants, new employees, and advisers to tell them how to seduce the Great Pumpkin. They then followed their various gurus' advice. Still, no Great Pumpkin.

By mid-1999, Citibank's e-commerce efforts had lost scores of millions of dollars. They had a great Web site, they had some great promotions and a big bunch of slick materials. But nothing had happened.

Earlier that summer, Citibank had issued an RFP (request for proposal) on providing an e-commerce infrastructure to serve their existing card members — about twenty million of them. Their requirements were tailor-made for Value America. Citibank wanted an online retailer with an extensive category of offerings that took in orders, not only over the computer but also over the telephone. On our end, the Citibank relationship would allow Value America to take the custom store model to the next level, using our systems to build an e-commerce infrastructure for another company. We could also share in some portion of Citibank's revenue while simultaneously accessing their database of customers. Internet companies were killing themselves for an opportunity like this.

Citibank never originally said they wanted to meet with Winn, but he wanted to meet with them. If there was one thing he knew, it was that if he could just get in front of people, then he could sell them. From a distance, companies all looked alike. One might sell books, another CDs, and yet another jockstraps. But in person, any sale could be expanded and finalized. In person, the relationship was forged. It didn't matter if someone wanted to meet with you or not, you always wanted to get in front of them. For Winn, this wasn't a principle, it was a way of life.

No one, Winn believed, was pursuing affinity marketing on the Internet. Companies like MBNA had made a mint by getting major corporations and not-for-profits to sponsor credit cards. United Airlines, the Pittsburgh Steelers, Tufts University, America's Promise, the American Bar Association — all these groups had branded Visa or Master-Cards. For the groups it was a way to make a little money. For MBNA, it was a way to make a mint. In a competitive marketplace, an affinity group could tilt a customer's attention and loyalty to the MBNA card over any other one. Craig Winn saw in the Citibank deal not only the Value America engine for Citibank's site but also a co-branded Citibank/Value America credit card. He saw cross-selling Citibank life insurance to Value America customers. He saw an entire suite of financial services for e-commerce customers. Value America would become not only the marketplace for a new millennium but also the sole e-commerce destination for top brands — retail, insurance, financial services, travel, everything. All he needed was the Citibank audience. And he was about to get it.

Winn knew that Citibank was facing increasing competition from other banks. He also knew that its recent merger with Travelers Group was causing the inevitable turbulence that putting two different corporate cultures together always brings. Finally, he knew that the singular goal of the Citibankers was to devise an Internet strategy so successful it would catapult them into upper management. He started walking them through their issues.

First point: Citibank's historic lead in credit cards was eroding faster than anyone expected, and faster than Citibank had let on publicly. The two Citibankers looked at their priorities list and checked off item number one on their "issues to solve."

Second point: The first priority wasn't to acquire new customers but to reduce losses of existing customers by increasing loyalty. The Citibankers looked at each other, nodded slightly, and checked off item number two.

Third point: Citibank believed that improving the value of their cards for existing card members was one of the keys to Citibank's success, hence the RFP.

For the next thirty minutes Winn elucidated all of Citibank's issues, all the avenues they were exploring to solve their problems, and all the ways that Value America could help them achieve their goals. As the Citibankers sat back in their chairs, jaws agape, Winn smiled, began assembling his papers, and informed them he had another meeting he needed to attend. "But, I might add, if you think we understand your particular predicament accurately, please let us know, and we'd be glad to try and work together with such a fine institution." In tandem, the Citibankers stammered that they were grateful and happy and overjoyed to have met him and to see that he understood their situation so well. They *did* want to meet again — soon. They would love to work together, really they would. Winn smiled, nodded, and strutted out. We followed our leader with a little confident bouncing of our own.

At that moment if someone had asked me how I felt about the earlier Saks meeting, I would have looked at them quizzically — as if they'd asked me how I felt about having blond hair. It simply would not have computed. Saks was a blip that had never occurred. Winn was just proving a retail point. The Saks people had been mean. We were just being educated. All I could think about was Citibank. The drive to the airport, the flight back to Charlottesville, the couple hours at night in my office were all tied together by this single thought: How does Winn do it? I couldn't figure it out. I didn't understand the world that he saw. How did he *know* what Citibank needed? How did he *know* how the deal would turn out? How did he *know* all these things before they happened? Whenever Winn displayed these moments of genius, I got recharged, reinvigorated, and reminded that we really were going to conquer the world.

The next morning, Winn walked into Morgan's office and announced the good news. "Citibank was *awed* by me." Morgan was speechless. He'd already heard that the Citibank meeting went well — I'd whistled in a call to tell him as much. He knew firsthand that no one could make a first impression like Winn. The problem from Morgan's perspective was that a good first impression and a good first meeting and positive feedback empowered Winn to go on and push the envelope. It was like the Henry Kissinger thing all over again. Winn believed, truly believed, that Citibank's credit-card division was now his to play with. It was a brand-new sandbox. It might not be 150 acres, but it was bigger than $150 billion. That made it worthy of his full attention.

Winn left Morgan's office, went into his, shut the door, sat down, and began plotting out the billions of dollars Value America and Citibank would make together. It was now nearly August. He was absolutely confident that a huge deal could be nailed down by September. He told me about the press conference that would ensue: Winn and the chairman of Citibank standing behind the podium at a prestigious New York hotel. The media would be packed in. Flashes would be popping, blinding him temporarily. He'd put his arm around the Citibank CEO, smile broadly, say something witty, and ponder whether his net worth that day had tripled or just doubled.

He hustled back into Morgan's office. "I forgot to tell you this," he said. "When we were leaving, they pulled me aside and said, 'We are *awed* by your genius. We've *never* met anyone like you. Tell us what to do. We think you are sent by God.'"

Morgan didn't have a clue how to respond. "Fantastic," he said. "Really, fantastic." He desperately hoped that Winn would leave quickly.

"*Fantastic!* I bring you news about what is undoubtedly the biggest deal in the history of e-commerce and I get *fantastic?*" Winn was frustrated. Sometimes he wondered whether this whole thing was going to work out after all. He and Morgan were so different. He wanted to grow things and buy things and build things. He needed to make those visions in his head become reality so that he could move on to the other things in his head — things like being the President of the United States, for instance. But Morgan was difficult. He wasn't quick enough. He didn't get things fast enough. He was careful, and that was good. But he was also cautious, almost timid. That was bad, especially in the Internet space right now. Winn knew he couldn't run the business himself either; he'd tried that way once, and it hadn't worked out. But . . .

Tom Morgan couldn't sleep. Every evening he'd sit out on the porch of his 150-year-old farmhouse, hold a glass of wine in one hand, a cigar in the other, and listen to the soft sounds around him growing softer. Sharp chirps and croaks became muffled and gentle — soothing. The cool night air blanketed his long sleeves and long pants. He'd set the glass down, balance his smouldering cigar on the edge of the railing, then open the door and tromp upstairs. Collapsing into bed, he fell asleep easily. But at some unknown moment in the night, his brain kicked into high gear. Dreams about work became thoughts about work. Fuzzy became real. Stop analyzing. Just go back to sleep. Sleep. Sheep. One sheep, two sheep . . . the SAP implementation . . . meeting revenue expectations . . . three sheep, four sheep . . . runaway costs . . . infomercials . . . Winn's exaggerations . . .

Shoot. He was wide awake.

The kind of night he'd never known was now his uneasy but regular friend. The crickets eventually stopped chirping. Birds stopped talking. Everything grew silent. All that was left were him and his thoughts. Too many thoughts. On vacation in Bermuda he had slept . . . hard and sound. He'd run four miles twice a day to ensure exhaustion and had had a quick glass of wine with dinner. Now, here, back in Charlottesville, in a place darker, quieter, and more peaceful, sleep just teased him.

He couldn't put his finger on just what was causing his insomnia. If he could identify that one thing, then he could deal with it. The company itself was fine. Sure there were issues, but it was a business, and he could resolve those issues. The board was killer and completely supportive to boot. Even troublesome Winn, with his constant sales pitches and frequent truth lapses, was OK. After all, hadn't Winn been amazingly reassuring that morning he got back from Bermuda, saying how much he appreciated all the work, all the effort, all the struggles? Theirs was a partnership, he said. They were a left and right wing working together. Yet sleep and peace still eluded him.

The bond between them was, however, part of the problem. Morgan and Winn had had many spiritual conversations, and to Morgan it was clear that Winn was a man longing for a more substantial relationship with God. But though Morgan was hearing the right words from his partner, he still didn't see Winn transforming his life, and that bugged him. How long was he supposed to wait to see that transformation? And if the transformation never came, would Tom Morgan's integrity be compromised? Morgan feared it would. That would be unacceptable.

At USOP, he'd had to deal with a difficult boss, too — John Lidecki. Lidecki, now partners with Michael Jordan and AOL's Ted Leonsis in the Washington Wizards and Capitals, was mercurial and demanding, but at least Morgan understood where Lidecki was coming from. But at

Value America everything happened so fast. Decisions and opportunities and challenges came at him — at the company — like machine-gun fire. Even at US Office Products, where it sometimes seemed that he rolled up companies approximately every eighteen minutes, the pace and the demands had been more predictable. The performance markers were similar: make money, drive revenue, control expenses. This wasn't rocket science, just basic business. But business wasn't supposed to move *this* quickly. In traditional business there were reports to study, research to evaluate, decisions to be reached. At Value America all of that had to be done on the fly. It was business by gut-level guess.

Even Winn's pronouncements about the success of his Citibank meetings didn't move Morgan like they used to. There was a time, only a few months ago, when Morgan lived for moments like these. There were so many billion-dollar-revenue projects that he'd now lost count. He was trying not to lose heart.

He was also starting to hate sheep. He'd said the Lord's Prayer dozens of times without any narcotic effect. Finally he got up and padded down the stairs of the old farmhouse. He flipped open his Bible and turned to Ecclesiastes, the book he'd been reading during his early mornings. "I made great works; I built houses and planted vineyards for myself; I made myself gardens and parks, and planted in them all kinds of fruit trees. I made myself pools from which to water the forest of growing trees. I bought male and female slaves, and had slaves who were born in my house. . . . I gathered for myself silver and gold and the treasure of kings and provinces; I got singers, both men and women. . . . I kept my heart from no pleasure. . . . Then I considered all that my hands had done and the toil I had spent doing it, and behold, all was vanity and a striving after wind, and there was nothing to be gained under the sun." He trundled back to bed, hoping to find sleep.

On Sunday night, August 1, Morgan found himself caring less about *where* it would end and more about *when*. We were going to announce our Q2 results the next morning. For every public company — exponentially more so for public start-ups — the earnings call wasn't just a report card, it was a report card, SAT score, AP exam, and complete recommendation file all rolled into one. It was the one moment in every quarter when the company had the world's attention. With that attention, companies can impress, mortify, or bore. We really needed to impress. The revenue figures were incredibly impressive — slightly more than $35 million, an increase of 600 percent from the same period a year earlier. The annualized-run rate was now pushing $150 million, and Value America was growing at nearly 30 percent quarter over quarter. Significantly, companywide gross margin had improved to a little more than 4 percent. That wasn't going to set any records, and it certainly wasn't the 15 percent Wall Street wanted, but it showed positive movement.

Very quietly, Value America had become one of the top revenue-producing e-tailers on the Internet. Amazon dwarfed everyone else's revenues by hundreds of millions. But aside from them, Value America was now selling more than Beyond, Egghead, Cyberian Outpost, and the whole slew of lesser players, like eToys, Pets.com, Ashford.com, and MVP.com.

Unfortunately, as Morgan sat in his office preparing for the earnings conference call, he didn't have anything he needed. In front of him was a list of key figures that needed to be ready by the 10:00 A.M. conference call the next day. He believed in giving his executives maximum freedom — he gave them maximum trust. But for Morgan, nights like tonight should *not* be happening. These were not higher-order questions he was looking to answer but basic ones. For instance, how many customers did Value America have? How many members? What was the repeat-purchase rate? He'd only learned the final bottom-line numbers late on Friday. The good news — the $35.8 million for the April–June quarter was well above analyst forecasts of $28.8 million, even though it was below the $48 million internal figure Value America had set in mid-April. Nearly $26 million of that total came from commercial and consumer computers. Another $4 million came from software and computer peripherals. The remaining $4.4 million in revenue came from the twenty-six other categories of products. There were $635,000 in office-products sales. $24,000 worth of books. $4,000 in pet supplies. $2,000 in apparel. There were $6,000 in specialty foods and $58,000 in revenue from Value America's automotive division — Tom Morgan had purchased a car for his daughter Jamie through it, as had one other Value America employee. The only other large category of goods was $1.9 million in consumer electronics.

In the old world when companies made money, EPS, or earnings per share, was a key metric. EPS was the basic computation of net profits divided by the number of outstanding shares. Higher numbers are good. In the new economy, however, EPS really meant losses per share; the number was expressed as a negative figure, and the general goal was to have lower, not higher, losses. Lower losses told Wall Street that expenses were under control and that the business was moving toward profitability. Higher losses told Wall Street the company was just trying to buy revenue. At one utopian moment in Internet history, Wall Street had actually liked bad EPS results, but not anymore. Unfortunately, Value America was still operating in that utopian world. Value America had higher losses. *Much* higher losses. As in $31 million in losses. The question was how *much* was it going to hurt?

Why this surprise wasn't revealed until days before the earnings announcement was a matter for discussion. Apparently Glenda Dorchak hadn't given Morgan the final ad and marketing expenses until late in the game. Dean Johnson evidently hadn't called analysts to have them adjust their expectations. Despite the Goldman report on the importance of gross margins and Amazon's indefinitely delayed profit announcements, Winn, Morgan, Dorchak, and Johnson still expected that the dramatic increase in revenue would overshadow any bad news, including a big EPS blunder.

NASCAR sponsorships, golf tournaments, and advertising had ballooned the expenses column. We had spent more than $20 million on advertising alone. More than $3.5 million in technology improvements. Nearly $5 million in general and administrative expenses. Wall Street consensus estimates were for a net loss of $.63 per share. Value America had a net loss of $.79 a share. This wasn't a near miss, this was Mondale versus Reagan, Godzilla versus Bambi.

To boot, we were burning through cash at an astonishing rate. With slightly more than $100 million remaining, Morgan and Winn realized that cash was going to have to be raised no later than late fourth quarter 1999 or early first quarter 2000. By that time, the company's burn rate would hit more than $20 million a month.

Down the hall, Morgan had convinced himself things weren't that bad. We hit revenues out of the park, we've got a lot more members — though membership is still free — we're building the technology infrastructure — it isn't going to be that bad. Of course, he still didn't have any of the numbers he needed. It didn't look like he was going to get them either. He'd just have to wing it.

After listening to the last conference call, Robinson Lerer Montgomery had implored us to rein in Winn and his pronouncements. The script he now held in front of him was perfectly acceptable, if not perfectly inspiring. But if RLM said to stick to the script, he was going to do it. After all, they were going to make Value America the next AOL.

At the opposite end of the building, Dean Johnson sat in his office, fuming. It was 10:30 at night on a Sunday. Why did *he* have to be there? Everyone else was talking about getting pizza and digging in like it was a campaign or something. This wasn't fun, this was hell. His stuff was done, there wasn't any need for him to be there, why couldn't he just leave? Why should he have to pay for other people's stupidity? He'd suffered these BS sessions for a couple *years* now. It was time for sanity.

In another small office, Mick Kicklighter was gazing at the pictures now hanging on his wall. He thought back to Vietnam and to how orderly it all seemed in comparison to the dot.com world.

In his office, Winn was preoccupied with preparing new "guidance" for the analysts. Based on the pending relationships with Citibank and the custom stores, he believed that Value America's analysts needed to dramatically increase their revenue projections for 2000 and 2001. He had prepared a memo explaining to them the new "demand generation" opportunities and advising them to *double* their revenue predictions. If nothing else moved the stock, surely the news that analysts were *doubling* revenue projections for Value America would send shock waves through the e-commerce world.

I headed for Kohr's. Kohr's was the single best excuse for Charlottesville. The original Kohr's had been founded by three brothers on the Coney Island boardwalk in 1919, but this Kohr Bros. had the same frozen custard with "the sinfully delicious taste of premium ice cream with the calories of frozen yogurt." Kohr's was the dessert equivalent of crack cocaine. There were moments when Value America employees were crazed for it. The size ordered corresponded directly to our stress levels. Small was for when it was just a little hectic and we needed a quick pick-me-up. Regular was for average days, like when we were ordered to double the stock price or store traffic or sales revenue or media exposure in the next two hours. Then there were the large days. Large days were when we felt the apocalypse to be close at hand. There had been a lot of large days lately.

That night I wanted Kohr's to just open up the lid on their little dispenser and give me a spoon.

I pondered Kohr's and Value America. There were significant differences between the two. Kohr's had a defined mission: They sold frozen custard. Four months after going public, Value America had no defined mission: It sold everything and anything. Kohr's aimed at turning a profit. Value America aimed at custom stores one day, government the next, and business the day after that, all while spending as much money as possible on anything possible. Value America seemed to think that a profit was something that God sent to the Jews in the desert. Kohr's had a nice little phrase to differentiate its product. Value America had a new mission and a new description every third press release.

I wondered if I might be able to make a future in frozen custard.

Part Three

HELTER SKELTER

CHAPTER THIRTEEN

"To the moon, Alice, to the moon!"

I had a bad feeling as I flipped on my computer early on August 2, went to the Nasdaq-AMEX site, and read the headlines from the wire reports: "Value America reports larger than expected losses," "Value America blames technology spending on losses," "Value America loss $.79 v. est. of $.63." The world had changed. It wasn't just about revenue anymore. It was about gross margin and controlled losses and growing revenue. It was like having to grow a real business. No one ever told us we had to do *that*.

Nearly three thousand miles away, Keith Benjamin sat at his desk, feet propped up, headphone adjusted just right, and watched the sun begin to cast its first light across San Francisco. In his left ear, Craig Winn was blathering on about upping Value America's revenue estimates. Benjamin was tired of Winn's promises. Even though another Robbie Stephens division was busily preparing a presentation for Winn on how they could help Value America raise more money — even with a deflated stock price — Benjamin wasn't going to budge. There was no justification for him to raise his revenue estimates. Looking at the press release, all he saw was red. The company's sales and marketing expenses were astronomical — it would be more beneficial if the company just hired a plane to skywrite "SHOP VALUE AMERICA AND TAKE 50 PERCENT OFF EVERYTHING ALL THE TIME." Sales and marketing expenses alone were more than 50 percent of the revenue. That didn't even factor in technology, administrative costs, or anything else. This wasn't a company on the road to success; it was a company on the road to implosion.

To Benjamin it seemed that no one inside the company had a clue. Despite his positive trip to Value America just weeks before, the Winn he was listening to and the press release he had read showed him that Value America hadn't changed. It was still the same company. It talked a lot and did very little.

186 · J. David Kuo

The world had changed. It was about a controlled revenue grab —
about gaining market share in an efficient and cost-effective way. Benjamin didn't see any evidence that Winn or Value America knew that,
and he wasn't going to pimp something just for the sake of pimping it.
If it was good, then he would sell it. If it wasn't good, he would remain
largely silent.

"Craig, at this time I'm choosing not changing revenue projections,"
Benjamin intoned.

Winn sat in the office, staring blankly at the conference-call phone in
front of him. What had he missed? Why was the little prick not following along? This was guaranteed stuff. This stuff was going to work.
Why wouldn't he raise the estimates? The estimates were too damn low.
Value America was going to be the biggest retailer out there. Winn was
fuming. These pricks were in Amazon's back pocket and couldn't get
out. Bezos, the opportunistic little turd, had everyone in a tizzy about
what they were doing. Even worse, the finance geeks were applauding
his move to spend hundreds of millions on building warehouses and distribution centers! Did they know *nothing?!* Warehouses and distribution
centers ate money, they didn't make money.

Well, if Keith Benjamin wouldn't do it, Winn reasoned, Derek
Brown would. Brown was the top analyst at Volpe Brown, a small Internet boutique bank that had helped with Value America's IPO. Like
Benjamin, Brown was soft-spoken, a nerd made good in a high-tech
world where IQ was more important than bicep size. But like his Robbie Stephens colleague, Derek Brown was not biting. There was just no
substance to the request. Why should he raise revenue estimates when
all he was hearing was speculation and hype?

As he put down the phone with Brown and struggled not to call the
other analysts, Winn saw what his new path of action would have to be.
He would rage against the machine. He alone could stand up to these
people and expose them to the retail truth. He would nail the treatises to
the church door — even if the door was virtual.

At 10:00 A.M., the earnings call was set to begin. The eight Value
America executives gathered around the little nineteenth-century-
American antique table that was Winn's conference center and spoke
into the little black electronic starfish. We had no idea whom we were
talking to or what their reactions were to what we were saying; AT&T

was going to supply us with a list of the callers, but it hadn't yet arrived. Outside, some maintenance workers were using weed whackers and blowers to spruce up the grounds. No one could shut them up. I stood up and started jumping up and down, waving my arms wildly to get them to zip it. Winn started flailing his arms, too. Tom Morgan got up and moved to the other window to try and get their attention. Cristal, excited by all the commotion, started barking. All the while the AT&T operator was repeating with ever increasing volume, "Hello? Value America? Are you ready to proceed?"

Finally, the dog stopped barking, the maintenance guys moved on, and the call commenced. On the other end of the phone were some day traders, several institutional investors, and the few analysts who covered us (tuned in to make sure they weren't missing anything). As our analysts listened, their colleagues were telling people to dump VUSA stock; indeed, they had been telling people this even before the call began. It was the daring new world of Internet banking and investing.

During the call, I walked over to Craig's computer, dialed up the NASDAQ site, and watched trading in our stock. It was dropping. It was dropping. It was dropping. For a company in search of momentum, we had finally found it. Unfortunately, it was strictly down, down, down.

Toward the end of the call came the request for questions. There was general silence. Finally Keith Benjamin jumped in, asked a couple questions, and bid everyone farewell. Derek Brown did the same. That sufficed. No one knew whether the silence was awe or just the sound of dead air as people rushed to sell their Value America stock.

Dean Johnson got up and left for his office. Tom Morgan stood up as if to say something but changed his mind. Winn silently gathered his belongings, reminded me to be at the airport in about twenty minutes, and left, with Cristal in tow.

Morgan went into his office, closed the door, and picked up the pen for the white board. He wrote down just a few words: "EPS," "Customers," "Expenses controlled." Those words would determine Value America's future in Wall Street's eyes. Since Wall Street controlled the purse strings, it would end up determining our entire future.

I raced off to the airport to head out to the Robbie Stephens conference, an orgy of people with money and people who wanted more money. It was the place to figure out who was hot, who might be hot, who had been hot, and who could never be hot. Everyone paid close attention to who spoke when, where they spoke, and who was speaking at the same time. This was the kind of conference designed for Winn: He could spend every hour of the day selling his vision and his company. But he gradually began to realize that this trip wasn't about schmoozing, it was about confronting.

Aboard the Hawker en route to San Francisco, Winn retreated to the lone seat on the last row port side. Mick Kicklighter, Rex Scatena, and Kathy Winn — along for the shopping — and I read newspapers and magazines and fiddled on our laptops.

I'd been on the job . . . how long? I honestly couldn't remember a time before Value America. I'd been on the job . . . I squinted my eyes in concentration . . . almost three months. In that time Value America had faced more crises and challenges and business decisions that fundamentally affected our future than I would have expected in a year. The dot.com world wasn't so exceptional except in that one way — speed. Everything happened all at once and never stopped.

The tech guys had pulled yet another all-nighter getting Winn's presentation ready for the Robbie Stephens conference. Somewhere over Kansas or Nebraska, he gave us all copies to read and review. He wanted to give the "idiots" at the conference a "retail revelation." "E-tailing," he posited, "is retailing." For Wall Street, the press, and investors to understand and value e-commerce companies, they first had to understand what retailing was — and what it was not. They had to measure e-tailing like retailing, understand what it takes to build a brand, to win a customer, to keep a customer. When they did, they would come to only one conclusion: Value America was the only e-tailer that mattered.

Our airborne discussion of Winn's speech was a microcosm of the company's dynamics. Scatena submissively affirmed that everything Winn was saying was brilliant and smart. General Kicklighter smiled and softly said he was impressed. I argued for Winn to get rid of the condescending tone in the speech but didn't have much basis for my argument. It was, at the end of the day, a gut call on my part. It was like a political convention, I argued — you've got to win people to your side with charm and grace. You've got to be Bill Clinton, not Pat Buchanan.

When you go negative, they associate the message with the messenger. Winn wasn't pleased.

"What do you know about marketing?" he barked. "Have you ever worked in marketing for a company before? I don't remember it from your resume. Trust me on this."

"I may not have worked in marketing for a company," I blew back, "but politics is all about marketing. It is brand making and image testing and messaging and constituent building. Last time I checked, that pretty much describes marketing."

Winn cocked his head to the side, smiled at me, and shook his head. "Nice try."

The decision was already made. He was going to say whatever he wanted to say. We both knew that marketing a candidate and marketing an e-retail company weren't the same thing. But we both also knew he was about to do something very risky. More than anything, it amazed Winn that I was brash enough and stupid enough to so regularly argue with him. He'd never come back and say I was right — even if I was. But if I was, usually in a day or two he'd make some oblique reference to having made a change in the exact area we had disagreed about. I hoped this would prove to be one of those times.

We rushed into the San Francisco Ritz-Carlton to change clothes, and then dashed out to meet the Robbie Stephens banking execs. They were young and hip and way too happy with themselves. Why shouldn't they be? They had a ton of money. These late-twentysomething, early-thirtysomething multimillionaires led lives that revolved around 3M — not the Scotch tape people, but weekend cottages in Marin County, the newest Mercedes in their collection, and the omnipresent merlot they sipped. Value America and the now countless dot.coms like us kept them indulging.

The nameless Robbie Stephens bankers greeted us at some hip joint at the foot of Nob Hill — each with a glass of red wine in his hand. They had studied our losses and *knew* we were coming to them for more money. While we were escorted to a table, Winn remembered again why he hated them so much. These were the vultures who raised money for you one day and sued you for your last dime the next if your business had problems. They had different names from the people who had come after him at Dynasty Lighting, but they had the same soul. He knew they didn't care about him or his company, they just cared about getting more, more, more. And at that moment he resolved that these people weren't getting any more of him. They hadn't come through. Just for fun, he'd play with them for a while, just to see if he could make them squirm.

"What's going on with Keith?" Winn asked the head Robbie Stephens man nonchalantly.

He started raving. "Oh, Keith, boy, he's becoming a star. He's got his own little following on the Web. He's in demand, and boy, he can move a stock, can't he?"

"Not ours," Winn replied. "You see, we have been . . . unhappy . . . with Keith. He hasn't fought for us. What's the problem?"

"Keith? No, never, not Keith," Mr. Robbie Stephens replied. "Want some more merlot?"

Winn moved on, drank their wine, ate their food, and planned the rest of the conference in his mind. He knew *exactly* how it would all turn out.

Back at the Ritz-Carlton, we strolled through a lobby and bar full of clutches of people peddling their wares, their ideas. Kids with bright faces and paper-thin laptops were eagerly describing their flawless business models to potential investors. Middle-aged former middle-management corporate types with big Internet dreams of their own had slide presentations and telescoping stainless-steel pointers. High-priced hookers lingered around the edges, waiting for a $1,000-an-hour (plus tip) quickie. It was the Internet economy on parade in one hotel, sipping fizzy water or designer martinis. The chattering ones were panning for gold. Those listening were the ones making the money.

In the 150 years since the first northern California gold rush, the biggest changes were cosmetic. Everyone smelled better thanks to deodorant, everyone looked better thanks to better food, everyone smiled brighter thanks to fluoride in the water, and no one was sweating, thanks to air-conditioning. But aside from that, the roles were identical. True, there were more services. Want to get laid? No need for a brothel — the ladies, or gentlemen, as the case may be, will come to you. Need a drink? Room service. Want to make some money? No need to damage your back, just pull out your thirty-ounce laptop and give your mouth a workout.

I staggered through the door of my room. It was awesome. Under different circumstances I'd have been dancing around in glee over its awesomeness. This time I lugged out my laptop, plugged it in, got on-line, and looked at our stock price. It was down 15 percent after our earnings announcement. I slammed my computer shut, stripped off my clothes, and dove for the comfort of starched sheets. I didn't want to be conscious anymore.

As some of the others sat in Winn's room preparing for the big speech the next afternoon, I scoped out the room where Winn's great en-counter session would occur. There were two big ballrooms for the fea-tured companies' presentations, where two were running concurrently. There were also six smaller rooms for the new guys to make their pitches in. The schedule made it clear that there was a hierarchy even between the two big rooms. One hot company would be featured in one room, and one not-so-hot company would be in the other. AOL was paired against some retailer of fine socks. Amazon was paired against an astrology company. We were paired against AskJeeves, the megahot natural-language search engine. There was already a line forming out-side their room.

Winn and his entourage of Kicklighter, Scatena, and an RLM press agent arrived and noticed the long line. Briefly their faces lit up. Then they saw me pointing to the room with no line outside it. They gri-maced. Winn burst through the door to find a room with few seats filled.

"It'll fill up," Kicklighter said to him with Bambi eyes, as Winn made his way to the podium.

Ever since my political days, I had adopted a stealth speech-watching strategy. I never sat up front or watched from backstage. Instead, I sat in the back row or mingled with the audience. It was the most instructive way to learn how a message was playing or what buzz it caused.

I positioned myself on one of the risers in the back, where a few serious-looking guys listened. They had that special smell of New York invest-ment bankers — old money in new cologne.

Craig revved up his presentation and launched into his critique of the way e-tailers were being evaluated. The startled bankers exchanged disapproving glances. It was folly, Winn said, to judge e-tailers using In-ternet metrics. Things like customer-acquisition costs and page views were great for a portal or an ISP but stupid for an e-tailer. The bankers next to me frowned. Winn was just getting started. A lifetime in retail, he said, taught him what mattered to measuring retailers. What mattered, he said, were things like revenue and ad-to-revenue ratio. Everything else was stupid. Nordstrom, he said mockingly, didn't measure things like how many people looked at their shoes or how long people lingered in their stores. What they measured, he said caustically, was how much money they made. The audience was silent. A few people walked out of the already sparsely attended presentation. Every other presentation was a rather dry overview of where a particular business had been and where it was going. They didn't know what to do with a presentation that *wasn't* boring. After all, these were investment bankers.

After twenty minutes, Winn turned from his industry criticisms to explanations of Value America. He covered the technology systems being implemented, the features of multimedia product presentations, the interactivity. The presentation was flawless and very, very slick. One of the bankers next to me mumbled, "Can you believe this guy? He's like a televangelist — all fluff, no substance." I winced. I looked at the name tag on his lapel and winced again: Goldman Sachs.

The presentation adjourned to a small upstairs conference room where a handful of folks asked follow-up questions for twenty minutes. Then everyone dispersed. Scatena, Kicklighter, and I were all thinking the same thing: We'd just laid a stink bomb. On the heels of an earnings report that suggested we couldn't control expenses, it was a nasty one-two punch. We debated what, if anything, to say to Winn, and each of us concluded independently that nothing should be said for a few days. We all knew what had happened here. We left the staging area and walked toward the elevators in silence.

Our next meeting was with the Robbie Stephens "convert guys." Convert guys specialize in offering convertible bonds on behalf of a company. These are offerings of debt, which are convertible into stock in specified circumstances — like if the company's stock price rises to a certain level. This attracts investors who prefer to have some sense of security about their investment being repaid, on time and on schedule, with interest, plus the option to turn their investment into stock if the company succeeds in its goals. Bonds were one of the only "good" ways we could raise money, since a new stock offering would depress the stock price, diluting the company's current total value as represented by the number of shares outstanding. No one wanted stock in a troubled company. This time, so far as the bankers were concerned, it would have to be debt — our promise to repay, with interest.

We wound our way through the halls of the hotel, a beautiful converted white marble courthouse, and arrived at our designated room to meet . . . no one. It was empty of people and full of old Coke bottles, half-eaten cookies, and crumpled napkins. I was hoping we weren't expected to bus tables to raise money. Finding no edible food or drink there, the general, Scatena, and I set out to find goodies to either pep us up or knock us over. Instead we found a phalanx of bankers meandering down the hall. Discovering that these were *our* missing bankers from Robbie Stephens, we shook hands on our way back to the room and introduced them to our awaiting chairman. Winn pleasantly shook hands and greeted the bankers as they unloaded enormous briefcases, pulling out pads of paper, calculators, pens and pencils, laptops, binders of information, and stacks of business cards. They passed out business cards and started arranging all of the other stuff on the table in preparation for what looked like a *very long* meeting.

On one side of the table, Winn stood, tightly grasping the back of a chair, while Kicklighter, Scatena, and I flanked him. He wasn't about to sit. Meanwhile, all but one of the bankers had arranged their areas, grabbed seats, plastered on big grins, and prepared to work. One loan banker, whom I recall simply as Ghost Banker for his pasty complexion, stood opposite Winn.

"Well, shall we get started? We've prepared a number of working papers to discuss — ways to structure the deal, as well as comparisons of other deals we've done recently."

"No," Winn replied coldly.

Ghost banker said, "Well, let's get started then." He sat down. We all stood.

Silence. The seated bankers shifted nervously and decided it was high time they checked whether those calculators were working. As they fiddled with their little toys, Winn and Ghosty just stared at each other.

Winn finally broke the straining silence. "There isn't going to be a convert deal."

The bankers instantly stopped playing. Value America *had* to raise money, Ghosty said. What options were available other than convert deals? With VUSA stock at $11 and falling, a secondary offering wasn't possible. They could always try to do a private round, but that wouldn't be easy either.

We all started shifting our weight back and forth, faces flushing, as

Winn stood rigidly. Our banker counterparts looked at each other and tried to figure out whether they should stand, too. Ghost Banker was clueless, too.

"We have decided we aren't going to raise any money right now," Winn announced.

"Well, why don't we walk you through these figures and projections?" another banker asked plaintively, perhaps hoping he could at least break the ice. The senior management at BBRS wasn't going to be happy about losing this deal. It would cost them millions in revenue.

Winn paused again, smiled playfully, and snickered. "No." He didn't seem to be in any rush. He wasn't moving toward the door, he wasn't moving to sit. Other than breathing and talking, he didn't seem to be moving at all.

Clearly desperate to get the hell out of the room, Ghost Banker looked at his counterparts and muttered, "OK, I see. Perhaps we should go find Todd [Carter — head of the Robbie Stephens Internet Banking Division] and talk to him about the situation." Maybe, just maybe, if Carter got in on it, things could be salvaged.

Winn again paused dramatically, looked them in the eyes and mouthed, "No, I don't think so."

The other bankers bustled about, putting their things away. Kicklighter, Scatena, and I had no real understanding of what had just happened. We were amused, we were uncomfortably self-conscious, but we were clueless.

Winn was pissed, but he had gotten some revenge. He hated those bastards. Keith Benjamin f———ed us by not covering us. They f———ed us at this conference. These bankers think we've already chosen them to raise any and all future dollars. F——— 'em. Besides, Winn knew, tomorrow was a meeting with Dan Case, brother of AOL's Steve Case and head of the elite boutique bank Hambrecht & Quist. Case understood what Value America was up to, he was smart, he got it. Maybe he'd even serve on Value America's board. If that meeting didn't work out, Craig Winn would just find someone else. He could raise money in his sleep. This wasn't a crisis, just a chance to prove to these pricks who was boss.

The bankers jerked up, we shook their hands, and they shook their heads. Then we strutted out, struggling to contain our laughter.

"No! No! No!" Winn chortled as he walked down the hall. Scatena and the general were both laughing as they recalled the shocked looks on the bankers' faces. We didn't actually have any other sources of money. The SF part of the trip had been a disaster thus far, but we felt jolly anyway. We'd identified an enemy and given them the finger.

Back in my room, I hopped online to check the market. It was closed, mercifully, but VUSA stock was already down 30 percent in just two days since we'd announced earnings. The next day it would drop another 20 percent.

The next morning we gathered downstairs for breakfast and another confrontation, this time with Tom Courtney, head analyst at Bank of America Securities. Courtney was initiating coverage of Value America and wanted to discuss the business in detail. Unfortunately, Winn's mood hadn't improved dramatically in the past twelve hours, and he wasn't feeling very cordial.

Courtney's questions were straightforward. How was Value America going to reduce its customer-acquisition costs? How was Value America going to achieve profitability? How was Value America going to reduce costs? Winn, who claimed he wanted to be a politician for the rest of his life, was tasting the drudgery of retail politics — the same questions asked different ways all day every day. No one likes giving the same answer over and over. But the greatest politicians smile every time they hear the same question. They impart a sense of, "Gee, that's a *great* question," and answer it like they've never heard it before. The not-so-great politicians roll their eyes and sigh and conjure up different answers, so they won't bore themselves to sleep with the same answers over and over and over again.

Winn particularly hated these questions. They were more proof to him that these analysts didn't have a clue what was going on.

"Tom . . . those questions won't tell you anything . . . they are meaningless . . . they are . . . worse . . . than . . . meaningless . . ."

Courtney looked around the table, looked down at his financial models and numbers, and put on a half grin. "Well, I disagree, Craig. I think they are fairly predictive of long-term success."

"I don't," Winn replied. "But I do think it is appropriate to tell you, confidentially, of some *very* big news that we'll be announcing in the near future."

He paused, looked at Courtney, and grinned. "I can't tell you who, exactly, but we are going to be entering into a historic partnership with one of the largest financial institutions in the world. It will give us exclusive e-commerce access to more than one hundred million affluent customers in the United States."

My ears perked up. I didn't know there *were* one hundred million affluent Americans! Bill Clinton and Alan Greenspan must have been doing one *hell* of a job.

Courtney's head leaned slightly toward Winn.

"That's right," Winn said with his trademark Cheshire grin *(now I've got him, he thought)*. "I'm prohibited from telling you who exactly, but they are the world's biggest player in consumer credit cards, and we are on the verge of a huge deal with them. It will mean billions of dollars in revenue and a completely new way of looking at e-commerce. It won't just be *electronic* commerce, it will be *everything* commerce.

"Our arrangement with this financial entity will mean the most efficient marketing spending you'll ever see. We'll hit their card members with catalogs and bill inserts, we'll have a special eight-hundred number for them. They'll have their own Web site. And we won't have to pay anything to market to them."

Courtney set aside the financial tables and listened intently. I did, too. Meetings like this with Winn, I'd learned, were either informative or entertaining. Sometimes, I had a difficult time distinguishing between the two. I was sure that at one point Winn's Citibank pronouncement would have absolutely shocked me. That morning, I just looked up at Winn, enjoyed my omelet, and listened.

Winn's latest ideas included a holiday catalog for the Christmas shopping season directed at Citibank customers. Every Citibank member would earn points from all their credit-card purchases that could be redeemed at Value America. It was, he assured Courtney, a *billion*-dollar-revenue opportunity.

Courtney didn't have the numbers he wanted from Value America, but he did see possibilities for the company's success. He wasn't going to hype the stock, but Winn persuaded him to just not trash it — for now.

Another departing victory came on the heels of the Courtney meeting. Winn and Kicklighter zipped over to meet with Dan Case to propose that H&Q help Value America do what Robbie Stephens would not — raise money. Case was appalled at the idea of a convertible deal.

It made much more sense to do a small $30 million private round, work to increase the stock price, and then do a secondary offering sometime in early 2000. Unlike most of the Internet financial world, Case was not enamored of Amazon and thought that an inventoryless model like Value America's had a chance. He was eager for his top analyst, Ginny Combs, to venture out to Charlottesville and take a peek at the company up close and personal. Case was the fairy godparent that Winn had been praying for.

The final meeting of the trip was with Visa International. One of Winn's longtime friends had arranged a meeting with one of Visa's top marketing gurus, Armen Kharciggian. Winn held high court, making a pitch to Visa similar to that which he had devised for Citibank — Value America as the infrastructure for a Visa shopping engine that would target Visa customers throughout the world. Kharciggian loved the idea. He thought it was a natural fit for Visa. He also thought it might be of interest to another friend of his, Tour de France champion Lance Armstrong. Perhaps, everyone speculated, Armstrong, fresh from his historic bicycling win after defeating cancer, would be a natural partner for Value America.

Winn tasked me and the general with the whole Visa project. Our goal was to devise an exclusive holiday deal for Visa customers and to work with Kharciggian and his team to strike a broader Visa deal, targeting their more than six hundred million cardholders worldwide.

We all headed back to the jet, where General Kicklighter had arranged for Winn and Kathy's favorite Rocket burgers and fries for dinner. It was now August 5, and the trip didn't look so bad anymore. There were new possibilities. No one was mentioning the speech — it was to be forgotten. But damn, the burgers were good.

I'd never nuked Rocket burgers on a private jet before.

Come to think of it, I'd never grilled burgers on my still missing Weber Platinum Series grill either.

CHAPTER FOURTEEN

Snake Handlers

I stumbled back into the office from the California trip to find an urgent note from Tom Morgan to see him immediately. I made the short, winding trip to his office and stuck my head in the door.

"You rang?"

Morgan smiled broadly, put his feet up on the desk in faux relaxation, folded his arms in front of him, and said, "I'm sorry you missed him."

"Missed who?"

"Well, does the name Dennis Connor mean anything to you? You know, America's Cup winner, head of *Stars & Stripes,* you know, Dennis Connor."

"Yeah, why?"

"He was here."

"Why?"

"We're thinking about sponsoring his America's Cup yacht. Sorry you missed him. Oh, well."

I was an America's Cup racing fan. I'd always wanted to watch the races in person. I knew the various syndicates, I knew how competitive the race was. And I'd always thought Dennis Conner was ultra-cool. And I'd missed meeting him.

"Don't get too revved up," Morgan said. "We probably won't do it. Nevertheless, he was here, khakis, Top-Siders, no socks. Looked cool."

Glenda Dorchak only days later talked to the *Stars & Stripes* team and negotiated a sponsorship package. For $750,000 we'd be one of Dennis Connor's big sponsors. He would even fly a Value America sail! I read the e-mail announcing the possible deal and sputtered.

$750,000? For *Stars & Stripes?* Much as I admired him, I knew that sponsoring Dennis Connor for nearly a million bucks was woolly-headed. He stood virtually no chance of winning. This time around he was viewed almost as a has-been. Besides, the races were in New Zealand! Kiwi outreach wasn't our top priority. If we wanted to sponsor someone, I shot off in an e-mail to both Dorchak and Morgan, we should have tried sponsoring the all-women's team or at least *America³,* which stood a chance of winning.

I waited for a reply.

It was now August, and I'd been waiting and waiting for some big news to announce. There were still no big deals. I didn't think sponsoring *Stars & Stripes* was going to help much.

Word had dribbled back to Tom Morgan before our return that the San Francisco trip hadn't gone terribly well. On top of my own reports about Winn's speech difficulties, a host of others told Morgan that Winn was becoming an impediment to Value America's success. He'd become so confrontational with Wall Street that people weren't investing in the company, just because they thought he was difficult and arrogant.

Value America couldn't afford a contentious Wall Street relationship. Not only did we need to get our stock price back up — it was now down around $12 — but we were going to need to raise more money toward the end of the year. On Friday, August 6, Morgan and Winn talked. Morgan told him he'd heard from various sources that California had been "difficult." Perhaps, Morgan suggested, Winn should take a breather from Wall Street interaction. To Morgan's surprise, Winn didn't put up a fight. Winn knew things weren't going well with the Street. Winn also knew he'd erred by making it apparent to the Street how much hostility he held toward those "idiots." Winn resolved to step further back from day-to-day operational control.

One early August evening, I drove to Winndom for dinner with Craig, Kathy, and the boys. As I drove up the winding driveway to the estate, I noticed what appeared to be two brand-new farm vehicles parked just off the driveway. Having grown up in the suburbs of New York City, I couldn't make an educated guess at what they were, but I was sure I'd hear about them soon enough.

Every so often Winn and Kathy invited me over to sample the latest in Value America's gourmet offerings. I loved it. Kathy was an amazing cook, and Winn and I loved talking business. At times he was like Bob Barker on *The Price Is Right.* He'd hold up a box of Near East Couscous and say, "You see this box here? Guess how much. Really. Guess!" I'd look at him blankly. "We ordered it on Value America for only seventy-nine cents. In the store it is, like, two dollars. We click, it comes! We've done a tremendous job building up the gourmet section of the store. It is going to be a big seller. It'll drive millions in revenue." Winn's enthusiasm was endearing even when it wasn't infectious.

As Kathy Winn's scrumptious dinner concluded and her orgasmically divine chocolate cake beckoned, Winn grabbed me by the arm and said he wanted to show me his new toys.

Winn's toys were like the Tonka trucks I had as a boy — just a lot larger and more expensive. He hadn't actually been tutored on their features yet, but he had some idea what the various buttons and levers and knobs did. These were not Old MacDonald's farm tractors. They had enclosed cabs with a stereo system, air-conditioning, and, I was pretty sure, a seat that massaged your back. There were headlights, floodlights, taillights, and spotlights. They moved up and down and sideways. Winn sat proudly in the plush cabs, utterly enraptured by his new gadgets. His big eyes and face-consuming smile were a blur as he spun the seat around, pushing and pulling knobs and levers and buttons like he was in a private video game.

I asked Winn how he knew so much about farm equipment. He replied smugly that he just liked to help clear the land. Then he led me down a hill to the cavernous barnlike structure looming behind clusters of trees, expounding knowledgeably on the John Deere line. Opening the doors to the shake-and-cedar barn, he showed me what appeared to be the entire line of John Deere products. "I don't have the combine," he admitted.

A combine is a mammoth machine designed to harvest, among other things, wheat, corn, and barley, and is primarily used by people with, say, a thousand acres or more of fertile land. Many new models have global-positioning-satellite monitors, yield monitors, weather monitors, stock tickers — the whole nine yards. I know because I got to drive one during my Fourth of July vacation with Kim in Kansas. You wouldn't think Winndom would need a combine, but you wouldn't want to say that to Craig Winn.

Of the tractor collection I said tactfully in tones as manly as I could muster, "OK, well, they're sure *damn* impressive." They were, too. There were huge tractors and cute little tractors with cute little pet names to match, like Katie. He had big backhoes and big steam shovels. I didn't ask if they were named Fred or Butch.

Tractors weren't Winn's only attempt to divert himself from the reality that other people had hold of his prized toy — Value America. While in terms of management we were much better off with Tom Morgan at the helm, we still needed Winn's deals. Apart from the flurry of press activity after I'd joined the company, Value America was still coming up dry on the news front. The SAP software implementation was at least a month away. We weren't buying anyone, and we didn't have any deals of any significance. My fear, voiced daily, was that Value America was being defined only by our omnipresent newspaper ads, which usually showcased cheap computer and electronics items. I didn't want us to wind up being the Crazy Eddie of the Internet.

My biggest hope was for Winn's Citibank deals and Starnes's government business. I also recognized that our systems could be used by any portal, ISP, or search engine to power their shopping capabilities. While companies like Yahoo! and AOL raked in money by charging retailers "rent" to participate in their malls, there were obvious flaws in the model. First, as Kim had told me from her AOL perch, the retailers weren't getting any bang for their bucks and were beginning to question the wisdom of paying companies like AOL or Yahoo! millions of dollars with no real returns. Second, portals like Yahoo! were losing hard-won customers by sending them to other sites to shop. By partnering with Value America, the ISPs, portals, and search engines could snatch a portion of that revenue rather than settle for placement fees. It would be a revenue and PR bonanza.

I moseyed down to Winn's office to share my genius. He listened to me, leaned back in his puffy leather chair happily, and gave me an approving look. "You figured it out," he said, sounding like a professor lauding a student's discovery. "You figured out that the Value America engine was *always* designed to be an infrastructure solution." Value America's greatness, he reminded me, wasn't just the inventoryless solution, it was the brand relationships. Once those relationships were established, Value America could leverage them on behalf of other people who wanted to sell. I left his office with a gold star happily affixed to my report card, and a charge to pursue these portal-type Internet deals.

Moments later I was busily scribbling away on my white board, trying to figure out who I needed to pitch and how I needed to focus my efforts. The list was actually not that long — AskJeeves, Go Network, Lycos, Excite, Inktomi, Yahoo!, AOL. The chances for enticing the latter two giants were slim, but hey, why not give it a whirl?

I called Kim and told her the news. I was now officially in "biz dev" — I was going to be driving deals. Kim was almost used to the random stories I spouted about my Value America work life. But having the communications guy doing business-development deals struck her as odder than most. Perhaps it was my *Fantasy Island* experience that prevented me from seeing this logic. To me it made sense — I was just becoming a little Winn clone. Craig sold to the media, and I sold to the media. Craig sold to other companies, and now I was selling to other companies. It made perfect sense — didn't it? Kim told me it might be good for us to talk over the weekend. I agreed — it was going to take her a little longer to see how much sense this all made.

Meanwhile, as I added business development to my list of Value America responsibilities, Value America was deep into infomercialism.

While the magic wrench had never taken hold — the owners apparently wanted Value America stock options — the infomercials were alive and well. The decision from on high was that our first infomercial offering would be for Proteva computers, at a bargain-basement price of $999 for computer, monitor, and color printer. Of course there were a few *issues* with Proteva. Apparently they weren't the best-manufactured computers in the world. A few of them had been known to overheat and catch on fire. And according to one of our guys, the units generated so much radiation, they weren't necessarily safe for women of childbearing age. Other than that, they were quality machines.

Word went out companywide for all hands on deck to take orders from the first wave of infomercials. We were all to endure sales training and then sign up for time slots over the weekend. I didn't believe people would actually buy these things, but once the clock struck 6:00 A.M. on Saturday morning, August 14, the hour when the first infomercial aired in Des Moines, the calls flooded in. It was my first experience as a telephone salesperson — again, not the kind of thing I had previously associated with being part of a dot.com. But since Value America needed revenue, and since infomercials provided such good gross-margin numbers, we were jazzed.

The goal was to up-sell. In short, up-selling means convincing people that they really want a more expensive item than they have requested. In this case, we were to persuade callers that they didn't really want the bargain-basement $999 computer. What they *really* wanted was the $1,299 computer with the larger monitor. If we were especially talented, we could push them up to the $1,499 system with the bigger monitor and the bigger printer.

A lot has been written about how the early days of the Internet separated people along class lines. Those with access to the Internet and its prodigious tools had access to virtually unlimited knowledge, experience, and shopping opportunities. Those without the right tools — a computer with Internet access — were simply shut out of those opportunities. The argument was largely intellectual for me until I put on that headset.

I quickly discovered the infomercial demographic. Callers weren't typically yuppies or dinks. They were lower middle class, the ones who dreamed about having things like computers. Indeed, person after person told me this was "a dream come true" for them. Their kids could finally learn to use a computer, and they could find information on jobs, education, and travel. They could learn what the Internet was and how computers could help them create resumes and put them in touch with a world they'd never seen firsthand. The closer we got to the moment when they had to give the payment information, the more quickly they talked and the more effusively they thanked me for taking the time to listen to them. When I finally asked for their credit-card number, about a quarter of the people just hung up. Others started to explain why they didn't have a credit card (a divorce, a bankruptcy, past financial mistakes). Value America had planned for this possibility. As part of a new financial-services division, we were also launching a Value America store credit card that day. With higher interest rates and lower credit qualifications, it gave consumers a chance to buy and Value America yet another way to make money. When I told customers about this alternate financing possibility, it was as if I had told them they won the lottery. There was a little shriek. They giggled. Then they would give me their Social Security numbers and tell me they were talking to Jesus about getting this credit. I would enter their number into the system and send it off into the great credit unknown. Within seconds, it would come back with an approval or a rejection. Fortunately, most were approvals.

The rejections are voices I can still hear: "I understand," "Thank you for trying for me," "Aww, we'll be OK."

The weekend was a booming success for Value America. We sold nearly a million dollars' worth of computers in two days, not counting what we were simultaneously selling online. Everyone was pumped. Morgan saw the infomercials as a short-term-revenue and gross-margin bridge to take Value America to the business and government market-places. But Winn saw it as much, much more. Infomercials, he informed us all Monday morning, were our future. He wanted us to quickly ready a series of infomercials for the holiday season — everything from DVD players to home-entertainment systems to super-high-end computers. We had gross margins in excess of 15 percent on the base-level machines the infomercials had pushed and more than 20 percent on the higher-end models. We were actually *making* money. Gadzooks!

Just like that, we were hot again. Tom Morgan had heard that Sears.com was buying national radio airtime for commercials that claimed they had more products for sale than any other online company, "including Value America." Dan Case of Hambrecht & Quist was sending his top analyst, Ginny Combs, to Value America for a prospective research report on the company; it seemed Dan was interested in helping finance and promote Value America.

Arriving in his office before the sun rose on the eighteenth, Morgan sat down at his desk and fired off a companywide e-mail:

Midway through Value America's third quarter — second quarter as a publicly traded company — I wanted to share a few thoughts about our business strategy going forward.

It is, in a simple thought, to execute a vision for retailing that Craig Winn has had for more than two decades — to bring consumers and manufacturers together in a convergent retail world. If this vision can be made real through world-class execution, I am convinced that Value America can do for e-commerce what Wal-Mart did for retail — revolutionize it.

To make that happen, we are committed to creating the most effective and efficient company we can. Too often in the Internet space some companies seem to think that the traditional rules of business don't apply. Long-held rules of managing costs and creating efficiencies are discarded because today investors seem to have patience with companies losing money as they build scale.

Value America has been committed to a different sort of approach. We believe fundamentally in creating a business that is a model of efficiency in everything that we do. That applies to our advertising, marketing, systems, operations and everything else.

This approach is one of the reasons that our last quarter numbers made me proud. As a percentage of our revenue, our operating costs decreased. That may not sound like a big accomplishment, but it is. While our revenues grew by nearly 30 percent, our costs actually declined. This is a path that we are committed to pursuing for the future — lower costs, higher revenue. And it is one that will lead us to profitability before anyone on Wall Street expects.

Specifically over the next few quarters we will be moving significant portions of our advertising away from mass-market approaches and to more direct-marketing approaches that play to our strengths with our demand alliances of non-profits, charities, foundations, associations and the like.

At the same time, we are ever more dramatically committed to improving the customer experience at Value America. We have done a great job in being "customer obsessed," but we are committed to being even better.

Finally, we are also dedicating resources to expanding the product offerings in our store. The merchandisers have done a tremendous job of bringing product into our store, and their hard work is paying off. With new deals and possibilities around the corner, however, we are going to have to increase those offerings. We will dedicate the resources we need to get that done. . . .

All the best,
Tom Morgan

From where I sat, it felt like the early August craziness was gone.

Perhaps not coincidentally, sporadically during late June and July, but regularly beginning in August, Craig Winn's Hollymead office was the site of weekly 7:00 A.M. Bible studies. The time was chosen so as not to interfere with the company's business. Neither Winn nor Morgan wanted anyone to feel participation or nonparticipation in the Bible studies would impact one's career within the company. Morgan hoped the group might help rein in Winn's erratic actions and personality. For Winn, there was something, too. He had surrounded himself with men who placed a higher priority on their faith than on anything else. It was something he wanted in his own life.

Winn's evolving faith rippled through the company. Most immediately it impacted people like Ken Erickson, Greg Dorn, and Neal Harris — friends with whom Winn had once caroused. As Winn moved away from occasional party nights and toward regular Bible and prayer meetings, Erickson and Dorn in particular were a bit incredulous. How could Craig Winn be finding God? they each wondered. To them, Winn was a friend with an affinity for mixed drinks and loud jokes. They didn't understand what he was doing, why he was doing it, or what their decreasing face time with the chairman meant for their careers.

I was one of the regular attendees at the meetings, which softened some of my own anger toward things religious. The legalism, judgmentalism, and narrowmindedness I'd feared were nowhere to be found. Instead, these meetings were about forgiveness and mercy and grace.

The August morning that Morgan fired off his e-mail, the group gathered to study Paul's Second Epistle to Timothy. The letter begins with Paul sitting alone in a jail, reminding his young friend Timothy that he alone remembered Paul in prison. Only Timothy brought him food and blankets, sent him letters, and visited. Paul, once the great Jewish leader and now the rebel Christian outcast, thanked Timothy for his faith and love. As everyone discussed the passage, Winn sat quietly, closing his eyes, saying nothing. Finally, as the meeting was winding down, he said quietly, "I wonder who will be there for me when I am alone."

He went on to talk about the dark days of his experience with Dynasty Lighting and the isolation that followed failure. He could, he said, relate to Paul's separation from former friends and supporters. He knew what it was like to sit across the table from bankers who once courted him and endure their curses. Worse yet, he said, he knew the pain of finding his kids and wife at home crying because of the way friends and neighbors teased them about *his* failures. There was, Craig said softly, no more desperate moment than when you find yourself totally and completely alone. Except, he added, when you find yourself totally and completely alone because of your own mistakes and missteps. No one said a word. The general, Morgan, Jamie Parsons, and I glanced furtively at each other. Of all the unpredictable things Winn had done, this may have taken the blue ribbon. We were all speechless. It just didn't fit our image of Craig Winn. He was many things — good-hearted, tough, visionary, difficult, egotistical — but we never saw him as vulnerable. I tried to reaffirm our loyalty to him. He wouldn't, I promised, ever be alone. We were a team here at Value America. We watched out for each other. We took care of each other. There wasn't going to be any abandonment going on. This company, we all pledged, was going to succeed, and these relationships, we promised, would last.

We all sat around the room, glancing at one another, forced by Craig to confront our own fears and wounds. We could hear the company coming to life all around us, but none wanted to join it. Soon, however, the silence grew awkward, a few of us started squirming, and we abruptly adjourned.

Fifteen minutes later we were preparing for Ginny Combs's arrival. The Combs meeting, Winn crisply reminded the same group that had been discussing theology moments before, was crucial. If Value America could find just one reputable analyst who *really* understood what we were doing and who really understood what retail was about, we would break through. Winn *knew* Combs was that person. She was really smart, not arrogant, and willing to learn.

I was again dispatched to Washington, D.C., to escort her down later that afternoon on the Hawker. Genuinely short, with short, straight, sandy hair, she reminded me of what the comic-strip character Cathy might be like if she were real — quirky, witty, and cute. Most important, unlike Keith Benjamin, Ginny Combs was duly impressed by the jet. As I escorted her to it, she asked, "You were just passing through, right — this isn't for me, is it?" I evaded the question, and when we were settled in our seats I tried to pawn off some nice shrimp on her. She liked the shrimp. She seemed a bit embarrassed by all the attention — and a bit worried. "I can't really accept any favors from the company," she gently warned me. "Oh, no," I stammered, "no favors, of course not, we aren't doing favors, no, not at all."

The next morning, Winn insisted his meeting with Combs wasn't a retreat from his partially self-imposed Wall Street quarantine. It was just a vitally important pitch he needed to be part of. Combs met with Winn for two hours. He told her about the burgeoning custom stores with groups like Jerry Falwell's, lauded the technological improvements under way, and expounded again on the potential for the Citibank relationship. In talking to her about the infomercials, he came up with a new moniker: They were "convergence presentations." Value America, he assured her, was going to be the leader in "convergence commerce" and the king of e-commerce. The only obstacle to Value America's success, Winn assured Combs, was the rush to get scale. Scale was Value America's fountain of eternal youth. With scale, Value America could charge manufacturers thousands of dollars for every product in the store. Brands would ship more quickly and more efficiently because they had more skin in the game. Scale for Value America, Winn told her, was like critical mass in a nuclear bomb — it was everything. Other than scale, Value America's only other problem, Winn said, was with analysts who didn't understand the revolutionary nature of Value America's business. For two hours, Combs nodded and smiled and listened.

Then, walking into Tom Morgan's office for her meeting with him, she said, "OK, I've heard from Craig. Now let me hear the truth." Combs knew exactly how entrepreneurs see the world. It wasn't that she thought Winn was lying, just that, well, sometimes guys like that get a bit carried away.

Value America, Morgan assured her, was looking hard at the business-to-business and business-to-government markets. It was a no-brainer. The consumer market was saturated, and it was only 10 percent of the business-to-business market. If Value America made the transition, he believed the company could win big. The management team represented a diverse mix of talent and was beginning to gel. Morgan told her he wanted to upgrade several of those positions, including the CFO and the CIO, but he also reminded her that the third quarter was the first that the whole team had worked together.

As they talked, Morgan and Combs reinforced for each other a single certainty: Value America was in a cutthroat race. No one knew where the finish line was, and no one knew who all the competitors might turn out to be. That meant that the only place to be was out in front — by a long shot. Amazon was in that position. Value America was fighting for the number two slot. It promised to be, they agreed with big smiles, a memorable ride. Combs headed back to San Francisco to continue her research and talk to Dan Case about Value America's prospects for success. She was high on the company.

She wasn't alone. There was, throughout the company, the very strong sense that the best lay ahead. Even the board was psyched. Fred Smith related a story to Winn about his longtime friendship with Sam Walton. Every year Fred and Sam went quail hunting, and every year Walton would tell Smith, "Fred, no one gets Wal-Mart. Wall Street doesn't like us, the press doesn't like us, I just don't get it." Every year Fred told Sam to have faith, keep executing, and eventually Wall Street would figure it out. And they did. Smith reminded Winn that Wal-Mart was the biggest and most successful company in the world and exhorted him to remember the uphill fight all great companies have. Federal Express had faced similar struggles in its early years, losing significant amounts of money as it grew to scale.

It was with that enthusiasm that I welcomed my relatives-to-be Scott and Heather to Charlottesville. Scott was in town to interview with General Kicklighter about working in the custom stores program. Heather was interviewing with Tom Morgan about serving as his special assistant — being his eyes and ears as well as an occasional enforcer on important issues like customer service. Kim was down in Charlottesville, too, taking a peek around with the family. The long discussions we'd had about potentially working together were now being forced toward some conclusion. Were we all to do this, it would be a risk (there's an old Chinese saying: Many eggs in one basket, make sure to have strong handle). But we also knew that if Value America succeeded, it would be like being part of AOL before it took off, and if Value America failed, we would all have Internet experience to parlay into new ventures somewhere else.

Sure, Value America wasn't flying. But Kim kept reminding us of AOL's 1996 access crisis that nearly demolished the company. For those few months when their phone lines were jammed, their stock was plummeting, and their people were leaving, AOL was widely perceived to be dead. Only the newly appointed CEO, Bob Pittman, and the chairman, Steve Case, could see the light. To them, a lot of people wanting the AOL product wasn't a problem, it was an opportunity. Too many people want what we've got, he said. All we've got to do is give it to them. They did. For those who persevered through the access crisis, there were the twin payoffs of psychological victory and secure financial futures. Even some of the janitors who stuck it out were now multimillionaires. Literally.

Our difficulties were hardly unique. Across the country, hundreds of thousands of people were debating whether to leave the safety of their established corporate jobs for the chance of winning the Internet lottery.

Kim and I both knew AOL had already made it. It was the king of the Internet. It would continue to grow, but its rocketlike growth was completed. At AOL, she would be a cog. But at Value America, she could be surrounded by family and help Value America win. The financial upside wasn't bad either. If Value America made it, we'd have Internet millions. Of course, we both realized, it could go bust. But really, what were the chances of that happening with such brilliant leadership? Not very high.

Scott and Heather spent a long weekend walking around the town, talking to people, getting a feel for the place. They were in. Kim was too — a nice coup for Value America. Luring an executive from AOL's communications shop could only be perceived as a plus.

We, a little group of retail revolutionaries — increasingly related — from Charlottesville, Virginia, were going to overcome the doubters, and we were going to win. When we did, we'd be able to say that we were there for the hard times, we were the original survivors.

Scott even volunteered to help me fill a slot in the communications shop. A good buddy of his at Junior Achievement was a press guru. Scott called him and told him the good news about Value America and suggested I hook up with him. That was perfect, because I needed to have a staff in place before I left for my honeymoon.

Whenever Winn was asked about familial ties within the company, he would chortle and say, "We have a company policy on nepotism: We encourage it." He envisioned Value America as one huge family. What better way to make that family stronger than to bring actual families to work together? Value America's buildings were filled with spouses, fathers, mothers, sisters, brothers, cousins.

Kim's new role was establishing an investor relations department reporting directly to Tom Morgan. She hadn't focused on IR per se at AOL, but because communications and investor relations were inseparable in a new-economy company, the transition made sense. Tom Morgan had been looking for a good IR person since he'd arrived at the company, and while I dabbled in IR from my communications post, Value America wasn't ministering either to its investors or to Wall Street. Kim's job was to change that.

From our perspective, investor relations translated into stock price increase. Not having a single point of contact for the financial community had hurt us as Wall Street changed its expectations for e-commerce companies from revenue to EPS. Kim would keep our analysts informed of what Value America was doing and make sure Value America knew the latest trends in Internet metrics, business processes, and general conventional wisdom.

She'd have her hands full. With Value America's stock decline, unhappy investors called Value America almost as frequently as unhappy customers. When I arrived, Dean Johnson passed them off to me. With Kim's arrival, I was happy to pass them off to her. A lot of these calls came from the high-profile investors Winn and company had brought on board late in '98 and early in '99. These people, like Charlottesville diva Patricia Kluge, were not happy that their dollars weren't magically transforming into millions. They were even unhappier that they were actually *losing* money. They demanded explanations for the decline, and they wanted reasons to hope the declines would be reversed soon. With a background as Jack Kemp's press secretary during his unsuccessful vice presidential campaign as well as Bob Dole's press secretary, Kim had honed her spinning skills, a talent essential for her new post. That both of these politicians had eventually disappointed their supporters had given her lots of experience that would be extremely valuable in the months ahead.

CHAPTER FIFTEEN

Here Comes the Bride

To someone from the not-for-profit and political worlds, bonuses were rarities. Perks, however, were common. There were occasional free tickets to concerts or football games. There were nice dinners and even nicer parties. But never in my relatively perk-happy life had I been flown to the Caribbean on a vacation. That, however, was exactly what our trusty $170,000-a-year Value America customer-service pilots were doing: They were flying Winn, Kim, Kim's friend Sheila, Winn's two boys, and me to paradisiacal Grand Bahama Island. Stretched out on the maroon seats, we talked about the scuba diving, jet skiing, and sunning we'd soon be doing.

I'd heard about our yacht for the better part of a week. It was supposed to be big. I sure hoped it was big, because seven people (Jamie Parsons would be meeting us) were going to be on it for the next five days.

We pulled up to the Atlantis Resort complex — a subtle hotel resort in sandstone pink with teal-blue dolphins on top — and proceeded to the marina. There I witnessed the naval phalanx for the Internet economy. Boat after huge boat bore stenciled dot.com derivations on their sterns. There was ".com dreamin'," "dot hot," and "dot me." Most, the marina workers informed me, were owned by Internet billionaires.

It was all a bit intimidating. This was *Lifestyles of the Rich and Famous,* and I was more comfortable with lifestyles of the middle-class and unknown. And I hated mooching off people, even off paper billionaires. (Actually, with Value America's stock in decline, Winn was now worth only about $350 million.) Plus, I had to be out of the office for the week. It occurred to me that others in the company might resent this token of Winn's Sun-Kingly beneficence and favor. But saying no to this trip would have required far more willpower than I had.

Kim was much more at ease. The trip had all the essential elements for her: fun, sun, ocean, and me! She didn't care if it was a yacht or a dinghy as long as she could work on her pre-wedding tan. She told me to relax and have fun. It wasn't too hard.

Our boat, *Charisma,* stretched along the dock for about ninety feet. It might not have been big by *über*-boat standards, but it sure beat the inflatable raft I'd had in college. There were four staterooms, plus quarters for the dating four-person crew. A pair of wave runners and a Zodiac pontoon were secured above. I'd always thought sailboats seemed more elegant, refined, and one with nature. But once you're on a yacht, you quickly forget about being one with nature; I just wanted to be one with the big HDTV while sipping margaritas after a day of wave running.

For the next four days that is exactly what I did. We'd wake up in the morning, devour a gourmet breakfast, engage in heated debates about whether to swim, dive, ride wave runners, go exploring, or tan first, and then end up doing all of them.

Sheila Howard, Kim's friend and Jamie's prospective date, kept commenting on how *much* she *loved* this Internet world. A Jodie Foster look-alike with mischievous eyes, she had taken to diving off the top of the boat into the water some twenty-five feet below. It was that diving — and enthusiasm — that led us inextricably to our encounter with Thunderball Cave.

One evening, somewhere between the conch fritters and the rock lobster, Sheila piped up that she'd heard this part of the Bahamas was home to Thunderball Cave. We didn't really follow. Thunderball Cave, she explained incredulously, was where James *Bond* had concluded the movie *Thunderball.* He got ejected from the top of the cave and went on to save the world — or something like that. It would be a blast, Sheila exclaimed, to plunge fifty feet from the top of the rocky mound into the fish-filled waters of Thunderball Cave — the inverse of James Bond's ejection.

For some inexplicable reason everyone agreed with her. We set our course immediately.

Thunderball Cave was inside Thunderball "Mountain," a mound of sharp, dangerous lava. Thankfully someone lent me a flipper. I put it on my right foot, which felt fine. The left was getting shredded on the lava rock as I climbed. Ahead of me, Sheila scooted up the hill without much trouble; in front of her, Jamie was skipping up the hill in his scuba socks, trying to impress her. Below, Kim was sitting in her bikini, sunning herself and trying to avoid the *huge* barracuda she was sure was stalking her. A little above me, Craig was carefully shepherding Ryan, his ten-year-old son, while mischievously looking back at my spastic limping and giving an encouraging shout or two.

Our little group huddled at the top, staring at the black water far, far below, each thinking, what the *hell* am I going to do now? We all *had* to jump. I knew I did, because Kim was gazing up at me expectantly, and my manhood was at stake. Craig had to, because Ryan was all set to go careening off the cliff and you just can't wuss out in front of your own kid. Jamie had to because he wanted to impress the hot-looking thirty-something businesswoman next to him. Sheila just wanted to. We shuf-fled around the rim of the opening for a good five minutes. Suddenly, Craig looked at us, mustered up a big grin, pinched his nose, and leapt up, bellowing, "CANNONBALL!" With frightening speed, the Value America chieftain plunged into the water below. We survivors blinked. Four stories below, a buoyant Winn tilted his head back and made the loudest damn chicken clucks I've ever heard. We looked at each other and jumped. Only wise-beyond-his-years Ryan decided to turn around and descend on foot.

That night as we prepared for our next day's adventure, Craig walked slowly up the stairs from his stateroom below. Ever since we'd arrived in the Bahamas, Winn had either been wearing long pants or had two sets of very large bandages covering his lower legs. They were, we'd been told, the result of a silly accident. As he unsteadily shuffled past our Scrabble-playing group toward the bridge, we noticed the bandages were gone and his lower legs looked shredded. From where we were sitting, however, we couldn't get a close-up.

We heard the captain's gasp. Apparently, the night before our trip, Winn had had a nasty encounter with chiggers. Chiggers are tiny bugs that bite like mosquitoes, bury themselves in your skin, and then pro-ceed to feast on your flesh. Craig was out shooting tin cans with his boys when he stepped on a nest of the critters, hundreds of which decided to immigrate to his ample legs. Winn fought back with reckless abandon, using sandpaper to scrape off his skin from ankle to knee and then pour-ing gasoline into the raw wounds. Nuclear annihilation to the damn bugs was his plan. It worked rather too well, not only for the chiggers but for his legs. They were turning purple and black. The captain men-tioned the word *gangrene.*

Hasty calls were made to a doctor. Given the description, the doctor implored the captain to get the patient back to Nassau ASAP. If it was gangrene, it needed to be treated immediately. Craig was in incredible pain, so we loaded him up with Percocet and encouraged him to wash it down with wine. That happily knocked him out for a few hours.

With Winn snoozing in the middle of the floor, I walked to the bridge to talk to our always-gregarious captain. He was studying his maps, his global positioning systems, and his instrument panels. Those were the only three things he looked at. The problem with the Bahamas, he explained with his eyes fixed on those objects, was the massive coral reefs that loomed below. Running during the day wasn't much of a problem, since you could see most of the potential dangers. Running at night, you ran pretty much blind with your instruments and a high-intensity floodlight. Worse, one of the islands we'd be cruising by was owned by a notorious drug lord. He tended to run his ships at night, since the Coast Guard wasn't so insane as to chase them through the reefs at night. Captain Jack was worried, because he didn't want the drug lords to think *we* were the Coast Guard and turn a rocket-propelled grenade launcher on us.

The captain turned all the lights off on the bridge to preserve his night vision. Jamie, Kim, Sheila, and the boys, meanwhile, decided it would help pass the time to play with Jamie's karaoke machine and sing the night away. The captain actually encouraged noise and lights, kind of like hikers in grizzly country. If there were drug traffickers around, we wanted to advertise the fact that we were just a crazy bunch of partying tourists.

After about five hours we saw lights far in the distance. Six hours or so after we had left, we pulled into the Atlantis harbor and breathed a collective sigh of relief as Craig was carted off to the doctor. He insisted on going alone. Jamie, the captain, and I hit the casino for a little gambling relief. Kim and Sheila hit the sack.

Craig, it turned out, was fine. No gangrene, just a nasty infection quickly knocked out with penicillin. We all flew back to Charlottesville on August 23. Perhaps I should have been wrestling with profound thoughts after our wild romp in the Bahamas. Somehow, though, it all seemed quite normal — as normal as urging most of your family to desert their homes and move to Charlottesville, as normal as working on biz dev one day and telemarketing the next, and as normal as dropping scores of millions of dollars a month on newspaper ads that encouraged phone sales. It was just another day at Value America to me.

For Kim, however, the trip was an impressive affirmation of her new life at Value America. The private plane, the luxurious yacht, the exotic food. And hearing Winn's endless chatter about retail's history and future and Value America's grand designs convinced her he was, if extremely eccentric, a true visionary. Winn constantly relayed his certainty that huge deals were about to break, that Citibank was on the verge of making the company billions, Saks could be huge, and the Falwell custom store was going to bring in millions of loyal customers. His bout of chigger annihilation revealed his toughness and psychotic will. Winn, Kim told me, was like Mary Poppins. As he described his vision, suddenly we all leapt through the sidewalk into a glorious new place. Value America was powerful and profitable, and we were all riding on cream-puff carousels.

Back in the office, we were greeted by new reports from the technology team that slow-loading pages were causing half of all visitors to the Value America site to abandon their shopping attempts before ever having a chance to purchase. Everyone flipped out at that news — well, almost everyone. Winn didn't believe it.

The biggest problem seemed to be the graphics-rich front page. With more than thirty graphics buttons on top of a hodgepodge of banner ads featuring "hot" items and other offers, the page was already top heavy. Hypothetically, that amount of graphics ought to take only forty-three seconds to load on a 28.8k dial-up modem. But that calculation didn't take into account Internet congestion, query time, database response time, or anything else. We were getting e-mails from customers telling us it was taking five *minutes* for the home page to load.

One problem was that too many people and departments had staked a claim to the Web page. Glenda Dorchak and the sales team wanted banner ads and flashy promotional buttons to generate revenue and draw people to the hot deals. Craig was wedded to the checkerboard of pictures. There were endless tugs and pulls — buttons for investor relations, information about the company, and press releases. Changing any of those individual items was a major undertaking because of the complicated proprietary software the Value America attic gang had developed and because getting Winn and Morgan to sign off on changes was even more cumbersome.

Complicating things further was the continued upgrading of Value America's internal systems. On top of the SAP implementation, the tech folks were trying — via other software upgrades and packages — to further hone communication with manufacturers in hopes of getting quicker shipping. We had programs from GE Information Systems, Siebel, and Netperceptions all stitched together, often with the seams showing. All of this combined with continuing the custom store development, executive presentations, and the daily work of maintaining a complex technological infrastructure had the technology team working twenty hours a day seven days a week.

So what did we do? We made it worse: We added yet another button to the front page, notifying shoppers of a special message from the CEO. "Value America," the note said, "is in the midst of creating a world-class e-commerce infrastructure, better than anything else online. As this building continues, there may be temporary congestion and slow loading periods. We apologize to our customers for any inconvenience."

Perhaps not surprisingly, on August 31, Value America's stock hit a new low — $10⁹⁄₁₆. It wasn't alone. Another company that went public the day before Value America, iTurf, was trading at around $12. Autoweb, another former highflyer, had broken through the dreaded $10 level and was trading at $9. Not far behind, TheStreet.com, a financial news site, was below $20 a share. And there were others. According to *Red Herring* magazine, of the thirty-three Internet-related stocks that experienced a first-day stock bump of greater than 100 percent in 1999, only nine were selling *above* their first-day close. The other twenty-four stocks were below that close, and seven were below their offering prices. To *Red Herring* and other publications, Value America was leading the pack of stock disappointments.

Internally, however, the third-quarter numbers looked very strong. Tom Morgan's $57 million revenue goals — including $40 million in computer sales, $8 million in peripherals and software, $3 million in consumer electronics, $1 million in office products, and another $4 million in general consumer products — appeared to be on target. Based on the sketchy reporting we were getting, it appeared we were also going to increase our gross margins to about 5 percent — maybe 6 percent.

The only real downside was the continued failure of the multimedia product presentations to generate the kind of revenue they were designed to produce. If we were lucky, the revenue from products with such presentations would reach $500,000, about what Value America had generated in 1996. Furthermore, only a handful of companies were contributing *any* cash to Value America's heavy investment in print advertising. In fact, the only real revenue generated from ads, so far as we could tell, came from selling ad space on our own Web site. Those spots generated nearly $1 million in revenue.

Because the budding executive team needed more physical space, Morgan arranged for a new suite of executive offices closer to town. The space would be nice, quiet, and more relaxing. It would also, I feared, further isolate the executive team. It wasn't, I told Morgan, how good campaigns were run. Politics, I maintained more emphatically than ever, was the only model for what we were doing. We *were* running a campaign — a campaign to convince Wall Street to love us, retail traders to vote for us with their dollars, and consumers to vote for us with their business. But my views were strongly in the minority.

My views were at least partially supported by the two people I'd hired to help create a killer PR operation. Kim Martin, a long-term Value American, had been assigned to me out of mercy a few weeks after I'd begun. Always friendly, always helpful, and always overwhelmed given my schedule, Kim was probably even happier than I was to see Jen Messmer and Kurt Stenerson — my future brother-in-law Scott's former work buddy — join the company. Their specific task was to chase every possible press lead, determine what deals were in the pipeline, and create a normalized distribution-and-checkoff process for press releases. In short, they were going to do what I thought I was going to do back in May when I was hired. Instead, I was busy with a hundred different things. Things like business development.

AskJeeves, the natural-language search engine billed as the first Internet butler, hosted me, Tom Morgan, and a couple other Value Americans in their New York offices. We proposed that Value America would create a branded AskJeeves store — perhaps called ShopJeeves — powered by Value America. We didn't have financial specifics nailed down but assumed we'd give Jeeves 3 percent to 10 percent of revenue. In addition, Value America and AskJeeves would share customer lists. Better yet, the store could be up and running and advertising in a few weeks.

My deal-making experience at that point consisted of watching the movie *Wall Street* and taking notes at a lot of Craig Winn meetings. But it all seemed to be going very well. The approach was radical from AskJeeves's perspective, so I was thrilled they didn't reject it out of hand. In fact, Frank Vaculin, AskJeeves's number two man, latched on to the idea instantly. As with most Internet dealings, he was working both ends: He was trying to convince us to buy the AskJeeves search engine for our site. Vaculin was also proposing a joint venture that combined the best of our shopping and the best of their search engine, or perhaps to swap technologies — for AskJeeves to enhance Value America's shopping site with its search engine in exchange for Value America's shopping engine on their site. He also pondered a different scenario: If AskJeeves stock increased significantly from its $33 position, he thought Value America would be an interesting acquisition target. He headed back to San Francisco to discuss all the possibilities with his boss.

Across town at Citibank, Winn and his team were again trying to finalize their deal. While the lower-level executives from both companies were working to finalize the original portion of the agreement — essentially a custom store for Citibank-card members — Winn diverted to higher levels. His latest focus was on creating a Citibank catalog for the CitiPrivileges program that was designed to serve its card members. Winn's lack of interest in the little things (and the original portion of the Citibank deal was now, in his mind, a little thing) meant that early September passed with numerous meetings but little progress in finalizing any deal.

Part of Winn's higher-order thinking was inspired by his other potentially huge project, an enormous deal with FedEx. Around the company, speculation had run rampant about a potential FedEx–Value America partnership ever since Fred Smith's son Richard came on board.

Richard was an offensive-line coach's dream — a big block of a young man who was smart, learned quickly, and knew how to throw his ample weight around. Winn was determined to make Richard a great salesman and businessman. The two spent hours together talking and strategizing.

One day Richard Smith ambled into Winn's office and pitched an idea. Value America needed to create a custom store for FedEx's hugely popular Web site. Winn loved the idea and immediately began fleshing it out with marketing, sales, and growth projections. His plan was to take Richard Smith (a Value America *intern*) with him to FedEx's headquarters in Memphis and have him pitch the deal to his father. Winn loved the symmetry of it all, as well as the fact that the deal, according to him, could be worth billions.

Following a much-needed Labor Day break, the Visa project began springing to life as well. After the San Francisco trip in early August, I had begun a dialogue with our Visa contacts there. The opportunity they were presenting was for us to be part of their 1999 holiday season campaign. Backed by television and ad spots, the Visa.com holiday promotion gave Visa cardholders who visited the Visa site special offers and rewards. Perhaps Value America could be the backbone of the site. No one quite knew what terms might be appropriate, since no one — not even Visa — knew exactly how many people would visit Visa.com. No decision was needed until later in September, so the various powers at Value America jockeyed. Neal Harris proposed offering Visa a selection of consumer merchandise, while Winn favored something incentive-based. Dorchak, Morgan, and the rest of the team were silent, probably wondering what I was doing managing sales and marketing projects. If I hadn't been having so much fun, I probably would have wondered that, too.

In fact, I was having so much fun that almost nothing could faze me: not the fact that the technology team hadn't yet debugged the SAP software and probably wouldn't by our target date; not the fact that the executive offices separated us from the rest of the company and brought the total number of Value America buildings to sixteen; not even the fact that Lloyd Ogilvie, Senate chaplin extraordinaire and the man who was shortly to wed Kim and me, had done the most inconsiderate of all possible things — he had had open-heart surgery and a quadruple bypass ten days before our wedding. Kim tearfully informed me that Ogilvie was on the shelf for at least a month and our wedding was in some jeopardy unless I found a preacher fast. She had hit her ceiling. To me it was *sort* of funny.

My preacher problem was scuttled to the back burner. Mick Kicklighter had requested my presence in Winn's office, and as we walked down the hall, I explained my predicament. Winn's new track-lit office was full of dark wood and glass. There, live and in grinning person with his arm around Winn, was Jerry Falwell. A *big* man, both in height and girth, Falwell smiled expansively at me as his doughy hand enveloped mine. Constrained by a dress shirt over the collar of which flowed his neck, Falwell glided about the place, commenting about how lovely the décor was, what a wonderful town Charlottesville was, and how great Value America was. He was probably pleased by the $1 million loan Winn had insisted Value America bestow on his preacher pal as well.

As I stumbled over what to say to Falwell, Kicklighter and Winn leapt into deep discussion. Winn beamed as he gravely asked me to leave for a moment. Bidding an awkward farewell to Falwell, I scurried back to my office to find a preacher.

Moments later, Winn positively skipped into my office. He beamed like a new father. "I've solved your wedding problem."

"Really?" I gasped.

"I just spoke with Jerry, and he's agreed to perform your ceremony. I'm going to pick him up in the plane, deliver him to the wedding, and fly him home!"

My heart stopped. "Gosh, Craig, wow, really, wow, I'm just speechless, wow. Thank you. Wow. Gosh. Really, wow. I'm overwhelmed, really."

After I was sure Winn was safely back in his office, I bit my cheek and grabbed the phone to call Kim. "You aren't going to believe this one," I began, struggling to sound chipper. Her reaction was worse than I imagined. After several unfinished exclamations, she ordered, "Just tell Craig I already found somebody. I'll do that now." With that, she summarily dismissed me of my previously assigned duties. I wondered how this would impact our wedding night.

Before I had a chance to hang up, Winn was back in my office, wondering if I'd talked to Kim yet. I used the phone in my left hand to emphasize my points. "Craig, I think that Jerry, while a wonderful choice, isn't quite what Kim had envisioned. He's just so . . . public that she's afraid it might distract from the ceremony." It was as good an answer as I could come up with on short notice. Deflated, Winn agreed it was the bride's day above all.

I felt genuinely sad for Winn. He so wanted to help and had been so excited to bestow his solutions on my problem. But he couldn't see Falwell was still Falwell. For all of Winn's brilliance, there was this massive blind spot: Even after forty-four years, he failed to realize that what he saw and pronounced to be good wasn't necessarily good for everyone else. What he believed to be true wasn't necessarily true.

Falwell was at Value America to receive the loan and also to discuss the new catalogs scheduled to be mailed to his constituents. Since the Falwell custom store hadn't exactly performed to expectations (it fell approximately $999,900,000 short of a billion), Winn had modified the plan a bit. Now, instead of pursuing Falwell's sheep online, Winn wanted to send catalogs to the faithful via the good ol' postal service. The "Falwell Ministries Store" would feature all sorts of goodies for Christmas — everything from a little bench for the backyard to a cheap, but quality, laptop computer. The catalog served several purposes. First, it gave Value America a new marketing avenue. Now, Value America could claim to be a catalog-distribution company. The catalogs also offered another opportunity to get merchandisers to pay for their products to be featured. Because the catalogs were going to targeted groups, merchandisers could be sure that important demographics saw their goods. Craig saw the catalogs, therefore, as a potential savior on both the revenue and profit fronts.

Winn had wanted catalog production to begin back in June. To date, however, there had been little progress. Every catalog from a competing company that appeared in Winn's home mailbox over the summer only compounded his frustration.

Winn was also branching out into direct online marketing via Value Dollars, which were one part coupon and one part frequent-flier mile. One percent of every customer's purchase accrued as Value Dollars. Each Value Dollar could then be used to reduce the price of a future purchase by the accrued Value Dollar amount — provided that the Value Dollars applied did not exceed 50 percent of the purchase price. Value America sent out electronic direct mail (EDM) with Value Dollar coupons, and the results were remarkable. While Value America's newspaper ads earned a dollar in revenue for every dollar spent in advertising, the Value Dollar EDM's were more like $7 in revenue for every $1 in spending. Where many other e-commerce companies were spending $2 or $3 in advertising for every revenue dollar generated, Winn saw the Value Dollars as remarkably powerful marketing tools.

Dean Johnson and Glenda Dorchak, however, thought Value Dollars were absurd. To Johnson, Value Dollars cost too much from an accounting perspective. Advertising was treated as a marketing expense and was therefore deducted as such. It was becoming increasingly clear, however, that PricewaterhouseCoopers, the company's auditors, believed Value Dollars when applied to specific items were not a marketing cost but rather a sales expense. That meant certain types of Value Dollar incentives would come directly out of gross margin, thereby crushing the company in Wall Street's eyes.

Dorchak detested Value Dollars because they reduced her ability to control the company's marketing expenses. Dorchak knew how to drive sales for computer and technology products using run-of-print advertising. She knew how sales responded to ads, and she knew how much it cost to get the revenue she needed. That approach would never, ever make Value America profitable, but it would drive revenue, and that earned her high marks on her report card. Tom Morgan sided with Dorchak. Her case to him was persuasive. She could virtually guarantee revenue targets with the newspaper ads. She couldn't do the same with Value Dollars.

What Dorchak really wanted was to bring in a high-power brand-consulting firm to overhaul everything about Value America. She wanted to change the company's name, logo, Web storefront, and newspaper advertising, and launch new broadcast ads as well. But she knew that so long as Winn remained Value America's power center, that wasn't going to happen.

Trying hard not to piss off his CEO but obsessed with garnering revenue, Winn finally tapped Ken Power to lead the catalog-production effort. For several days, Winn and Power worked together to draft catalogs for both Citibank and Falwell. For Winn, the time with Power was a reminder of what Value America had once been — a place where he knew everyone's name and where his hopes and their hopes were one grand hope. Now, as Winn looked around his company, he saw people he didn't know speaking a language he wasn't comfortable with. It was all about marketing briefs and sterile analysis. There was no room left to improvise. It was, Winn believed, a company in danger of losing its soul.

Winn knew the shadow his personality cast. He knew that people were intimidated by him. In some ways, he *wanted* them to be intimidated. But he also longed for the moment when his executives became tough enough to lead despite him — to show the kind of determination and passion required to make Value America great. He wanted to butt heads and conflict and come out a unified team.

He was concerned about the board, too. It was an awfully powerful group of men — chiefs of major corporations, the top finance guy for one of the kings of the Internet age, a former member of President Reagan's cabinet. They were going to start asking more and more questions. He knew he didn't have good answers. On one hand, Value America was still *his* company. Everyone knew if Winn wanted something, Winn got it. Yet Winn knew less and less about what needed to be happening. He was losing touch. He hadn't been to an executive management meeting in months. He didn't monitor the day-to-day operations of the company. He was up to his elbows in various deals, he was constantly promoting the company in public, but he was operating on what was happening in his head. He was in a netherworld of his own creation.

The Visa promotion highlighted all this. After failing to assemble Dorchak, Harris, Morgan, Kicklighter, and Winn to discuss the opportunity, I did the next best thing. I stood outside my door until I saw both Harris and Winn and grabbed them for an on-the-spot meeting. Before I left for my honeymoon, I announced, we needed to finalize Visa. Harris hadn't been successful in devising any new consumer-product promotions. Winn wasn't entirely sure what had been offered previously or what I wanted. As he listened to me describe the Visa.com holiday promotion, however, he lit up and suggested we offer an aggressive Value Dollar promotion. Every Visa customer visiting the holiday site would get one hundred Value Dollars, to be used on purchases over $500. It was a compelling idea, but Value America's systems couldn't handle it, since the system was programmed to redeem one Value Dollar for every $2 purchased. That didn't matter to Winn. It's simple, he said, we just put that offer on the Visa site, and that's what people will think the deal is. Harris and I reinforced that it wouldn't work. After many sighs and much eye rolling, Winn agreed to the standard Value Dollar promotion — one hundred Value Dollars, to be used on purchases over $200. Winn knew people wouldn't spend exactly $200 and thus weren't going to get exactly 50 percent off. He figured they'd average about $300 per purchase, which was a good deal for Value America. He still preferred the other strategy, however. It was a superior marketing idea.

Five days before our wedding, Kim officially started at Value America. Three days before our wedding, she hit the road with Tom Morgan and Dean Johnson for investor meetings in New York. The road show was a blunt attempt to communicate the company's true value to key people making investment decisions for big funds. The clear objective was to raise the company's $11 share price and build momentum, so that raising money — which Value America would be forced to do by early 2000 — would be easier. The other message was at least as important: Value America wasn't just Craig Winn's toy that he could manipulate at will. Tom Morgan was the front man. He was reserved, understated, sophisticated, and logically persuasive — perfect for Wall Street. His challenge was to build legitimacy among the financial crowds who had listened to Winn for eighteen months.

Conventional market and media wisdom by late September echoed what Starnes, Morgan, and the rest of the executive team had discussed in late June, that the business-to-consumer market was too competitive, too fractured, and not profitable enough. People started commenting that it took way too much money to create an Internet brand and that ultimately only one or two of the exciting e-commerce retailers would be standing in a year or two. Onsale, Beyond, eToys, Pets.com, and the rest plummeted daily. The fact that these declines occurred as companies neared what analysts projected would be a record-setting holiday season was particularly alarming.

The Value America trio headed to New York and Boston on September 22 to meet with financiers already trafficking in Value America stock and those who might consider investing. Among the things Kim had envisioned for her celebratory wedding week, being stuck on a commercial puddle jumper for a pre-dawn flight to New York crammed between her new boss, Tom Morgan, and her new colleague, Dean Johnson, wasn't one of them. Still, she was eager to see the Value America team in action. AOL was run by a bunch of overachieving geniuses. There was Ted Leonsis, who ran macrostrategy. He had been responsible for all of AOL's key acquisitions, from ICQ to Spinner to MapQuest. There was Barry Schuler, who ran the interactive-services division that developed AOL Anywhere and other brain-bending technologies. Bob Pittman was the most ruthlessly brilliant manager she'd ever seen; he made Newt Gingrich look like Big Bird. Throughout

AOL, executives were the engines of the company's growth and success in a viciously competitive space.

She hoped Value America's leaders were the same way and knew her next two days of meetings would educate her about the company's strengths and weaknesses. The groups the team visited — Blue Ridge Capital, Spear, Leeds & Kellogg, Knight Securities, Fidelity Investments, Pioneering Management, and the Yankee Group, among others — provided a great cross section of how the company was viewed and what needed to change in order for Value America to regain Wall Street's favor.

Morgan was thrilled to have Kim along. Doubts about the company's future increased almost daily. The unsolicited reports Morgan received from friends and colleagues indicated that Winn was an ever-increasing drain on the company's internal morale and external reputation. Morgan didn't know how to break that news to his friend and colleague. He had once confronted an employee who had been increasing her sales productivity by giving blow jobs to prospective male clients — that was awkward. But telling a man you prayed with, a man who owned the largest part of the company, that he was a detriment to that company? That was a tough mission.

Morgan's other pending crisis was evaluating the papers that had anonymously landed on his desk the afternoon before his New York trip. Someone had run a Lexis-Nexis search on Dynasty Lighting Classics. Virtually everyone at Value America knew the company had declared Chapter 11 and never recovered. Unknown to everyone at Value America, however, was that Dynasty's rise and fall seemed to mirror Value America's. The articles splayed before Morgan reported that Dynasty "burst onto the lighting scene. Under the guidance of Craig Winn, founder and chairman, the company was lauded for its innovative strategies for marketing lamps to consumers, which consisted of bringing the housewares approach to packaging. And, the company grew quickly from $17 million in sales in 1987 to $94 million in 1991."

The articles pointed out that although Dynasty's sales had increased, net income had decreased. Industry sources attributed high overhead, too much product expansion, and an inability to ship on time as reasons for Dynasty's financial slide. "Dynasty had an extremely high overhead," said one lighting supplier. "They had very extravagant offices, a huge warehouse, a company plane, and hired too many high-paid executives."

Dynasty's problems were attributed to "a lack of structure and discipline. You had an entrepreneur who grew the company very quickly, then he hit a brick wall." The articles went on to detail how Dynasty lost focus and began diverting into random product lines such as wall art and ceiling fans.

The same articles landed on my desk, and I read them with increasing panic. For the first time I was objectively frightened about Winn's corporate control. If *that* was what he'd done to his last company, what was he going to do to Value America? And, by extension, to *my family*. I smashed the articles in a drawer and decided to ponder that question *after* my honeymoon.

Kim's meetings in New York the following day repeated those haunting themes. Despite nearly $100 million in advertising spending, the public didn't know what Value America was about. It was a mystery e-tailer. One vice president asked how the paid membership was going. Morgan and Kim looked at each other with bulging eyes. Other potential investors raised concerns that the vast majority of Value America's business was tied up in IBM and HP. Others just wondered why they should invest in an outlet mall on the Internet. How, they all wondered, could a clearance house for closeout technology and electronics products make money? Those were just the points of confusion. The points of criticism were starker still. Although Value America steadfastly refused to release its customer-acquisition costs, they weren't too hard to figure out, since it released revenues and average order size. The numbers turned out to be pretty staggering, and one analyst asked how any company could hope to make a profit if it cost upward of $1,000 just to *get* the customer. Amazon was getting customers for less than $20. Dean Johnson attempted Winn's typical rebuttal: Customer-acquisition costs were dependent on how much the customer spent. If Amazon got a customer for $20 but average order size was $13, it wasn't as good as if Value America got a customer for $1,000 and that customer spent $1,300. True enough, the investor responded, but Amazon has about ten million customers, and by our calculations, Value America has a small fraction of that. Silence.

The other criticisms were similarly fundamental to the business model. The product categories were a mile wide but barely an inch deep. This violated the cardinal rule of sales; it overpromised and *underdelivered,* instead of the other way around. If all the ads showed second-rate computer products, then people thought Value America was a closeout closet for electronics. The store's navigation system was antiquated as well. And, everyone chided, no one could have any confidence in a company with negligible *gross margins.*

Despite their dire line of questioning, most said that if the company could solve some of those problems, it could present an interesting investment opportunity. The unspoken requisite was getting control of the spiraling company, something not even Tom Morgan knew for certain he could accomplish.

On the return flight, Kim looked out the tiny jet window. This was doable. This was really, really doable, she thought. Sure, there were problems. But they were mainly image problems — well, and some operational problems. But Tom could handle those. It was just a matter of focus. Reviewing her notes, she found lots of reasons to be optimistic. Some of the analysts and investors had expressed a great deal of interest in several of the company's projects. Everyone was eager to see what Morgan could do. He was the company's best hope, as far as the financial community was concerned.

On September 25, I looked out onto the rapidly filling church and began to count all the people with Value America connections. There were Craig and Kathy Winn, Tom Morgan and his wife, Dianne, Bill and Elayne Bennett, my brother-in-law Scott and his wife, Heather, Jamie Parsons, Neal and Gabrielle Harris . . . the list went on and on. I wondered briefly if I could deduct the wedding as a business expense. We were very long on Value America.

As the reception buzzed along, Bill Bennett grabbed me in the midst of the craziness and said, "All the Value America people here at your wedding tells me more about the company than a presentation ever could." I looked around and saw all their gleaming faces. Morgan and Winn were talking to George and Mari Will. Jamie and Kathy Winn danced. Neal Harris and his wife mingled with our other friends. Value America had become an integral part of my life and a part of my family. It was encouraging to see the camaraderie before we left it behind for two weeks.

Then Kim and I were off. We left the world behind and headed to the wilds of South Africa to play with elephants and lions and hippos. For two weeks, we would know nothing, absolutely nothing, about what was happening at Value America.

We boarded the Air France jet, lugging bags full of *Forbes, The Industry Standard, Business 2.0,* and *Fast Company.* What could be more perfect, we thought? We had hours and hours of uninterrupted plane time to catch up on our business reading. We'd read them all cover to cover, rip out the important articles, and chuck the rest. We reclined our seats, raised the footrests, and toasted each other with our champagne. About thirty minutes into the flight, as I tried to care about Amway's new e-commerce strategy, and Kim tried to focus on management strategies for the Internet, we looked at each other, looked down at our glossy pages, and hurled every last one of the magazines onto the floor. Kim went a step further. She gathered them all up, marched to the bathroom, and shoved every magazine, one by one, into the little trash bins.

CHAPTER SIXTEEN

DefCon3

As much as Richard Smith liked being an intern at Value America, and as excited as he was about his idea for the Value America–FedEx relationship, he hadn't expected Craig Winn's offer. One day in late September, as Kim and I gallivanted around the South African bush, Winn called Richard into his office and asked if he wanted to "own" the FedEx relationship.

To Winn it made perfect sense. Who else should run the project but the guy who thought of it? That the guy was a twenty-one-year-old kid was offset by the fact that his dad ran the company Value America was striking the deal with. Who else had a better chance to get Value America exactly what it wanted?

Down in Memphis during the first week of October, Winn, Kicklighter, Smith, and a small team of other VA executives, including my newly hired brother-in-law, Scott Carter, arrived at FDX headquarters to discuss the young Mr. Smith's idea.

Winn was buzzing with excitement over the potential FedEx deal. In every way it trumped the Citibank relationship. Citibank was, of course, the kind of miracle deal that breathed life into Internet start-ups. Citibank was a fine institution, and Value America's deal with the legendary bank would be worth billions. But the *FedEx* deal was really, *really* big.

FedEx had a busily traveled Web site that attracted more than ten million people every day. FedEx customers visited the site to track the status of various packages. Because of the technological advances FedEx had recently implemented, customers could find out *exactly* where their packages were at any point in time. It was addicting, actually, following the extraordinary journey little letters and big boxes took.

To Winn, since FedEx had the eyeballs, it made sense to do more with those eyeballs than tell customers that at 11:11 P.M. their letter went from a warehouse to a container bin in Memphis. Winn envisioned a "FedEx MarketPlace by Value America" backed by the promise that FedEx would deliver every order from the marketplace to the purchaser's doorstep the very next day. Off the top of his head, he could name twenty well-known companies ranging from Williams-Sonoma to Gap that didn't have a solid Web presence and that he figured would clamor for this kind of opportunity. If the product was bad or in any way offensive, FedEx would pick it up and return it free of charge. For Winn, part of the genius behind this plan was that the FedEx name helped overcome any latent consumer fear of e-commerce.

But the MarketPlace was just the start. Winn knew FedEx wasn't a shipping company; it was a logistics and distribution company. He recalled that Fred Smith loved to say he was the "maid to every major corporation in America." He was. FedEx got inside its business partners' logistics and helped them operate more efficiently, effectively, and profitably. Winn reasoned that if FedEx combined that expertise with Value America's e-commerce expertise, it would be lights out for any of Value America's e-commerce competitors.

Winn's *other* FedEx idea was even bigger: This new partnership could go public as a separate entity. He even had a name for it — Serve America. This Serve America was a derivation of the Serve America he had proposed earlier that year. In its tweaked form, it would primarily be a business-to-business retailer. This made sense. FedEx's biggest margins were not in residential delivery, where drivers trekked door-to-door to drop off single packages. FedEx made money when it delivered one hundred different documents to the same business address. Now, instead of just shipping stuff for other people, FedEx could ship stuff and take a percentage of the revenue as pure profit. Value America, of course, would be the engine making it all run. Eventually it would work internationally as well.

FedEx, Winn reasoned, needed this kind of shake-up. Once a Wall Street darling, it was under increasing pressure from rival UPS, who was contemplating a massive IPO. Even worse, FedEx didn't seem to have anything to say about how it was going to change things.

On that crisp October day, Fred Smith and his top deputy, Dennis Jones, met with the Value America team and listened to Winn's presentation. Winn thought it was an especially nice touch when Rick handed his newly printed Value America business card to father Fred. FedEx was a bit concerned about diluting its shipping and logistics focus by venturing into retail, but Smith and Jones both liked the ideas and wanted Winn and team to meet with the FedEx Internet team.

The reception there was not quite so rosy. One of the FedEx Internet executives, David Roussain, was deeply troubled by the idea that FedEx might become a retailer. Roussain had been developing a small FedEx mall for some time. But, he recognized, there was a big difference between providing space on the FedEx site for retailers that FedEx served and having FedEx become a retailer itself, potentially competing with the very people it was serving.

The Value America–FedEx discussions progressed significantly for a single day's meeting. The goal of each company was to implement *something* no later than the end of October, just four weeks away. FedEx established a working group of about a dozen people, representing all the company's major divisions, to hammer out a deal. Value America did the same. Richard Smith was named captain of our little team.

Winn was jubilant. Now there wasn't just Citibank to talk about, there was also FedEx. It was what Winn referred to as the *Fortune* 100 strategy. He would build alliances with the biggest and best businesses in America to drive revenue and credibility for Value America. The FedEx deal proved that Value America — Winn's "marketplace for a new millennium" — wasn't just about the Internet; it was about shopping morning, noon, and night, shopping as recreation, shopping as therapy, shopping as sport, shopping as divine calling.

Morgan decided to build on the relative success of the New York–Boston trip by meeting with key investors, analysts, and opinion leaders in the Bay Area. After they finished their questions, Morgan asked each one why he or she thought Value America's stock was under so much downward pressure. The answers he expected — not enough product offerings, bad advertising, no clear message — never came up. Instead, meeting after meeting closed with a similar answer: Value America's chairman, Craig Winn, was a problem for the company. The responses were the same: "No one trusts him." "He's like a used-car salesman." "People out here remember him from the last company he bankrupted." Hearing the same sentiments Morgan had read in the articles about Dynasty, the team was told that "Die-Nasty," as others called it, was all huff and puff, a lot of talk and no delivery. Winn's Dynasty, they were told, *never* made a quarter's numbers.

One individual met Morgan, Dorchak, and Johnson at the door, red-faced. "Are you," he asked, barely constraining his rage, "affiliated with Craig Winn?"

"Yes," Morgan said steadily. "He's the chairman of Value America."

"Then," the beet-red investor screeched, "I don't want a f——ing thing to do with you." He hissed, "That bastard cost me ten million dollars. Your problem" — he glared at them — "is that we all know Craig Winn. We know his games. We know his act. No one out here believes the guy. If you want to turn things around, you've got to get rid of him."

Wrapping up our South Africa honeymoon after not having contemplated too much of Value America for two weeks, Kim and I found ourselves partially dreading and partially giddy about our Charlottesville return. Our excitement, however, overcame our doubts. We were going to work together and live together — all the time. We'd be working with Heather and Scott. We'd learn more about this new economy that was supposed to rule the world and change all our lives forever. Plus, Kim said, handing me a copy of the *International Herald Tribune,* Value America is an America's Cup sponsor now. Maybe we'll all get to go to New Zealand. There, smaller than life, was a picture of Dennis Connor's *Stars & Stripes,* limping back to the docks after a punishing loss. It was flying the Value America sail.

Winn, Morgan, and the Kuo honeymooners all arrived back at Value America on October 11. The wonder of modern travel is that one day you can be getting an aromatherapy massage on your private deck, listening to elephants trumpet in the distance, and the next day you can be sitting at a plastic desk in Charlottesville, Virginia, feeling like a chewed-up impala. After seventeen hours of wonderful French hospitality aboard an Air France jet that rocketed us from Johannesburg to Washington, D.C., via Paris, Kim and I now sat in adjoining offices wondering where this adventure was going to take us. Down the hall was our sister Heather. Downstairs was brother Scott. Heather and Scott were enjoying their Value America transition. Heather was becoming Morgan's right-hand person and was tasked with — among other things — getting to the bottom of the customer-service debacle.

Scott was helping manage the FedEx relationship. We looked forward to evenings of dinners and weekends of hiking, biking, and relaxing. We were just one cozy little family.

Jennifer Messmer dropped in and told me she almost hadn't made it through the two weeks of my absence. It wasn't because she missed me. She'd tried to get advertising numbers from Glenda Dorchak and had gotten her head bitten off. She'd tried to accompany Winn on a D.C. speech he gave and was told to "leave him alone." During a magazine interview, she'd tried to correct Winn when he told a reporter that Value America had signed deals with Citibank and FedEx. He told her not to interrupt him during interviews. She told me her husband had quit his teaching job and taken a job in merchandising at Value America, and they were now both wondering why. I told her not to worry and to give me a few days to straighten things out.

As she left, Tom Morgan dropped by, closed my door, commented on how relaxed I looked, and, after a few moments of pleasantries, cocked his head to one side and announced, "David, I'm going to have to resign."

"What?" was all I could manage, as my face flushed, my eyes narrowed, and my body was once again awakened by that familiar flush of stress-induced adrenaline.

Morgan was fried. He couldn't take the sleepless nights or the stress of trying to run a company despite the chairman's constant meddling in business decisions. More than that, however, Morgan was now convinced Winn was a devastating liability to the company.

Reclining in my little chair in my little office, I could tell Morgan was only partially convinced it was time for him to go. Maybe, he said, he wasn't cut out for this Internet world. Maybe he was just an old-fashioned business guy who believed in controlled costs, reasonable revenue growth, and real profits. For Morgan, trying to run Value America wasn't business management — it was riot control.

I wanted to tell him to suck it up and make it all work somehow. We'd laid our lives on the line. We'd moved in family and friends. He hadn't even moved his family down from McLean, Virginia. I wanted to see that he was passionately committed to making Value America succeed, damn the costs. Instead I saw waffling.

As we sat looking at each other, pondering our next moves, the door swung open and a beaming Craig Winn burst into the office. "Looks to me like our young Mr. Kuo is a much happier and *relaxed* man since the honeymoon!" He nudged Tom and winked. "I've got to go give a speech in Phoenix and then hustle to Memphis for a FedEx meeting. Why don't you come? We're going to leave in about an hour." He turned and left before I could express my displeasure. I'd been trapped in a flying steel tube for the last twenty-eight hours and had no interest in returning to one — not even to the Hawker. Morgan calmly eyed Winn's exit, looked at me, and said, "That's *exactly* the problem."

I went on the trip. Inbound to Phoenix for his speech at the Phoenician in Scottsdale, Winn excitedly filled me in on the incredible happenings since I'd left. All smelled like roses. The third quarter closed with *stunning* numbers. Revenues exceeded $55 million. Gross margins doubled compared to the second quarter, to about 6 percent. It was hard to predict EPS yet, but it looked like there would be no unpleasant surprises. The Citibank relationship was developing. And FedEx portended to be bigger than Citibank. Things couldn't be more positive, he gushed.

As I listened to Winn I realized I'd crossed some bridge. I saw the brightness and the world he was describing. I just wasn't sure that I believed in it. I wanted to, more than anything. But I'd heard all the same stories. I sat back, chugging a six-pack of Diet Cokes, hoping the caffeine would kick in, wishing I was back with my new bride.

Our first stop was the Office Products International (OPI) convention. We pulled up to the Phoenician in our long black limousine like movie stars at an L.A. premiere. Our geeky entourage of Neal Harris and Greg Dorn greeted us. No flashbulbs erupted, but we were certainly the center of attention. The duo whisked Winn off ahead of Mick and me, presumably to ensure the adoring masses didn't crush him as they pressed for his autograph.

Dorn could barely contain himself. "We may have f——ing won the E-tailer of the Year Award from OPI! It was f——ing unbelievable! Those shits from Office Max and Office Depot and even Staples are all vying for the award, but we may have won it."

To date, Value America's office-products sales amounted to less than $1 million over the previous nine months. Sales of pencils and paper and Post-its weren't exactly skyrocketing. But as with everything Value

America–related, office products had "potential." To the Internet-crazed OPI crowd, that potential beat everything else.

Winn was pumped up by the award possibility and by the crowd. Taking the stage like a prizefighter, he roared through the Value America road-show presentation. Unlike in his ill-fated Robertson Stephens speech, he didn't criticize anyone. His mission was convincing the thousands gathered before him that Value America was the most revolutionary retail presence of the age. It worked. The crowd applauded enthusiastically time after time, as Winn worked them over. He closed his speech with new charts showing Value America's dramatic revenue increases over the past twelve months and projecting even more dramatically impressive charts for future quarters. He wasn't divulging exactly what Value America's Q3 numbers were — that would be illegal — but anyone looking at the unlabeled bar graph could unmistakably conclude that revenues had reached about $55 million. "There is no limit to what Value America will be," he said solemnly, surveying the crowd.

Then, as he was about to step off the stage, Winn raised his arms to subdue the applause. Just between us friends, he said, I want to give you a preview of a little announcement we'll be making any day. We are going to announce a major relationship with FedEx that will revolutionize e-commerce. Not only will Value America be shipping products free of charge via FedEx, we will also be creating an online marketplace that will revolutionize b2c [business-to-consumer] and b2b [business-to-business] e-commerce. The audience exploded, chattering, laughing, and clapping like teenagers.

I was thinking maybe my lack of sleep was causing me to hallucinate. As I stood in the back listening to Winn speak, it sounded like he just announced a deal that didn't exist yet. It wasn't the first time such a thing had happened — actually far from it — but this time it was so damn blatant.

"So, nice move on your part," one of the OPI dupes standing next to me whispered. "I just hope I can buy first thing tomorrow before the news hits."

I silently prayed that no SEC flunkies had overheard what sounded to me like a possible violation of federal securities law. The SEC had strict rules about how and when companies could and couldn't make announcements. Bottom line: If there is a "material" event for the company, it must be disclosed to the world through a press release, not just to a few people in a room. According to those rules, we'd have to issue a press release the next morning or even that night to let the rest of the world know what the OPI participants knew. When I broached this to Winn, he just rolled his eyes and asked me if I knew *anything* about sales. It was clear to him that among my talents wasn't the ability to create a new multibillion-dollar e-tailing operation. He forgave me only because he figured I was exhausted.

Landing in Memphis at 3:00 A.M., I saw the alternate FedEx universe at play. Plane after purple-and-orange plane lined up to take off for destinations far and wide. The entire place was lit up like a movie set. Even the customer-service pilots were impressed.

The next morning began with Winn excitedly banging on my door. "We won, we won!" I greeted him in a towel, wondering *what* on earth he was talking about. "We won, we really won! This is big! Get a release out!" Then he spun around and disappeared.

"Craig?!" I called with considerable volume. "What did we *win?*"

"The Office Products E-tailer of the Year Award," he said, skipping away.

"Oh."

I called in to the press shop. OPI had beaten us to the punch. Not only had they issued a release announcing the award, they also posted on their Web site a notice that Value America and FedEx were entering a long-term relationship that guaranteed free shipping via FedEx for all Value America orders.

I immediately called Morgan and gave him the details. He sighed heavily, paused, sighed again, and hung up without saying much.

Pulling up to the shiny steel-and-glass operations center at FedEx, Winn, Kicklighter, and I prepared for our meeting with Laurie Tucker, the top-ranking Internet-strategy executive at FedEx. According to Winn, Tucker actually wanted to work for Value America, heading up this project. I thought that strange. Maybe, I wondered, she wanted to work for Richard Smith?

The meeting, held in a purple-and-orange conference room that adjoined Tucker's office, went well. Winn described to Tucker his department-store vision with a single promise and single checkout and common customer service, all supported by the Value America platform. Instead of just featuring Value America products, however, FedEx and Value America would jointly approach all the leading niche merchants — everyone from Victoria's Secret and Williams-Sonoma to Home Depot and Athlete's Foot — to be part of the store. For the merchants, this was the ultimate solution to a vexing e-commerce question: how to parlay the Internet into more revenue. It also enabled them to get in the game quickly and play without bearing the up-front costs of building their own infrastructures.

In Craig's mind, Value America and FedEx would profit greatly. Each merchant would pay for a spot in the store — along the lines of $1 million to start. There would then be a revenue share on all sales, which Value America and FedEx would split. The upside for both companies was profit without any great expense. The key ingredient for Value America was the FedEx name, which was strong enough to make the whole thing happen. To emphasize Value America's commitment, Winn told Tucker, Value America would offer free shipping on every order from the company's store. Laurie Tucker, and apparently Fred Smith, supported the ambitious plan.

There were internal politics to deal with, but with Fred Smith on board and with Smith's son heading the Value America team, success was a real possibility. Craig was gleeful.

"Excuse me, phone call for Mr. Kuo," Tucker's secretary broke in. Odd — why on earth would someone be calling me now?

"David? Tom. We have a major, major problem. *What* is going on with Visa?" Morgan demanded.

This was an ominous start. I calmly explained to Morgan that Neal Harris, Winn, and I had decided to provide a Value Dollar promotion for Visa customers who shopped on the Visa Holiday Rewards site. All new customers would get one hundred Value Dollars to use on their first purchase. Given that our customer-acquisition costs were so high, we all figured getting a customer that cheap was a bargain.

Things weren't exactly going as planned. Apparently tens of thousands of people flocked to the Visa promotion. (It was a uniquely Internet phenomenon that so many people could learn of an utterly unadvertised deal so fast.) But that wasn't a bad thing. The bad thing was that Value America's internal systems couldn't keep track of the customers. That meant a single customer could open up an unlimited number of Value America accounts and use the Visa promotion to get up to 50 percent off many, many purchases. To Morgan, Dorchak, and Johnson, this spelled financial disaster. Money tied up in Visa Value Dollars wasn't available for regular run-of-print advertising unless Value America wanted to incur even greater losses. That might mean compromising the holiday advertising plan.

It was exactly the kind of reckless business decision making that was driving Morgan berserk. Things had to go through proper channels. Morgan realized Winn had no confidence in Dorchak, but designating advertising dollars was still her responsibility. To have the communications guy, the chairman, and his chief of staff making advertising decisions was unacceptable.

As the corporate trio ranted about how this promotion spelled disaster for Value America, Winn walked out of the FedEx conference room to inquire about what had caused the interruption. As I relayed Morgan's concerns, Winn's face flushed. The coffee cup in his hand slowly crumpled, and somewhere from his depths he bellowed a guttural, "They . . . don't . . . have a clue! This is the best advertising we have going!"

As patient as Winn tried to be with the other children playing with his toys, he'd reached his breaking point this time. The advertising plan for the entire year absolutely sucked. The Visa deal at least moved in the right direction. Under worst-case conditions, if everyone used their one hundred Value Dollars to purchase $200 worth of goods, the advertising trend would be reversed overnight to a positive 2:1 ad-to-revenue ratio. According to Winn's calculations, our newspaper advertising was 1:1 at *best*. To Winn, the idea that anyone on the executive staff could be anything but thrilled by this turn of events was positively ludicrous, especially considering the upside. Chances were that anyone using Value Dollars would probably spend $300 to $500 per order, which yielded an advertising-to-revenue ratio approaching 5:1. At 10:1 Value America was profitable. His patience was running thin.

If his management team could so thoroughly botch something so basic, how on earth could they be trusted to do anything right? With FedEx poised to catapult the company to e-commerce legend, Citibank ready to roll out a groundbreaking program, and now Visa revving into a revenue engine, things were beginning to take off. Winn would be damned if anyone was going to screw things up now. It was high time, he said, to hop back — at least partially — into the saddle.

We puttered to the airport and jetted back to Charlottesville amid the rants.

When we arrived, we each peeled off into our offices to drop bags, check messages, and prepare for an all-hands meeting. I tried to sneak down to Morgan's office to warn him of the impending storm. There I found Dorchak, Johnson, and Morgan huddled together crunching numbers. Dorchak and Johnson looked at me and said, "Thanks for this deal, it is just...*great*." I successfully fought the temptation to snap back.

Gingerly I warned Morgan of Winn's anger. "I don't care," was all he said. He didn't appear to be joking. "I'm tired of his crap. Things need to change."

I just blinked at him, thinking of nothing constructive to say.

Fifteen minutes later, we convened in the conference room. Tom Morgan emerged from his office, a stack of papers in his hand, with Dean Johnson huddled behind. Glenda Dorchak was preparing documents showing Visa's negative impact on advertising in her office. Winn's fuse had been burning for months. Now, once and for all, he was ready to blow a canyon-size hole through Dorchak and her ridiculous, probably book-cooking schemes. She'd "blackmailed" him once, before the September 1998 IPO. He'd wanted Morgan to fire her days after Tom started. Now Winn was determined to take her out. With the new third-quarter numbers in hand, he could pummel her into oblivion. It was revolting how she cozied up to Tom Morgan, and perhaps more ridiculous still that he allowed it. Now was the time for reckoning, the time for truth.

Winn stalked into the conference room, looking much like those hungry leopards we'd photographed a few days before in South Africa. Jennifer Johnson, the Amazonesque Internet sales guru, skittered in, eyed Morgan, and said, "Tom, I've called the lawyers, and our exposure is limited —"

"You did *what*?" Winn exploded.

Jennifer, who hadn't seen Winn, spun around and stammered, "Glenda wanted me to call —"

"I don't give a shit what Glenda said. The only people who can call lawyers in this company are Tom and me. That's it. Is that f——ing clear? Now get out of here!"

No one breathed.

Johnson slinked out of the office. Morgan knew he'd have to console her that evening. Another Winn clean-up job for his to-do list.

As people crawled out from under the table, the meeting precariously commenced. Dorchak arrived and with Morgan started laying out the issues. More than twenty thousand people had signed up for the Value Dollar promotion between October 9 and October 12. There was a total Value Dollar liability, therefore, of $2 million already on the books. Because of the recent auditors' rulings that $2 million must remain on the books through the end of the year, it was imperative to eliminate the program immediately.

Winn listened, but the numbers went right past him. It was, he said, entirely irrelevant how many people had signed up or what our "liability" was. What mattered was figuring out exactly how productive advertising had been and then evaluating the Visa promotion against our existing ads. If the Visa promotion was less effective, then it was a problem. If it was more effective, then we faced a far different problem. He laid out a series of questions he wanted answered. How much was spent on newspaper advertising? How much revenue was generated? How much of it was repeat revenue? How much of it was business revenue? Winn posited that Value America had about forty thousand unique visitors per day and a tiny fraction of those visitors purchased. That meant that the Visa promotion alone likely increased store traffic at least 25 percent — and that was just one promotion. Next, he predicted that b2b business was about 25 percent of the $54 million Q3 revenue, and repeat customers accounted for about 35 to 40 percent of all online purchases. To Winn, newspaper advertising (personally solicited by Value America employees) didn't impact b2b sales, and it didn't drive repeat customers since they already knew the site from earlier purchases. Therefore the $20 million spent on advertising in Q3 had actually resulted in only about $20 million in revenue — at *best* a 1:1 advertising-to-revenue ratio. By all logical accounts, therefore, it would be best to eliminate the entire advertising department and devote the entire advertising budget to online marketing, utilizing, among other things, Value Dollars. Over time, the Value Dollar ratios could be changed to 3:1, 5:1, even 10:1, but the bottom line was that Value Dollars worked and nothing else did.

Morgan, Johnson, and Dorchak gnashed their teeth as Winn "educated" them on the way Value America should work. But here, he was right. Winn's high-horse methods were as appealing as castor oil, but the essential truth remained: Value America's advertising spend was bleeding the company, conveying a confusing if not negative image about the brand, and producing negligible revenue returns. And things were not getting better. If anything, things were moving in a negative direction.

Morgan tried to respond. "The question here, Craig, isn't about newspaper ads. The question is about two million dollars' worth of Value Dollars that may have to come out of our holiday ad spending."

Winn thundered back, "The newspaper ads are the *only* issue, Tom. If Value Dollars work better, then f—— the ads." Winn paused a beat. "And I guarantee they work better. I want the numbers tomorrow. We'll reconvene then."

It had been only thirty-six hours since Tom Morgan had sat in my office and told me he was going to resign. From both a business and a soul-searching standpoint, it had been the most treacherous thirty-six hours of his life. Closing his office door, he plopped onto his beloved tan leather Arnold Palmer couch and tried to remember what sanity was like. He'd managed quarters most of his adult life. He almost always beat expectations and improved results. Never, never had this kind of pressure and shifting standards of judgment impeded his ability to perform. He felt like a figure skater ordered to skate a free program in Olympic competition while being told to intermittently interrupt the well-honed routine with new spins, jumps, and twirls. It was impossible. He wished he could refute Winn point by point, but he couldn't. All he could really do was wait for the Visa numbers to come back and try to manage the fourth quarter as best he could.

In his office, Winn felt the world opening up again. For the first time since before the IPO, he saw the big picture again. He remembered the true genius of *his* company — its ability to provide the inventoryless e-commerce infrastructure, friction-free commerce, to other companies. It didn't matter whether it was shopping services for Citibank, Web customers, or FedEx trackers; what did matter was the engine. Sure, people could shop at Value America's online store — that wasn't going away. But the revenue streams were going to multiply. There would be implementation fees and revenue sharing with companies that used Value America's infrastructure to open their own stores. This would accelerate the company's race to profitability and its rendezvous with destiny to succeed splendidly.

Feeling buoyant after the Visa confrontation, other decided to take other things into his own hands. Winn had a long-standing phone interview with Anne Pollack of Bloomberg News to discuss Value America's plans for the upcoming holiday season. For Winn, the holiday shopping season was interesting but hardly as important as the groundbreaking deals about to blossom at Value America. Of course, he couldn't tell Pollack any specifics of those deals — not technically, anyway. He could and did, however, talk circles around them. He started by announcing he'd moved up the earnings announcement to after the market close on November 4. The executives were debating that date, but Winn had decided there was no reason to put it off. Pollack didn't really care; she liked the company, she was intrigued by Winn, but this was a ten-minute interview to get a sound bite on a holiday shopping story. It was not a feature-length interview about the history and future of the company.

But history was exactly what she got.

Winn wanted Pollack to *understand* Value America, to understand the incredible journey that he began two years before. It was impossible, utterly impossible, to understand the company's possibilities without understanding its history. That history, of course, began twenty years ago, when he was working at Costco and had written the business plan that would become Value America. Holiday shopping? She wanted holiday shopping? That wasn't a problem — this year holiday shopping was going to be four or five times what it was just a year ago. Four or five times! Sure, that may be higher than what analysts were predicting, but they were idiots, and considering Value America had Citibank, FedEx, and Visa, 400 percent growth was conservative. And don't forget Falwell — those catalogs would be huge this holiday season. Jerry's people always came through.

Winn liked Anne Pollack, he really did. She listened. She wasn't like a lot of other reporters who tried to cut him off or show him up. She showed respect for his knowledge, his achievements, and that made her a heck of a lot smarter in his eyes. He figured the best thing to do was reward her. So he offered her an exclusive on a *major* announcement the next day.

As Winn waxed poetic about the company, the exclusive news offering, the revenue projections, and everything else in the Internet universe, Lauren Hurvitz, our RLM contact who'd arranged the interview and was listening to the call, started hyperventilating. She didn't need this. She was going to have a baby. For the past two months she'd been busting her hump trying to get reporters interested in this company without a real brand, without a real message — this company with a babbling, unmanageable chairman. Now, when the *New York Times* and the *Wall Street Journal* had finally expressed some interest, he was telling a Bloomberg reporter he would give *her* some damn exclusive? What the hell?

Hurvitz fired off an e-mail in a near panic to me and Kim, describing the disaster now occurring and imploring us to do something — anything. It was too late. Pollack called Hurvitz after the interview and offered an olive branch. "I like the guy. Heck, I think the company has an interesting story, but this is the second time I've interviewed him, and he is out of control. He doesn't stick to any message, he gets bogged down in random details, even after you ask specific questions. Then he gets defensive if you follow up. By the way, I'll expect news on the exclusive tomorrow."

Back in his office, Winn was pleased to finally connect with someone who *got* it. He was excited to give Anne Pollack an exclusive tomorrow. Problem was, there wasn't anything to announce yet. There *would* be. There certainly *would* be. That was the important thing. She'd understand. He'd call her tomorrow and tell her about the general terms of the deal. That would be, he figured, sort of an exclusive. She'd like that.

I had been back from my honeymoon for forty hours. I hadn't slept but a few of those hours. I didn't know which end was up. But with what little coherence I had, I realized that Winn was now scaring me. I pulled open my desk drawer and reread the articles about Dynasty's demise. Winn always told me that Wal-Mart had screwed Dynasty by withholding a $28 million payment. These articles told a very different story. Dynasty's demise, they suggested, was the result of a CEO named Craig Winn who overpromised and underdelivered. I saw the same happening to us at Value America. With Kim, Heather, and Scott on board, I had too much at stake.

Later that evening, Tom Starnes and I sat with Tom Morgan on his porch to discuss chaos control. Morgan figured he could call board members and tell them the developments — the exaggerations, the lack of credibility on the Street, the abuse of employees. Or, he could step down and spare the company an ugly fight. He wouldn't say anything negative about the company or Winn and wouldn't even ask for the severance package guaranteed in his contract — he'd leave quietly. Or, he figured he could try yet again to make something work with Winn. But that seemed a mountain far greater than he was capable of climbing right now. He'd been trying since his first day in February. He tried soft selling, hard selling, even God selling. Nothing worked for more than a few days. Craig Winn was like a hurricane that might shift its course from time to time but continued to move lethally onward.

My life's goal at that moment was to avoid high noon, where the CEO and the chairman met in the street to shoot it out for ultimate power. I still believed Morgan and Winn working together was best for Value America. But if someone had to go, I knew it had to be Winn. Morgan might lack the grand vision, but the grand vision was largely in place. Morgan could build a business, and he had credibility on Wall Street. Value America couldn't survive without those things. There would be battles no matter who was in charge, but better to rally against the competition than to implode from chaos. Right?

CHAPTER SEVENTEEN

Controlling Legal Authority

On Wednesday morning, October 13, Value America's store crashed. Again.

When analysts and potential investors asked about the risks involved in a massive systems overhaul, we always said that problems were expected, prepared for, and would be handled. Just how they got handled was a different matter.

Every morning at 5:00 A.M., someone in technology would systematically reboot all Value America's computer servers. It was, the tech team discovered, one way to minimize the chances of a total store outage. All told, fifteen servers were rebooted every morning.

Rebooting is a fancy term for turning a computer off and then on again. Of course when dealing with complicated segments of an online store, rebooting isn't that easy. For some undetermined reason, that morning's rebooting hadn't gone well and the whole store was down.

Instead of confronting Winn as planned, Morgan assembled an early-morning meeting to figure out what the problem might be. This was the third outage in two weeks. The obvious answer was that Value America's systems overhaul was hitting some glitches. That morning's glitch was a big one. Value America hadn't yet fallen off its precarious knife-edge, but Morgan knew it was close. Any sustained outage would create even more problems for the company — fewer shoppers, more Wall Street skepticism, more bad media coverage.

The crisis meeting didn't focus just on getting the store up and running. The bigger question Morgan faced was whether to push back the new systems integration until after the holidays. There was no way to ensure Value America's current systems were up to an onslaught of holiday shopping, but launching new systems this close to the holidays might unleash devastating *new* bugs and glitches. Ultimately, Morgan's team decided the implementations should continue, with some additional outside help. Another technology firm was enlisted to smooth the transition. It was likely to be another $1 million bill, but there was no choice. Without the upgraded technology, Value America wouldn't exist. Technology spending now approached $2.5 million a month.

News of Winn's blowup at Jennifer Johnson in the great Visa Value Dollars confrontation had blazed through the company and the outside world. Johnson immediately fired off a resignation letter, which Morgan asked her to rescind. He apologized repeatedly for Winn and promised her nothing like that would happen again. Throughout the company, and across Charlottesville, mutterings about Winn's explosion were confirming his legend. His comments were plastered by a company insider on the Yahoo! message boards within minutes of the occurrence. Yahoo! messengers speculated Winn might be having a nervous breakdown. Most message-board posters concluded Value America was clearly falling apart. Johnson agreed to stay for two weeks but said she couldn't continue working at a company run by Craig Winn.

At 1:15, the store was back up. Neither Jerry Goode nor Joe Page nor anyone else could figure out what had happened. Everyone went back to crossing their fingers and hoping the store stayed online. Goode assigned two people to constantly monitor the server's capacity load. If at any time it appeared that any server was bogging down, they were to rotate that server out, reboot it, and bring it back online. Jerry hoped that such hands-on intervention would help.

As Morgan juggled crises, Winn was plotting his own political future. I had arranged for political and *Fortune* 500 corporate strategist Ralph Reed and his colleague Tim Phillips, one of Virginia's top political activists, to visit Winn and discuss two items. First, Winn's potential run for office in Virginia. Second, any consulting that Reed's firm might provide for Value America.

For Reed, the former head of the Christian Coalition, the visit with Winn was not about finding the next Ronald Reagan. He hoped Value America would be a dot.com pony. Reed could endure the world's biggest blowhard for years on end if it meant he could increase the size of his corporate client list. Reed knew Value America had its problems but he also knew Value America had Fred Smith, Gerry Roche, and Paul Allen on its board. Helping Winn win, therefore, could have positive payoffs for Reed with the all-star board.

Winn greeted Reed and Phillips and ushered them, Kicklighter, and me into his sanctum sanctorum. For the next forty-five minutes, Winn offered his ideas, plans, and ambitions without taking a breath. He expounded on his policy ideas — welfare moms working in lunch rooms, Internet-enabled PCs for the poor, adoption incentives to make abortion more rare. Reed and Phillips nodded and scribbled down notes.

The discussion then turned to practical questions. When would Winn run? For what office? What was he prepared to spend? How long had he lived in Virginia? Winn suggested he might run for lieutenant governor in Virginia in 2001. Reed and Phillips thought it was an aggressive first step for a novice politician with no record and limited residency in the state. Winn saw it as his lowest possible first step and an inevitable victory on his road to higher positions. "This campaign will *not* end in the Virginia statehouse, you know," he said gravely.

Reed and Phillips nodded curiously.

"I *intend* to go to the White House. I'm only doing this to serve, you understand. I already have plenty of money and a home that is *much* nicer than the White House. I'm building my own version of Camp David up in the Shenandoahs. It'll actually be much more luxurious than Camp David. I'm going to fly world leaders and corporate leaders there for conferences. I am willing to do this even if it means a step down in my lifestyle."

Winn's Camp David was a nine-hundred-acre tract of land called Rocky Bar, next to Walton's Mountain. Now in the early stages of its design, it would eventually include numerous customized cabins and one central meeting lodge. He fancied it a center for gathering the world's great political and corporate minds.

Reed and Phillips glanced at each other, nodded in sync, and contemplated how much money would be required on the corporate side to make the political side more palatable. The pair were supremely experienced political operatives, but they were also intensely patriotic. They were appalled by the arrogance of a man who thought that 1600 Pennsylvania Avenue was merely a house and Camp David merely a cabin in the woods.

Perhaps sensing his guests' discomfort, Winn turned the conversation quickly to corporate matters. Value America could use Reed's and Phillips's help in reaching the Christian marketplace through radio ads and direct marketing. Reed promised to report back to Winn in a few weeks on both the political and corporate fronts.

I escorted Reed and Phillips out to their car. As I bid them farewell, Ralph Reed looked at me and burst out with a long, hearty laugh that bounced off the buildings around us. "Are you sure about this guy?" he asked — exactly the question Fred Barnes posed months earlier. To my dismay, this time I didn't have an answer.

Thursday, October 14, dawned with Morgan, Kicklighter, and me huddled on the porch at Winn's customized log cabin in the heart of Winndom. The chilly morning air reminded us of winter but still smelled like summer.

This was the first time Morgan and Winn had been together since the Visa Value Dollar crisis. My goal was to bring peace to the setting.

Winn acted like nothing had ever happened. Instead he said quietly that he now knew Value America was on the cusp of *greatness*. With Citibank and FedEx brewing, we'd survived the valley of disbelieving analysts and were now preparing to ascend the mountain of Silicon greatness. No one in this group, Winn said, could do it without every other one. God had clearly brought everyone together for a grand purpose, and he was sure Value America was just the beginning of a bigger plan. There were greater things to accomplish — perhaps, Winn said, even the White House. He went on to recount his extraordinary meeting with Ralph Reed the day before.

This was the Winn I believed in — which is not to say I believed *what* he was saying. But in the early morning Winn hadn't yet found his bluster. Whether it was from tiredness or just because of the morning's quietness, Winn was softer around the edges. This Winn you could actually talk to and hope to be heard by. I hoped Morgan would say some of the things I knew were bothering him.

But Tom Morgan was tired of the sales, tired of the talk. He didn't believe a word Winn uttered. Integrity, Morgan believed, wasn't about how well you sold something — it was about how you lived every day. Morgan waited to hear Winn express remorse for how he had treated Jennifer Johnson. He waited to hear if Winn would apologize for going around him on the Visa deal. He wanted to hear Winn say he was sorry for talking publicly about the FedEx deal that wasn't even a deal yet. Faith, for Tom Morgan, was about repentance — about changing the path of one's life. It was about letting actions speak louder than words. For Morgan, all Winn had were more empty words. Morgan didn't bring up his problems with the chairman. What, he figured, was the point?

"Remember," Winn reminded us as we bundled up to leave, "we are never closer to our greatest failure than at the moment of our greatest success. We have to be vigilant," he continued. "Satan will try to bring us down and tear us apart — now more than ever."

Big and happy news came the next day. Citibank had approved stage one of the Value America–Citibank relationship. The deal was every struggling start-up's wet dream. The program would increase revenues and membership while decreasing marketing costs by leveraging Citibank's information-rich database. For Citibank, it meant new cardholder acquisition, greater cardholder retention, and incremental revenues. One million CitiPrivileges catalogs, produced by Value America, would be mailed in November, and three hundred thousand billing-statement inserts would be distributed in December. Full-scale program roll-out was set for January 2000, targeting all forty million Citibank cardholders via catalogs, direct-mail pieces, billing-statement inserts, printed messages on monthly billing statements, voice-prompting on Citibank's 800 number, and imprinting on the back of all Citibank credit cards.

In return for all of those marketing benefits, Value America agreed to extend its return policy from fifteen days to thirty days for CitiPrivileges shoppers, guarantee the lowest price on quality products, and institute personal shopper and concierge features. Much of the delay in launching the Citibank program came as Value America struggled to prove it actually had the capacity to fulfill those promises.

Winn waited for Citibank to approve the press announcement that would mark the beginning of Value America's road back.

I was back on the roller coaster. That Citibank had finally happened was something of a surprise to me. I'd convinced myself it was all bluster and no substance. But now it was real. I couldn't wait to get the press release out and sell the story.

I popped into Kim's office, next to mine, to tell her the good news. She stared at me. "And?"

"And?" I asked.

"Yeah, where is the *news*?"

She had a point. Craig had talked about the Citibank deal to so many people — analysts, potential brand partners, FedEx, board members —

that *no one* would be surprised by the announcement. It was, she said, air pudding.

A big, deflated me shuffled back to my office to pout and wait for Citibank approval. A week later we still didn't have it. I wondered anew whether the deal was actually going to happen. I wondered, too, whether the same thing was true for the FedEx deal.

With the Citibank deal seemingly in hand, Winn, Rex Scatena, and their families took off on a ten-day Tuscany vacation. Winn tasked Richard Smith with making sure the FedEx relationship progressed to the next level while he was gone.

During Winn's absence, every afternoon at 5:00 P.M., the Value America and FedEx teams held a conference call to iron out the specifics on a potential deal. FedEx insisted they didn't want the comprehensive Winn plan, wherein FedEx would essentially become a retailer. Instead, they just wanted a simple online shopping portal on their site featuring brands that shipped FedEx. Richard Smith bristled when FedEx insisted it preferred this shopping portal to the FedEx-powered Value America department store featuring great brands. Day by day, the calls got more and more intense. "Shopping portals are nothing more than malls, and Internet malls are for idiots," Richard Smith bellowed at his father's employees. On the other end of the phone silence screamed, until one of the FedEx operatives calmly retorted, "We're just going by what our boss told us." At that, Rick stormed out mumbling expletives, stomped down the hall to his own office, and called his dad.

As the negotiations continued, another small problem arose. Since Winn had announced that Value America would ship purchases free via FedEx beginning almost immediately, the company scrambled to transition its brand manufacturers to FedEx. But a whole lot of Value America's suppliers didn't use FedEx. As the operations team reported who did and who did not ship via FedEx, a lot of us discovered an uncomfortable truth: For all the hype about Value America shipping brand-direct, it didn't. Value America had virtually *no* brands that shipped direct. They were all routed through suppliers or distributors. Not even my *still*-missing Weber grill came from Weber. It came from Harco — a distributor. I knew distributors had been essential to getting the company started. I just hadn't realized we were still hooked on distributors. It made the whole story feel just a bit fake — or maybe faker.

Since I was the person charged with communicating Value America's revolutionary inventoryless model to the media, I found this reality somewhat perturbing, if not a calamity. I broached the subject with John Steele, now the EVP of operations. It was just standard, he droned, smiling and weaving his head in a familiar figure eight. Value America wasn't big enough to have everything come directly from the brands — but it *would* happen . . . eventually. I made a mental note to hammer Winn on this point.

In Charlottesville, Morgan tried to fathom the impact of Winn's edict to shift to free FedEx shipping. First, he tried to reconcile how Value America could guarantee free FedEx delivery when most vendors didn't *use* FedEx. Second, he pored over financial projections that suggested that a full-tilt shift to FedEx shipping would increase the company's costs — and therefore losses — by as much as 25 percent. Third, he had to figure out how to tell ULLICO — the union that owned a good chunk of Value America — that we were going back on our word to use only UPS. In fact, when Morgan informed Mike Steed of the *possibility,* Steed threatened to send an army of union boys down to Charlottesville to organize the company on site and "shut the f——ing company down."

By the last week in October, as Morgan continued to juggle ticking technology, FedEx, and personnel time bombs, unbeknownst to him some senior executives were in discussions with Value America board member, outside counsel, and investor Gary LeClair about Winn's erratic behavior. One executive complained Winn undermined her ability to implement effective programs by constantly micromanaging and capriciously overriding decisions he didn't like. The same executive complained that Winn didn't treat her with the respect or dignity required. Other executives were more oblique in their condemnations: "I heard that x or y happened," "You might want to take a look at this or that part of the 10Q," "You must ask x or y person about what happened regarding this or that issue." No one wanted to specifically undermine Winn. It was more of an "education" campaign. They merely wanted to lead others to play witness to Winn for the jury of the board.

That same week, answers to some of Winn's earlier questions regarding Visa trickled in. As of October 25, the day the report was prepared, Value America had 45,238 unique visitors to its online store every day. By comparison, Amazon's unique visitors numbered in the *millions*. Of those visitors, only a fraction of a percent actually purchased. During the entire year, we had 28,084 total online customers — this after spending more than $50 million in advertising over the first nine months of 1999. So, all the systems, all the technologists, all the software, all the staff, all the executives were supporting a site that had less than 30,000 customers, whereas Amazon had hundreds and hundreds of thousands. By comparison, nearly 50,000 people signed up for the Visa promotion within about two weeks. Winn's assumption had been correct — the Visa Value Dollars promotion ran circles around Value America's other advertising and marketing efforts. That wasn't necessarily reason for jubilation, but it was sweet affirmation for the chairman.

Neither Kim nor I had ever seen these numbers before. Kim's sister Heather, who was Tom Morgan's eyes and ears in the company, hadn't seen them. Tom Starnes in business development hadn't seen them. In fact, not even Tom Morgan and Craig Winn had seen them. They'd been sent out by accident. One of the technology guys, in his zeal to answer Winn's questions about advertising and the store, had taken it upon himself to get the answers from various segments of the sales and marketing team.

Kim and I sat in our offices analyzing the numbers further. For every person who purchased on the Web, two people purchased via the telephone. Even more shocking, according to those numbers, about 86 percent of Q3 purchases were from repeat customers. All the massive newspaper advertising — $20 million for the quarter — had brought in slightly more than $6 million for the quarter. It was . . . staggering. That these numbers were just now being divulged to the executive staff was even more amazing. What, everyone wondered, were we doing?

As bad as the Q3 membership numbers were, it was still the overall numbers that were shocking. I had envisioned hundreds of thousands of people buying. Instead, there were just tens of thousands. In August we had announced to the world that we had more than four hundred thousand members. Now it appeared we had only a fraction as many customers. This was a discrepancy of the highest order.

We got e-mails from people in the company saying the numbers weren't technically correct. They were low. Numbers were lost in the system. A lot of people hadn't been counted.

The problem was, as we looked more closely, the numbers really did make sense. The only way to explain our not showing up on various lists of top Web sites was that no one came to the store. The reason the Street always pounded us for customer-acquisition costs was that ours were stratospheric. Those ads we'd always hated really weren't working.

Winn was right that high-cost Value Dollars were more effective than our existing advertising. But Morgan was right that it was next to impossible to project Q4 expenses, because he didn't know how much Value Dollars were actually going to cost. And Johnson was right because it was highly probable the Value Dollars were going to come out of gross margin. Morgan and Johnson knew the program — effective or not — would be deeply damaging to Value America's bottom line and therefore to the company's stock. They had to shut it down.

On Friday, October 29, Gary LeClair called Tom Morgan. LeClair told Morgan he'd been hearing lots of rumbling from inside Value America about Winn and needed verification on some issues. Morgan, as he'd done in the past with board members, said he wouldn't say anything negative about Winn. It wasn't his place. But this time, LeClair persisted. Unless Morgan told him otherwise, he was going to present allegations of Winn's mistreatment of employees, dangerous exaggerations to the investment community, and bad business practices — like the Saks meeting — to the entire board for censure or worse. Morgan relented. He would not specifically detail Winn's problems, but if LeClair relayed what he knew, Morgan agreed to either confirm or deny the claims.

LeClair began. Did Winn, he asked, curse out an employee in front of other executives the week before?

Morgan confirmed the incident.

Did Winn regularly talk about business deals like Citibank and FedEx publicly before they were finalized?

Morgan confirmed the statement.

Did Winn regularly hint at future Value America business matters, including confidential performance issues, like earnings?

Morgan confirmed again.

Did Winn mingle his own political ambitions with Value America's business?

Morgan said quietly, "Yes."

Did Winn regularly state as fact things that weren't materially true? For instance, the number of brands in the store, the return percentages, the number of vendors, etc.

Morgan again confirmed, wondering how on earth LeClair had collected such detailed evidence.

LeClair proceeded through his long list of allegations. To each one Morgan said, "Yes."

There was, LeClair told Morgan, no choice in the matter. He was calling Fred Smith to raise these matters at Value America's November 4 board meeting. Unless something drastic happened, there would likely be a humiliating reprimand and a motion for Winn's dismissal.

Morgan did not want that to happen. No matter the nature of their disagreements and Morgan's frustration with Winn, he couldn't knowingly allow Winn to be humiliated in front of his own board. Morgan asked LeClair for time to confront Winn on Monday morning with some of these issues and work out a transition plan that would enable Winn to save face and remain involved in the company, at least superficially.

Monday morning, November 1, at 7:30 A.M., Morgan walked into Winn's office and told him they had to talk. Winn, back from his Italian vacation, was a bit jet-lagged but quite relaxed and ready to ease back into discussions with Citibank, FedEx, and the host of other business opportunities blossoming at Value America.

"Craig," Morgan began, "there are some things we need to talk about. They aren't pleasant things. They pertain to you. I am willing, however, to say right now that I'm prepared to resign and not bring up these issues."

Winn was irate. Here he was, fresh from a blissful vacation, just back in the office, and Tom Morgan was talking about unpleasant issues and his resignation? What was going on? If Morgan resigned, Value America was doomed. Winn knew his CFO was out the door. He'd heard rumblings that his CIO, Jerry Goode, was leaving as well. If Morgan left, it would be absolute chaos. What the hell was Morgan thinking?

Winn gathered himself and calmly told Morgan he obviously didn't want him to resign.

Morgan tried to ease into the issues. He didn't want to overwhelm Winn, and he also didn't want to hurt him. So he talked about general problems — that Wall Street still didn't trust Winn and Value America. There was resentment from employees who perceived Winn as imperious.

Winn got even more pissed. He was just back from Italy and now he was being slandered? That was crap. What the hell was Morgan thinking? There was a board meeting coming up, too. Why the hell was Morgan bringing this up before a board meeting?

Winn ranted for another few minutes, but Morgan looked at him fearlessly. Morgan was prepared to resign and walk away with no severance or get fired and walk away with two years of salary. Either way, he was calm. He wanted things to work out with Winn, but if they didn't, he knew he'd survive.

Eventually, Winn calmed down. If Morgan needed to talk to him about stuff, he'd listen and then refute *every damn little point.*

Morgan recommenced, with the Saks meeting.

The Saks meeting?! In New York?! What the hell did Morgan know about that? Winn reminded Morgan he was just giving the Saks folks a much-needed lesson in how to run a retail operation. There wasn't anything wrong with that.

Morgan told Winn that Saks had been prepared to do a deal with Value America. After that meeting, they pulled the plug.

Morgan brought up Citibank. Winn had promised Citibank dedicated technology staff, dedicated servers, and specific encryption technology. Value America had none of it.

That was bullshit. Winn pointed to a contract. There was no legally binding promise. There was only "our best efforts."

For the next four hours, Morgan and Winn wrangled over every point.

For the first two hours, Winn angrily denounced every point Morgan tried to make. Did he shout at employees? Maybe, occasionally. But he was actually sorry. Then, suddenly, halfway through, Winn stopped. The thunder clouds around him dissipated, and he suddenly grew calm. Winn, too, had a revelation. Perhaps, just perhaps, he *didn't* need Value America. Maybe, just maybe, Morgan was right. The criticisms echoed the condemnation he had endured during the Dynasty debacle. Maybe it *was* time for him to step away from his company.

Winn recalled a moment on the Air France jet from Italy. He'd been reading a commentary about the Bible, when some mystical force descended upon him and spoke to him. The force, the Spirit, told him that he would make a *significant* contribution to America's future. The Spirit didn't explain what, exactly, that contribution was, but it filled him with peace. Value America wasn't everything. It was a platform. And maybe, just maybe, this was his signal to leap from that platform.

He didn't mean to do all those terrible things Morgan sat accusing him of. He loved his company and believed in it and got frustrated when it didn't perform like it should. It was true, sometimes his emotions got the best of him. He always needed to make just one more sale, have one more fix. But the next deal always seemed *bigger* than the last. And every deal had to happen his way because, as Visa clearly proved, he really did know best. But now he knew it was time for him to go. He would step down. Not immediately, but in January.

Of the many things Morgan was prepared to hear, that wasn't one of them.

"There are places for me to go above and beyond Value America. There are important things I want to pursue, things I *must* pursue," Winn stated imperiously. Compared to building a company like Value America from nothing, it was a small step to mobilize the friends already in place and from there to establish the infrastructure of a campaign. He started running through the list in his head. With whom would he need to connect? Where would his campaign be based? He already had Mick, and with me he had an experienced political player. Plus, there was Kissinger and Bennett and Reed and . . . Of course, he still had important work to do with Value America — he needed to close those deals. No one else was capable of that. And it would take time — months. He could do both for a time. He could be chairman and founder of Value America and still run for public office . . .

Around noon, the plan was confirmed with a hug. Winn would remain with the company through the end of the calendar year. Effective immediately, however, he would cease all contact with Wall Street and the media — hardly a sacrifice from his perspective. On January 1, 2000, he would vacate his Value America office and pursue whatever he wanted to pursue. Morgan would do everything in his power to help Winn achieve his lofty dreams, but Morgan's resolute focus would be on running the company — in his mind, for the first time. That wasn't going to be easy. There were relations to repair with Wall Street, morale to build within the company, wounds to heal throughout the executive offices and the scattered staff. But as the weight of Winn's presence lifted from his shoulders, Tom thought his dream of growing old, dying, and being buried on his Charlottesville farm might come true.

Morgan called Gary LeClair and walked him through the outcome of the Winn confrontation. Both Morgan and LeClair heaved a heavy sigh of relief. They agreed, however, it would be wise for a board member to request clarification of the transition plan at the Thursday board meeting.

Shortly after the meeting, Winn called me into his office. "The reason we were brought together had nothing to do with Value America and everything to do with America," he announced. "I am going to be leaving Value America and am considering running for office earlier than planned."

Morgan had already briefed me on the meeting, so I clumsily feigned surprise. Winn had already informed Ralph Reed the timetable for his political campaign had been pushed up — to now. Winn was ready to write the next incredible chapter of his life.

Winn and I left to grab lunch. On the way to our favorite gas station/ hamburger joint, Winn shared not only the morning's conversation with Morgan but also his revelation. He felt something, a Spirit, a force, God, telling him He was going to take him in another direction. He was preparing Winn to do something great for America.

That afternoon, the executive team that now officially included my wife and sister-in-law gathered in Winn's office to discuss strategy for announcing our terrific Q3 numbers. Johnson, Morgan, Kim, Heather, Dorchak, and I sat around the round conference table in his office, while Winn busied himself doing other things.

The numbers were solid. From July through September, $57.6 million had poured through the company's virtual doors. It reflected an annualized-run rate approaching $240 million a year. The company's gross margins had improved to 6 percent — still below the level we needed, but well above the figure we'd gone public with. The net loss for the quarter was $31.6 million, a few hundred thousand dollars lower than the second-quarter loss. That didn't suggest we were close to turning a profit, but it did suggest we had hit bottom in the loss category and from here on the sailing would at least be smoother. Business-to-business sales of nearly $12 million were extremely encouraging, especially because they were achieved with minimal effort. The planned shift away from the consumer market into the business market would save Value America upward of $80 million a year. By Starnes's computations, if the company could capture 1 percent of the business marketplace — based solely on price and reliability — within eighteen months it would yield annualized revenues in excess of $2 billion.

Kim's preliminary discussions with Wall Street analysts were extremely positive. Business-to-business was all the rage on the Street, much of the enthusiasm stemming from increasing skepticism of consumer e-tailing. No one, with the possible exception of Amazon, had proven to consistently serve consumers and generate the revenues necessary to make a profit. Even Amazon was now facing enormous problems. Amazon's decision to diversify its product offerings earlier that summer by launching into toys and electronics while building warehouses to store inventory suggested one thing to all our experienced retailers — they would lose a ton of money during the holiday season. Because Amazon had no experience with across-the-board merchandising, it could never guess how many kids' binoculars to stock, let alone whether to stock red, blue, or purple ones. Sure, they had people with that experience, but none of them knew what people wanted to buy from *Amazon*. The solution? Stock them all.

That, to us, again displayed the beauty of the Value America model. No inventory. No overhead. No need to guess. No punishment for guessing wrong. Of course the company was hardly a fully functioning inventoryless retailer. But as far as I knew, things were moving in the right direction. There was even word from the customer-service shop that things were improving remarkably on that front.

Kim's sister Heather wasn't convinced. Heather's background was auditing, first for the big accounting firm Coopers and Lybrand and later for the U.S. Olympic Committee. As the press made abundantly clear, the USOC wasn't exactly scrupulous in its financial dealings. The hockey team trashed hotel rooms for fun, the execs chartered jets, the prima donna athletes demanded and received special perks. (It was, in short, a lot like dot.com life.) Heather's job was to straighten out the Olympic divisions one by one and figure out where the bodies were buried, so she spent countless hours in glamorous places like Cleveland auditing the teams. After looking over Value America's numbers for about a month, she had that auditor's hunch that the story execs were telling didn't match the story the numbers told. So she started digging.

Her first test was in customer service. She tasked several individuals at various levels of authority to report back on customer-service satisfaction. All the reports came back glowing. "We're doing great, fantastic! Everyone *loves* us." Then she asked for reports from the phone center.

She flipped through the numbers. Number of inbound calls . . . more than one hundred thousand in sales and about the same in customer service. The "close rate" of 25 percent suggested that twenty-five thousand callers actually bought from Value America over the phone. That was fine. It was the customer-service numbers that staggered. Of the one hundred thousand calls received during the past three months, hold times varied from nine to ninety-nine minutes with an average wait of about forty-five minutes. Forty-five minutes! To get someone — anyone — to answer a call from Value America, an average customer waited nearly an hour! The only fact more amazing than the hold time was that they actually waited instead of trekking down to Charlottesville to blow us all up with rocket-propelled grenades — bought from Amazon.com's warehouses.

How pissed does someone have to be to wait ninety-nine minutes on the phone to complain? Most people I know would only wait on hold for ninety-nine minutes if they were missing a body part. But Value America had *thousands* of customers waiting. Nearly every Internet outlet where people gathered to discuss Value America was filled with messages warning the world not to buy from "Valueless America." If the Visa Value Dollars promotion spread like the Ebola virus, then customer-service complaints zoomed through cyberspace like the Plague. Not even millions of dollars in advertising could compete with that kind of negative buzz.

But customer-service problems were a relatively minor concern as we sat around Winn's conference table rubbing our hands together, certain, absolutely certain, that *this* time we were going to rock the Street. Every single metric was better than expected. This was our bottom-of-the-ninth-inning World Series home run.

The only slight damper on the event would be Dean Johnson's resignation. After two years as Value America's CFO, he was done. Rather than issue a press release announcing the departure, we decided to mention it off-handedly during the earnings conference call. It was crucial that the outside world realize this was *not* a big deal and that Johnson would be quickly and seamlessly replaced.

Try as he might, Winn could not stay out of things. He insisted we release the earnings announcement in the morning before the markets opened and then do the conference call in the afternoon after the market close. He posited the good news would make the stock tick up and drive interest for the afternoon call. It was going to be the cherry on top of the perfect cake we'd spent three months baking.

A couple hours later, around 6:00 P.M., Dean Johnson raced into Kim's office in a panic. "Come here, we've got to call the analysts and get them to change their EPS numbers," he bellowed. It was Q2 redux. Value America had once again failed to advise the analysts about our quarterly progress. Most of the analysts predicted us losing only about $.68 a share, not the $.71 loss we were actually announcing. Johnson's mission was to force the analysts to adjust their estimates to about $.75 per share, to give the public the impression that Value America was doing better than expected in every category.

Kim listened to Johnson's reasoning with alarm. He was insisting we convince analysts to change their numbers, the night before earnings, to well below where we knew the final numbers would come in, just to make it appear things were going better than expected. (Unbeknownst to anyone in the company, Johnson had plans to sell virtually all of his remaining shares in the days following the earnings release. It behooved him, therefore, to make Value America look as strong as possible.)

The first call was the toughest call, to David Trossman. Trossman, now with First Union Bank, still held a dim view of Value America. With Kim scurrying around to collect phone numbers, latest reports, and recent models, Johnson loaded his bullshit cannon.

"David, Dean Johnson calling from Value America," Dean drawled as casually as possible.

At 6:30 P.M. on a Tuesday night, Johnson was about the last person David Trossman wanted to talk to.

"David, we're calling to advise you on numbers for Q3."

It was less than forty-eight hours from Value America's earnings announcement and Johnson was advising *now*? This was the far side of bizarre.

"On what basis?" Trossman asked.

"We, uh, well, we are expecting to come in above your EPS."

"So?"

"Well, we thought it would be much better for you to have those numbers more in line with reality."

"Why?" Trossman didn't care if he was off. He especially didn't care if he was estimating Value America to be more frugal than it was. He knew this bird didn't fly, and he didn't mind saying so.

"We really think it would be best if you revised those numbers up."

"No," Trossman replied, snickering. He wasn't about to be duped into changing his model just to save Johnson's sorry ass.

Dean sat in his chair blustering like a bloated baboon. "But you've got to, you've got to, you see, because —"

"Thanks for calling, Dean, I look forward to your release and conference call. I'll be on it. Good night."

Dean Johnson slammed down the phone, muttering to himself. But he didn't give up, and over the next two hours, he and Kim dialed and bullshitted and succeeded in raising everyone else's EPS estimates.

As we prepared to launch the press release across the wires, we were encouraged by a rising stock price. In the days leading up to the announcement, the stock had climbed steadily, by nearly 20 percent, to just over $13 a share. If things went properly, it might pop over $20 and maybe even higher.

Hopefully that would break through the greatest downward pressure on our stock — an enormous short position. In essence, there was an entire community of investors betting tens of millions of dollars that our stock would drop rather than rise. As many shares of our stock were being shorted as those of Cisco — a company more than one hundred times our size. The potential upside was that if we could ever break through about $20 a share, we'd create a short squeeze. In essence, that meant forcing those betting the stock would decrease to buy more stock to cover their positions. The result could be a quick shot up to above our historic $55-a-share high. It would take a lot of good news, but the potential was there.

We anticipated a bang-up morning.

CHAPTER EIGHTEEN

"Houston, We've Got a Problem"

Kim and I arrived in our offices at 7:00 A.M. on November 4 with analysts' angry tirades in our voice mails. Everyone wanted to know why on earth Value America had distributed its earnings press release *before* the market opened, without giving them an advance copy. And even more perplexing, why was the conference call delayed until after the close? How were they supposed to advise their sales staff without guidance? Their own brokers were looking to them for an explanation of what the numbers meant — and they had nothing! What did the numbers mean for the future? How much cash was left? What did the all-important holiday season look like? Did they know how *stupid* this made Value America look? Didn't Value America have a *clue*?

No one inside Value America knew we had blundered. If someone sent us a memo on how such earnings calls were supposed to happen, it had gotten lost in the mail. We were doing what everyone in the Internet world was doing — we were winging it.

We were learning a hard lesson in the ways of the Internet economy: Make sure the analysts get their information *before* anyone else, so they can advise their firm's sales managers based on the "not yet disclosed" information in their hands. The information is technically "embargoed" so that no SEC rules are breached. But the advance copies allow analysts extra time to digest the facts, ask questions, discuss the information with their firm, and then publish reports the moment the release crosses the wires. Without that special treatment, the analysts are as ignorant as the masses. That isn't acceptable.

Lauren Levitan, recently promoted by Robbie Stephens to be head e-commerce analyst — in place of the departed Keith Benjamin, who had left to head up a venture capital firm — was screaming at Kim over the phone. Levitan's assistant was furiously dialing Dean Johnson and Tom

Morgan so she could scream at them, too. Problem was, Morgan and Johnson, along with Winn and Scatena, were at the board meeting across town at Keswick Country Club.

It was the first in-person board gathering since July, and it was deemed important enough that Bill Savoy flew in from Seattle to hear firsthand how Paul Allen's (and his own) investment was faring. The agenda began at 8:00 A.M. with a report on Value America's Q3 numbers and a look ahead to the all-important fourth quarter. On both fronts, things were progressing nicely. The Q3 numbers, Morgan informed the board, were staggeringly good on every front. Value America expected its stock to rise significantly on the good news that crossed the wires at 7:00 A.M. He continued that the stock should rise again tomorrow based on the news of the 5:00 P.M. conference call that afternoon. If everything continued as planned for the rest of 1999, both Morgan and Winn believed Value America could achieve a $100 million fourth quarter. Neither believed it was inevitable, but both believed it was possible if everything came together just right. In addition, the predicted rise in our stock price, accentuated by news of impending deals, would make raising money in January or February 2000 relatively easy.

Kim's frantic pages pulled Morgan out of the meeting. Informing him of Lauren Levitan's erupting anger, she discussed damage control with him. It was now 8:45 A.M., and the market would not open for another forty-five minutes, so technically Value America could still try to get a conference call together. But with an important board meeting in progress, Morgan could not make that happen. His only option was to walk Levitan through the numbers privately. At this point, he had no choice.

After enduring his own shrieking condemnation from Levitan, Morgan walked her through all of Value America's numbers, fully expecting the Robbie Stephens analyst to applaud the company's efforts. Instead, she sniffed that they were "nice" but she wasn't changing her rating on the company — it was still just a "buy."

Morgan slipped back into the board meeting at about 9:20 A.M. and prayed the market's reaction would be more positive than Lauren Levitan's.

While the analysts continued to scream in her ear, Kim and I stared at the Nasdaq real-time quotes that revealed how the Street was reacting to Value America's announcement. At 9:30 A.M., VUSA ticked up $.50. A minute later it was up $1. We cheered! By 9:45 A.M., it was up $1.25. We snatched a moment of elated hugging. This could be the *breakthrough!*

Kim called Morgan to tell him the good news, which he joyfully relayed to the board.

At Keswick, the board was experiencing something new — Tom Morgan running a meeting. While Winn chimed in occasionally to discuss pertinent issues, like the FedEx relationship, Citibank, and various other deal possibilities, he deferred to Morgan throughout the day's discussions. By the end of the relatively punctual and precise meeting, Gerry Roche asked the question Gary LeClair had planted the previous week: "Can you please tell the board," he queried as he twisted his bushy brows, "what transition plans exist between Craig and Tom?"

Winn didn't hesitate. There were *not,* he assured Roche and the rest of the assembled board, *any* transition plans. There was no need for any transition plans. Value America, Winn said emphatically, was Tom Morgan's company to run. Tom Morgan was the CEO, and what he said ruled. Winn praised Morgan effusively and hailed his achievements. Morgan was, Winn assured the board, the *right* person, the *best* person to handle the job. Roche was impressed. The board departed, congratulating both Winn and Morgan on their outstanding job navigating very tricky waters.

But as the board meeting closed, Kim and I were watching VUSA stock decline. By noon, the stock was down more than $1. Unbeknownst to us, the downturn reflected that the world had changed *again.* If Q2 had been all about EPS, Q3 was all about losses. Wall Street was no longer enamored by potential and possibility; now they really wanted profit. Posting $31 million in losses on $56 million in revenue was not the direction they wanted to see.

Not surprisingly, the Street's conventional wisdom echoed something that Bill Savoy had said during the board meeting. E-commerce, he warned, had been transformed from a race for big revenue to a race for profitability and survival. Only one or two of the hundreds of companies out there would make it — and those companies had to have billions of dollars of cash in the bank or they had to make money. Value America, he preached, had to find a money tree or the righteous road to profitability. And like the boy perpetually crying wolf, Winn had so often predicted billion-dollar revenue opportunities that were unfulfilled that few people believed what he said now.

By the time the conference call started after the market close, the mood around the company was decidedly downcast. Grand expectations had been dashed. Winn, who was constrained to a thirty-second scripted introduction, was trying to figure out how to amuse himself during the rest of the conversation. Morgan, Johnson, Kim, and Dorchak were the quartet responsible for explaining the wonder of the numbers to the world. But by the end of that day, everyone was preoccupied with the diving stock price. What could we possibly do better?

Winn left the conference call after his introduction — including the fleeting announcement of Dean Johnson's departure — and plopped down in my office. His toys were gone now, and he was in search of new ones. He had listened to the call for a few minutes and was pleased Morgan and company weren't screwing up. It was just that they weren't saying what *he* wanted them to say. But this, he remarked, was part of letting the company go and hopefully letting the company grow. After fifteen minutes of chattering with me, he bolted up and started roaming the halls.

The Q3 earnings report was important for another reason. It signaled the end of the six-month management stock lockup, meaning executives could now start selling their stock — even if it was trading at less than $10. Starting the day after the earnings report, Dean Johnson sold 270,000 shares and walked away with more than $2 million. Rex Scatena sold half a million shares and loaded more than $5 million into the bank. Glenda Dorchak cashed in nearly a half million dollars' worth. The message, announced to the world through SEC filings that invariably ended up on the Yahoo! message boards, was unambiguous: Despite executive rhetoric that VUSA stock was poised to rebound, three of Value America's officers were dumping. If they really believed Value America was going to recover, why would executives be selling their stock at such a deflated price?

Winn was none too pleased with *anyone* selling stock. While he'd been told by Robbie Stephens that selling 1 percent was a common move for executives, he'd chosen not to sell during that trading window. As much as he would have liked to cash in 150,000 shares for nearly $2 million, he thought it would send the wrong signal. Besides, he thought, when Citibank and FedEx broke, the stock would go through the roof. Why, he wondered, would anyone sell now?

The next morning, Winn strolled into Tom's office early and shut the door. While Winn had agreed to leave the company on January 1, he now felt that perhaps April 1 was a better date. His first reason for delaying his departure, he informed Morgan, was his desire to teach Tom everything he needed to know about running Value America. Winn felt he simply could not teach him the necessary curriculum by the end of December. His second reason was that Value America was in the midst of finalizing several monumentally important business deals — in most of which Winn played an integral, if not leadership, role.

The third reason Winn wanted to stay was one he didn't discuss with Morgan. In Winn's discussion with him last Monday, Tom sounded like he was launching a coup. When Gerry Roche asked about the transition at the board meeting the previous day, Winn grew even more suspicious. He didn't actually believe Morgan was plotting, but he was nervous enough that he wanted to push back his departure date just to be sure. Winn had birthed and nurtured this company. It was his lifelong vision, and he couldn't turn it over unless he knew it was going to be well loved and well cared for. Suddenly, he wasn't so sure that was going to happen.

Morgan wasn't thrilled by the news. As Winn left, Morgan scribbled in his calendar, "Craig gives first sign of changing his mind." Morgan fully expected other mind-changing episodes to follow.

Across the country, Comdex was under way. Comdex is the world's largest computer and software convention, always held in Vegas and always the center of the computer world's attention. It is where Bill Gates and Michael Dell make big product announcements. It is where new hardware and software are unveiled.

Glenda Dorchak and her team had spent August, September, and October preparing for Value America's presence at Comdex. The million dollars that we spent on people and exhibits was expected to deliver us one hundred thousand new members, great press coverage, and general industry buzz about how *hot* Value America was. More than thirty Value Americans had headed to Vegas for the show.

Kim and I were supposed to go, but the more I read about Comdex and reviewed the press lists, the more I questioned our presence there.

Granted, it wouldn't ordinarily take a whole lot to convince me to spend an all-expenses-paid week in Vegas with my wife. But this trip sounded like an enormous waste of money. The press lists were long and *very* computer heavy. Had we been purely a computer company, our presence would have been a no-brainer. But since we aimed to be a comprehensive online retailer, I couldn't imagine we'd be too successful competing with Microsoft, Apple, Compaq, and HP for media attention.

I was right. Value America had a big display enticing people to sign up by entering a contest to win a $15,000 Value America shopping spree. Few bothered to enter. Worse, the Value America booth was passed over more often than the ugliest boy at a dance. Kurt Stenerson, the press-meister I'd sent out there, couldn't get anyone to talk to him about anything.

For the staff, however, it wasn't a total loss. Value America had reserved fifteen Lincoln Town Cars to make traveling between venues easier. The staff, not busy staffing the empty booths, used the cars for all sorts of novel adventures. Some took guided tours of the Vegas area. Others entertained female companions in the backseats of the cars. Still others picked up female companions — or male companions, depending on preference — for a quick "get to know you well" drive.

As the convention entered its final days, Value America didn't exactly have one hundred thousand new customers. It actually had a little more than ten thousand. Whoops.

Meanwhile, back in Charlottesville, a sandstorm of rumors was spreading through the company about executive infighting and departures. At various moments almost every executive was rumored to be on his or her way out. Amid this turmoil, the technology upgrades were scheduled to be implemented. While this was happening, the AskJeeves team flew in to follow up on our New York discussions and gently inquire if we might be for sale. AskJeeves was hot. Their stock had increased from $33 to $190 in the past sixty days, and they were looking for ways to grow. We were a possibility. Unfortunately, with all the turmoil, we had little time for them. After a few hours they shrugged their shoulders and went home to explore other partnership targets.

Hours after the AskJeeves team departed on Monday afternoon, November 8, I was sitting at my desk, bloated from yet another greasy Amigo's meal, when an e-mail from Winn popped into my box:

SENT: MONDAY, NOVEMBER 08, 1999 1:38 P.M.

TO: EVERYONE@VALUEAMERICA.COM

SUBJECT: MESSAGE FROM CRAIG WINN REGARDING SENATOR JOHN
MCCAIN'S VISIT

Dear Value America Team Member,

As many of you know, Senator John McCain is visiting us in Charlottesville this evening. However, he has been required to attend a committee meeting on a bill he is sponsoring in the Senate today prior to his arrival in Charlottesville. This unforeseen delay will make it impossible for him to tour Value America as planned. Therefore, any Value America team member who would like to meet Senator McCain and have dinner with him at my home this evening is cordially invited.

The press conference is scheduled for 6:45 to 7:00 outside our home. It is followed by a cocktail reception in our home at 7:15. Dinner will follow in our carriage house at 8:15. Dress is western, cowboy boots, if you have them, and jeans.

There is room for up to 40 additional people. This is a $500/plate dinner to thank and honor Senator John McCain. If you are interested in coming, we ask that you donate $100 to $250 per person, depending upon your comfort level. Please respond to Mick Kicklighter at extension 4330 or reply to this e-mail if you plan to attend.

Senator John McCain has dedicated his life to serving our country and is one of America's military heroes. After his military career, he has continued to serve our Nation as a distinguished United States Senator.

Also attending this evening is Robert McFarlane, the National Security Advisor for President Ronald Reagan. He was the principal architect of the strategy that won the Cold War.

Thank you,
Craig Winn

Craig had decided several weeks before to host a fund-raiser for Sen. John McCain's presidential campaign. That meant using his publicly traded company to sponsor a fund-raising event. Kicklighter, his shared assistant Sue, and a business-development staffer worked full-time to pull off a lavish fund-raiser at Craig's estate. The executive suite's printers were jammed with personal letters from Craig to potential supporters. There were twice-daily strategy meetings to ensure appropriate progress was being made — quality catering, elite guest lists, and Winndom primping. As the blessed event approached, Craig sent out this company-wide e-mail "inviting" employees to attend for a reduced donation.

Kim and I tried very hard not to notice any of the political happenings. Having spent our lives around politics, we knew when to keep our heads down. We worked very hard to not see or be involved in anything related to the fund-raiser. Plus, being Bush supporters, we cringed at Winn's misguided fund-raising loyalties.

Winn's e-mail was the perfect insight into his mind. McCain's Washington meetings had prevented him from getting a Value America tour. That disappointed Winn greatly. He desperately wanted to escort the senator from building to building and show McCain just how magnificent Value America had become. Because he was genuinely impressed by the senator's message, he wanted to sprinkle his fairy dust to as many commoners as possible. But just as important, he wanted to raise his new friend more money. Winn had pledged to raise at least $100,000 for the senator. Unfortunately, he was a good $50,000 below that figure. He hoped his flock of Value Americans would make up some of that gap. There was, in his intention and in his e-mail, no ulterior motive — he was not using his position to intimidate or encourage people to attend. He just really wanted them there — and especially their admissions fees.

Many Value Americans showed up at Winndom that night, but few of us brought any money. Kim and I gave nothing.

The senator was more than an hour late arriving from the airport, and as the delay lengthened, Craig paced around the cramped reception nervously, smiling broadly, as he did when excited . . . or nervous . . . or selling. When McCain finally arrived, Winn was on him like a lobbyist on pork. Craig led him through the crowds as the two shook hands with adoring fans together, sipped spiked punch together, strolled into Winn's barn for dinner together, and when dinner was served, sat side-by-side surrounded by Winn's family in a private room upstairs.

Winn was as starstruck as a fourteen-year-old with a Britney Spears calendar. Kim and I sat at a remote table with Tom Morgan and a few other Value America executives. Everyone commented that they hadn't ever seen Craig as excited as he was that evening playing host to Mc-

Cain — not even on IPO day. It was true. Craig had the same slightly flushed face of a teenage girl screaming for her favorite rock group. Just as the baked beans and cornbread were getting cold, Craig called the scattered diners' attention to the fireplace. He effusively introduced Bud McFarlane, who glowingly introduced McCain, who delivered the same stump speech Winn and I had heard earlier that summer on Capitol Hill. But McCain's folksy, candid style enthralled his audience. By the evening's close, most of Value America's team was enamored by McCain. His no-nonsense anti-Washington rhetoric prompted rowdy cheers but no great cash influx from the Value Americans.

The next morning, Tuesday, November 9, there was a FedEx frenzy. Winn had long had a vision of how Value America and FedEx would announce their historic relationship. They would rent a prestigious New York theater, fill its seats with media and celebrities, and eerily light the majestic stage. A thick, velvet curtain would hide a FedEx delivery truck, with the image of "FedEx MarketPlace by Value America" emblazoned on the side. Ascending to festive orchestra tunes, Craig would take the microphone, beam at the assembled horde of reporters, squint in the popping flashbulbs, and introduce "the Babe Ruth of American Business, Fred Smith." Then he'd linger as Fred praised Value America and its brilliant founder and heralded this revolutionary deal. It would be perfect.

But that morning, FedEx sent me an e-mail telling me that Fred Smith had resolutely decided against supporting anything more than a shopping portal on FedEx's site, featuring FedEx retail customers. Value America would be highlighted on the page, but there would be no more than that for now.

I was told that Smith had grown increasingly concerned about the project and the e-commerce company he was now inextricably tied to. It was nice that his son was working on the project, and he certainly liked Winn. The visionary concept on the table seemed quite strong as well. But something just wasn't clicking. Smith's gut had guided him through a relatively successful career in business. His gut was telling him to go slow, prove the concept, not bite off the whole cheeseburger. There was no upside for FedEx in cobranding a retail site with an obscure start-up when it could establish the FedEx MarketPlace brand on its own and retain all the potential revenue benefits.

I broke the news to Winn.

He paused and then spewed. His baby was being ripped apart! Instead of a revolutionary partnership with FedEx by which businesses could access from FedEx a one-stop marketplace of all the world's top retail brands with a single checkout, Value America was becoming a part of an *Internet mall* — the exact thing Winn had hated about Internet shopping when he started Value America back in 1995. How stupid could they be to have a joint-venture opportunity with Value America and choose instead to open an uninspiring Internet mall?

Value America and FedEx issued a press release on Wednesday, November 10, announcing a significantly smaller than expected relationship.

Value America Enters into New E-Commerce Marketing Agreement with Federal Express

CHARLOTTESVILLE, VA (November 10, 1999) — Value America (NASDAQ: VUSA), the Internet superstore, today announced a new e-commerce marketing agreement with Federal Express Corp. (NYSE: FDX).

Under the terms of the deal, the "FedEx MarketPlace presents Value America" site at *www.va.com/fedex* will have premier placement on the FedEx Web site (www.fedex.com) that receives more than 32 million page views per month. FedEx couriers will also be delivering 500,000 "FedEx MarketPlace presents Value America" catalogs to FedEx customers along with packages in the next few weeks.

The "FedEx MarketPlace presents Value America" Web site and catalog will feature 300 items that will be shipped free of charge via FedEx delivery services. This unique value proposition ensures that consumers will be able to get many of the best products by leading brands delivered by fast, reliable FedEx delivery services.

"I believe that Value America has one of the best business models I've ever seen," said Frederick W. Smith, Chairman and

CEO of FDX, Inc. "FedEx is working with Value America because together we can offer consumers an extraordinary value."

"Merging FedEx's shipping prowess and Value America's turn-key e-commerce solution serves consumers by giving them the quality assurance of the world's best brands and the delivery assurance of the world's best shipping and logistics company," said Craig Winn, Chairman and Founder of Value America. "Together, Value America and FedEx are the best choice for holiday shopping."

Fred Smith's quote was the source of some internal Value America consternation. Many employees repeated in their sleep Smith's affirmation of Value America as the "best" business model he'd seen. Now, suddenly, it was "one of the best." What was next? To Wall Street, the media, and industry analysts who had been hearing for months about the "great FedEx partnership," the press release was greeted with a collective yawn and a flat stock price. My attempts to pitch the story were shot down with questions: "What about free freight?" "What about a joint-venture company?" "Is this it?" "Craig was making this deal sound *much* bigger — what happened?"

As we fruitlessly pitched reporters, Winn spoke before hundreds of vendors gathered across town. Vendor conferences, like the ones that Winn had orchestrated to launch Value America in 1996, were designed to get more brands into the store — to drive more depth of selection.

Morgan was tucked in the back row, taking notes. If he needed to learn about retail, Morgan reasoned, then he should listen to Winn lecture. Winn always wound up giving "Retail 101," no matter who the audience was.

As his selling engines revved up, Winn stirred up the crowd with "friction-free" commerce and "inventoryless" selling. He really lit up the crowd of brand representatives when he maligned Wal-Mart's and other big retailers' abuse of brands. Representatives of forty different companies continually applauded Winn.

Then, suddenly, it seemed like Winn entered another, very alternate, universe. He told the audience about a recently signed contract with

IBM that was going to be huge. Morgan didn't know of any such contract. Odd.

Then Winn talked about how the efficiency of the Value America model resulted in less than one-half of 1 percent returns. Morgan was thunderstruck. Value America returns exceeded 5 percent — a good return rate but not close to what Winn claimed.

Winn started lauding the product-presentation team. "One hundred people, all journalists, all published authors" writing multimedia product demonstrations.

Then, about Value America's computer systems he said we had as many Cisco 5500 and 8540 servers as the Pentagon and AOL. Winn said he had a meeting scheduled next week with Cisco head John Chambers.

Morgan scribbled down what sounded to him like inaccuracy after exaggeration after bold-faced lie.

Winn effused about Value America's customer service. If someone indicates that they are displeased with a previous purchase, a Value America representative calls that customer and has the item replaced — within a two-hour window, using FedEx NetReturn, which no other company uses.

Morgan's leg started jerking up and down. Virtually none of what he heard Winn saying was true.

Winn lauded the custom store program by displaying a page of charities like the Girl Scouts, Habitat for Humanity, the American Heart Association — groups we had no relationship with. Then he described the catalogs we were sending out on behalf of these groups.

Winn talked about Citibank and said that analyst estimates for Value America's third quarter were "way, way off." Then he preannounced earnings.

Morgan was now way beyond irate. Energizer Winn just kept going and going and going.

Morgan had had enough. He had come to Value America to build a company with *integrity*. Now he was listening to the founder of the company lie about the company that Morgan was supposed to be running. That was enough. He stormed back to the office, composing his resignation letter in his head.

That evening, Morgan came into my office and shut the door. He was, he wanted to inform me, resigning in the morning. The reasons were the same as the ones he gave me ten days before. This time, though, it was clear his resolve was absolute. This was not a discussion. This did not require intervention. He was gone.

Morgan would stay only if Winn agreed to nine very strict conditions.

One, Morgan would have all control over the company: advertising, deals, technology — everything.

Two, Winn would sell the plane immediately.

Three, Winn would resign as chairman.

Four, Winn would have no more involvement in business affairs at all.

Five, Winn would vacate his executive office immediately.

Six, Rex Scatena would leave immediately.

Seven, there would be no free FedEx freight from the Value America store.

Eight, there would be no new Value America office park built in Charlottesville or anywhere else.

Nine, custom stores would be dramatically curtailed, because they were out of control.

Neither of us believed there was a chance that Winn would agree to all nine points.

I didn't want the balance of power to change. I didn't want Kim and my new brother- and sister-in-law to go through the upheaval of a bloody change of power. More than anything, I wanted us all to prosper. I had brought my family into Value America. I was now responsible for them.

That night, Kim, Heather, Scott, and I commiserated over dinner. Heather and Scott faced a tough decision. They were scheduled to sell their Colorado Springs home the first week in December. Should they sell that house and move to Charlottesville? Or, given the tumult, should they store their belongings in Colorado and wait to commit to Charlottesville? None of us had a clear answer. Finally we all agreed it would be best to hold on and see what happened. I reminded everyone that these conflicts had been going on for months — I was sure that they'd go on for months more. Like Lennon and McCartney, it was a competition that would create a marvelous result.

Somehow, rumors were already whirling around the company. Everyone knew Dean Johnson was leaving, and now rumors ran rampant that Morgan was leaving as well. Employees started polishing their resumes and flooding online job sites.

The next morning, Winn and Morgan were behind closed doors

early. The meeting began the way it had ten days before. Morgan offered to resign. Winn declined. Morgan marched forward. He had assembled a list of twenty items that called Winn's integrity into serious question. Morgan had donned kid gloves for their first conversation the week before. Now he wore brass knuckles. He confronted everything from the New York Saks meeting to the million-dollar Falwell loan to the dictum on free FedEx freight. Morgan told Winn the Whirlpool executives secretly mocked him for his bullshit and verbosity. He told Winn that Fred Smith called on several occasions to investigate the rumblings he heard about Winn's wild exaggerations. He told Winn he was reluctant to introduce Value America to his contacts because he was afraid Winn might mistreat them. Morgan attacked Winn's tall tales from the vendor conference the day before. And without revealing names, Morgan told Winn of the complaints about Winn's behavior that oozed from every executive, day after day. For two straight hours, Morgan discharged every single problem he had with Winn.

Outside Winn's office, executives circled around like parents awaiting a verdict on their child's surgery.

Winn remained shockingly calm. Inside, he was horrified. The litany of alleged abuses dug into the still vulnerable Dynasty wound. Value America was supposed to exorcise those demons, but Morgan was feeding them. Winn prided himself on consummate preparation for every meeting. He was always prepped to overcome any potential problems. But as Morgan called him a liar, told him he lacked integrity, said that none of the people around him trusted him, and laid out his evidence to prove every point, Winn appeared to crumble.

Around noon, I gingerly poked my head in and asked if they wanted lunch. Winn was misty-eyed, as was Morgan. It would be another three hours before they emerged. I started pacing the halls, hoping to nab one of them "accidentally."

Winn feared Morgan was right. Did Neal Harris really despise him? Was Rex criticizing him behind his back? Was he really a liar? Morgan's confrontation presented Winn with a complex decision — to believe Morgan and therefore believe everyone else was pandering to him, or to disregard Morgan as a power-hungry competitor. Morgan was either betraying him or telling him a bitter truth out of love.

After a total of six hours, Winn instructed Morgan to issue a press release the next morning, informing the world he was no longer a part of

Value America. Morgan told Winn to sleep on it, there wasn't any need to rush, the press release could wait until Monday. Winn had agreed to all of Morgan's nine demands. They hugged vigorously, like teammates after a final victory.

On his way to the door, Morgan turned back to Winn. "Craig," he said intently, "if you change your mind on any of this, call me." Morgan didn't want to wrest the company away from Winn against his will, even though he did believe it was Value America's best hope of survival.

I watched Morgan leave and walked in to see Winn. He sat blankly, like someone whose wife has just been murdered in front of him. The razzle-dazzle was gone. There were no flashing lights above the marquee anymore, just a few glints from its last flickering bulbs. He informed me of the nine conditions. I nodded. I tried to reinforce Morgan's points while giving him some soft place to land.

I gently told him about my dad. Like Winn, my dad was a tough, hard-driving genius who sometimes alienated people. A professor, my father nearly lost his department chairmanship at Columbia University. He spent a summer deeply discouraged, fixing up an old car in the backyard, after he'd been falsely accused of improprieties. But ultimately the truth won out and he was vindicated. Though truth to my father was more sacred than breath, he was like Winn in his intensity.

"You aren't made for this corporate world," I strained to convince Craig. "You will love the political world. I can tell it's in your blood."

His shoulders slumped forward toward his belly, and he nodded quietly. The speeches before adoring employees, the spirited road shows, the media interviews all flashed before him. It had gone so fast. Now, what was left for him? Not much. He looked around his office, wondering where all the plaques and pictures would end up. Then he walked out without a word.

I found Morgan bolting as well.

"Where are you going?" I asked.

"I've got to go see my daughter's cheerleading competition in D.C. tomorrow."

"You are leaving *now*?" I asked, somewhat incredulous. He'd just confronted Winn on every major issue, gotten Winn's OK to run the company full-out, and now he was disappearing. That made no sense to me.

Of course I had to go to D.C., too, for meetings the next day. But I wouldn't be so vital to the next day's happenings. The Winn I'd seen might not even come into the office the next day. Maybe we all would benefit from some space and distance.

Kim and I sat in her office and commiserated. The company had survived the bloodless transfer of power. Morgan could finally run the company unencumbered. We'd now see exactly how good a CEO he could be. But there was, we both sensed, a certain vibrant energy that had escaped the office like helium from a balloon. There was an uncertain haze choking us. We faced a Value America without Craig Winn. That was, despite my frustrations with him, incomprehensible. It would be stranger than Kentucky Fried Chicken without the Colonel.

Winn drove back to Winndom, stumbled through the door, and groped his way to his second-floor office. He collapsed into his big green chair and closed his eyes. He couldn't actually recall the drive from the office to his home. The world didn't make sense.

Who, he wondered, was Tom Morgan? What, he wondered, could all those people in the company be thinking? He hadn't run the company. He tried to make it clear he wasn't running the company. He was just trying to get brands and partners and new allies. What had he said that was so wrong? He'd gotten a few percentages wrong, a few facts off. He was going to leave his company for that?

His company. He didn't like his company anymore. It wasn't what he had envisioned. And all these people who were supposed to be running it, managing it. What had they done? They'd created systems that didn't work, ads that didn't matter . . . When he had run the company, Value America had succeeded. He'd raised more than $250 million. He'd created the technology. He'd brought in the brands. He'd guided it through an IPO. Then he'd passed it off — to . . . what . . . end?

Maybe, just maybe, he *shouldn't* be the one leaving the company. Maybe Morgan needed to leave. Maybe Morgan just couldn't cut it. The guy didn't know retail. The guy didn't know advertising. The guy didn't know technology. What the hell *did* he know?

Winn sat in his chair for hours. Head back. Eyes closed. Replaying everything he could remember, reliving every conversation, every moment. Soon it was dawn, and he had a full day ahead of him.

Late the next morning, as I was preparing for lunch with a potential new PR firm, my cell phone buzzed. "Things have changed," Winn informed me. He'd held meetings all morning long. John Steele, Paul

Ewert, and a bevy of other executives all denied what Morgan told Winn they had said. They all claimed to have no problems with Winn — never had had *any*. Even John Steele, who complained tirelessly about Winn to anyone who would listen, sang his praises to his face. They all confirmed that Winn was loved, respected, needed, esteemed. He was the father of the company. They said he was clearly the most important person at Value America.

Winn told me that John Steele said Morgan had done the same thing at US Office Products — maneuvered to oust the entrepreneur and snatch the CEO job. Tom Morgan, Craig Winn informed me, was a liar, a crook, and a deceitful manipulator. If Morgan wanted to resign from the company, Winn would happily oblige. He bid me farewell and told me he'd call me on Sunday with his new plan.

Winn got to work on a new organizational structure based partly on talent and partly on loyalty and trustworthiness. Paul Ewert was named president. John Steele was COO. I was SVP of strategic planning and business development. Winn would resume his role as CEO. Glenda Dorchak was demoted.

I called Morgan to fill him in. He was unfazed and Buddha-like. "Whatever will be, will be," he said. "It's in God's hands, not mine." He wondered where his next job would come from. Morgan had spent twenty years at one company and then had worked at USOP for only eighteen months. Now it appeared he'd be leaving Value America after nine.

Back in Charlottesville, Winn was in nonstop meetings. He conferred with everyone from his foreman to Neal Harris. The message everyone delivered was the same: Everyone loved and trusted Winn, no one had a problem with Winn, Winn shouldn't leave. He was a genius, and the company couldn't survive without him.

Winn even decided to reach out to Glenda Dorchak, who was still out at the Comdex Trade Show.

Dorchak informed Winn that Morgan was probably not that trustworthy, recounting all the times he had said critical things about Winn. Winn took notes. He ordered her back to Charlottesville immediately. Winn hated Dorchak, but he figured she could be controlled. After all, despite their difficulties, he knew he'd always been able to work with her and get things done. Since he was consolidating power and reasserting his control, he needed as many people on his side as possible.

That Sunday Kim and I drove down to Charlottesville to partake in the next stage of the drama. On the drive down, Winn rang. "There's a draft press release on the cabin table. Take a look at it," he ordered. Then, like an FBI informant, he disappeared.

We drove to Winndom, placing bets on what scandal or trauma could possibly await us. There, on the table, inside the log cabin were four handwritten pages announcing to the world that Craig was coming back as CEO of Value America:

> *Value America, in Charlottesville, Virginia is empowering members of its management team to strive more rapidly towards achieving profitability. Craig Winn, the company's founder, chairman and leading shareholder said today that he is returning to serve fellow shareholders, employees, brand partners and customers as CEO. Winn said, "Value America is entering the fifth phase of its strategic plan to improve <revolutionize> retail.*
>
> *In Phase one we conceived a radically innovative plan to serve all Americans, making the e-commerce world more inclusive by converging the personal computer with the telephone and television to serve all, not just the privileged few with internet access. We set out to concoor [sic] the digital divide that separate our nation by providing credit and linking customers directly to great values on internet enabled PC's. Our plan sought to revolutionize the engine of e-commerce, as well, by empowering leading brands with a turn-key on line solution that enabled Value America to reach and serve consumers in a more efficient, direct and inventory-free model. We sought to replace warehouses with technology and invest in systems rather than inventory so that we, working together with our brand partners could sell the best for less.*
>
> *In Phase two we brought together a bright, dedicated and talented team. We are all committed to working together to enable our shared passion to improve retail by serving brands and creating genuine value for consumers. Today, many members of our management team are being promoted, their just reward for their dedication and remarkable accomplishments.*

Reorganizing, it takes three things to positively change our world, great ideas, great people and a great deal of money. In Phase three we sought to raise capital. Working together we raised $131,000,000.00 in private equity and an additional $145,000,000.00 with our IPO this March.

In Phase four we sought to <endeavored to> execute our plan. In what may be record time, we have built one of the largest and fastest growing etailing companies. Our recently released Q3 results are proof of our scale and growth. They also reflect positively on our unique inventory-free model and innovative demand generation strategy because operational, technological, promotional and fulfillment costs are continuing to decline as a percentage of revenue.

In Phase five, we are committed to becoming profitable. We are aware of no company in business to business, or business to consumer etailing e-commerce that has achieved this goal and recognize there are many who doubt if any ever will. We believe we can and as a result have promoted today many members of our management team. They are responsible for our success in phases one–four:

Neal Harris to EVP, Supply and Demand Alliances
John Steele to EVP and COO
Paul Ewert to EVP Merchandise
Greg Sharer to EVP and CTO
Steve Tungate to SVP Operations and Fulfilment
Marcus Nucci to SVP of Systems Development
David Kuo to SVP of Strategic Planning
Nick Hoffer to SVP Advertising
Melissa Monk to SVP Sales
Aaron Schidler to VP Member Services
Steve Saltzman to VP Marketing
Kim Kuo to SVP Communications and IR
Ken Power to VP Creative Director

They will join Glenda Dorchak EVP Sales and Marketing, Mick Kicklighter SVP Chief of Staff, Joe Page EVP and CIO, Richard

Gerhardt SVP and President of the Consumer Products group and Jamie Parsons, SVP of Value America and CEO of the Automotive group on Value America's executive committee. The bios of each of these dedicated leaders is attached to the release.

In addition, the company promoted Wolf Schmidt [sic] Vice Chairman of Newell/ Rubbermaid to the Executive Committee of the Board. Mr. Schmidt [sic] joins Fred Smith, CEO FDX, Tom Casey, Co-Chair of Global Crossing, Bill Savoy, President of Paul Allen's Vulcan Ventures and Craig Winn.

If you are a shareholder, investor, analyst or journalist and would like to see for yourself how Value America is changing retail and how we intend to achieve profitability, you are invited to join us in Washington DC at on or in Charlottesville at on . Please call or email Kim Kuo to reserve your place at this investor forum. You will gain access to question each member of our Executive Committee on their role and contribution following their presentations. Come join us and discover what makes Value America different and perhaps better.

As I read through the draft release, my stomach filled my throat and blood flooded my head. I was facing a despicable but fundamental choice. Take the release, make my edits, return them to Winn, and turn against Tom, or take it to Tom, turn against Winn, and let the chips fall where they may. There was no longer any middle ground.

The incentives for me to stay and serve Winn were high. I'd break through to big-think strategic work and business development. I'd stay in a lavish inner circle and enjoy enviable raises and bonuses. Kim would take over both public and investor relations. It would be good for both of our resumes. As we stood motionless in the cabin, reading the release and looking blankly at each other, we sorted through the same facts. On a visceral level, Morgan was easier to like than Winn. He listened, he was kind, he was humble, he had a generous heart and impeccable integrity. But Winn *was* Value America. And in many ways I loved him more than Tom. No matter how hard he'd tried to give the company away for others to run, it was like separating Siamese twins. And

visionaries *do* matter. They make or break companies. They revolutionize industries. They crush naysayers.

We snatched up the press release and decided to drive. We didn't
know if we were driving to Morgan's farm or back to our apartment.
With the late autumn leaves still falling from the trees as we weaved
through Winndom's little forest, we breathed in the cold air, hoping for
clarity and the strength to make the right decision.

We wrinkled our noses, tried to joke, and slowly realized what we
had to do. I cranked the wheel left, called Morgan, and told him we had
to talk . . . now. I wondered if I'd ever see Winndom again. I knew
Winn would view my giving Tom the release as an act of betrayal. But I
hoped someday he would understand why I did it. To me, both men
were friends and mentors. I had dug deep to learn and respect each
man's strengths and fought hard to stay free of each man's weaknesses. I
steadfastly refused to admit that an unbridgeable chasm had developed
between the two men — that there wasn't some hope of bringing them
back together.

We drove along the creek-bordered dirt roads that led to Tom's
cabin, opened his front door, and found him standing next to Dianne,
casually talking about the night's dinner options. I didn't say a word as I
handed him the release. For the next hour — which passed as briskly as
five minutes — he read and reread the release. Then, still not speaking,
he walked outside to his back porch. Kim stayed with Dianne as she
ranted, and I followed Tom.

He sat in his high-backed rocking chair, eyes fixed on an invisible
something in the distance. "Well," he said, "I suppose this one is over."
There were, he said, things he was now obliged to do since he was in
possession of this press release. He'd have to call Value America's counsel Gary LeClair. The board would have to be notified of Winn's attempt to reestablish control of the company. There was no telling,
Morgan said, what would happen now.

CHAPTER NINETEEN

Coup du jour

No answer was the right answer. Kim and I both felt we had done the right thing in sharing the release with Morgan. He was, after all, still CEO. I was, however, haunted by the feeling that I had betrayed Winn's trust. But, I tried to reason, I made my decision for the good of the company — for my wife, for my Value America–employed relatives. I'd answered the question about who should rightfully run the company. I'd abided by corporate rules of conduct in reporting the proper information to the proper person, Tom Morgan. We needed focus and leadership. Now.

I had to tell Winn what I'd done. I'd tried to call him the previous evening, unsuccessfully. I couldn't imagine the wrath I'd face or the feelings I'd have.

Pulling into the Rio West parking lot before 7:00 A.M. the next morning, November 15, I found I wasn't the first one there. Winn's big truck, Mick Kicklighter's little truck, and Rex Scatena's maroon Ferrari were all cooling outside.

Inside Winn's office, the three men sat planning their new future. Scatena, who'd been a virtual ghost at the company during my tenure and who had allegedly been angling to extricate himself from Value America for months, was relieved to find the new plan didn't demand any more of his time.

Kicklighter sat at the table somewhat bewildered, nodding his head and wondering how all this had come to pass. He'd seen coups before but always from the outside. During the late 1970s, he was inside the Shah's Iran, advising the military. Every morning his driver arrived in a different car wearing different clothes and took a different route to headquarters. The only constant was the driver's very powerful revolver that rested in his chest holster and the shotgun perched on the seat next to him. It had seemed normal at the time; only later upon reflection did the absurdity of the situation strike him. Vietnam was the same way. Casualties and losses were accepted almost indifferently. It was only later that the gravity of the situation broke through the consciousness. Then, as now, his role was solely to execute orders, not to make his own decisions and certainly not to question the judgment of his commanders — at least not in front of others.

For Winn, it was easy to reclaim the commander's role; it was like he never left it. Of all the complicated situations he found himself in, this was a relatively easy test. Tom Morgan had resigned twice, and while Winn had rejected both resignations, he now realized he should have accepted them. After all, why would he want a CEO around who so clearly didn't want to be there? For Value America to succeed, it required a crew who was utterly, insanely, committed to its success. Behind those mild-mannered Clark Kent mannerisms, chic clothes, and smooth talking, Morgan, Winn now knew, was a reptile, cold and calculating. Morgan's most disgusting tactic was claiming this was all about "truth." He made it sound like some heroic sacrifice to tell Winn the "truth," but hell, it was a coup. What was it with these religious guys? Winn angrily wondered. When Dynasty Lighting was thriving, there was that pastor. Just like Morgan. He'd "confronted" Winn with a list of purported "truths." How absurd. It was nothing but brazen betrayal. Kathy and Rex were right — religious types were the most devious and deceitful types of all. It was foolish to ever get involved with them. Besides, it was very clear to Winn after talking to Rex Scatena, Mick Kicklighter, Neal Harris, John Steele, Greg Dorn, and a host of others that no one had *any* problems at all with him. It was time for their beloved leader to lead. He knew he'd have to delay his political destiny, but that was OK. After all, destiny couldn't be altered, just postponed. Besides, this crisis was a chance to show everyone else that when things were their toughest, he was the best.

As the three hammered out their grand plans, I was quietly typing my epistle. My letter asked Craig to focus on one thing — our mutual pledge to work together, to remain loyal to each other above all else. We all once agreed we were on a mission together. But now, if both Winn and Morgan persisted in their demand for ultimate power, we'd all fail. I explained that I had shared Winn's draft press release with Morgan because I thought the release was a mistake, and because I thought Winn should have dealt directly with Morgan instead of going behind his back. It was, I said, the least he owed him. Morgan had dealt with him face to face. Shouldn't he do the same?

I printed my discourse and walked slowly toward Winn's office. Closing my eyes, I gulped in a gallon of air and knocked vigorously on the door.

A harsh voice ordered me to enter. I marched in spine straight, apologized for interrupting, and announced I had something to say. Kicklighter, Winn, and Scatena were seated clockwise around the table. They showed me a chair. I sat to face Winn, who looked at me like I was standing in the way of a thousand more important things he had to accomplish.

There was something very important I needed to share before the day's events were finalized, I told the group. I stared down at my paper and read. Value America, I stammered, had responsibilities beyond the bottom line. There were six hundred people who depended on the company to feed their families. There were thousands of investors who trusted us as management to do the right things. I feared we were engaging in some juvenile pissing match and that everyone who depended on the company would be caught in a most unpleasant crossfire.

As I spoke, the three men sat stone-faced. Soon I got my rhythm going and read through the letter with increasing resolve. I *knew* I had done the right thing. I implored Winn to step back and remember that despite all their differences, he and Morgan were better together than either could be separately. Winn was a stunning visionary and business intellect, but Morgan was the manager and the facilitator he needed to make things work.

I concluded my monologue by revealing I had shown the draft press release to Morgan. There was momentary calm.

And then there wasn't.

"You did *what?!*" Winn exploded, enraged.

Pale and pasty, Scatena whispered, "That was stupid." It was eerily *Godfather*-like. I wondered if he was cracking walnuts with his hand.

Winn gripped the side of the table as if he were about to tip it over and took the floor back. "In all of my business years, I have never, ever seen or heard of a decision so profoundly stupid in all my life. That was stupid. Stupid! David, that was stupid and an act of ultimate betrayal."

Scatena pursed his lips, raised his eyebrows disdainfully, and nodded. The general sat motionless and silent.

"Get out. Get out of my office right now!" Winn roared. He was suddenly standing and pacing furiously, as if to exorcise the hatred welling within.

My eager attempts to defend my actions were stomped on. I went back to the letter, back to my thinking, back to those times in the cabin when we all pledged to stand together.

I figured my promotion and raise were likely on hold.

I stood and looked at Winn, Rex, and then the general. I waited for the general to come to my defense — he, I thought, would bring reconciliation to the moment. I waited. Scatena coolly reminded me that it was time for me to go.

I turned to leave, but the room felt like it had shifted. I felt like I was trying to walk on the walls. I staggered to the little kitchen area that adjoined Tom Morgan's office and the conference room. I was having a near-death experience — of the dot.com kind. Images of Winn promising me riches over burritos at Amigo's and of me sipping wine in Morgan's cabin, recruiting friends and family to the can't-miss company, and private jetting from meeting to meeting, munching on catered shrimp, all blurred past me. There was no light at the end of the tunnel. It was very, very cold.

The door opened, and a hazy figure walked through it. It was Tom Morgan. He looked at me, puzzled, and asked gingerly, "How are you doing?"

Somewhere between the near-death flashes and Morgan's entry into the kitchen, a very large lump lodged itself in my throat, a tingly sensation invaded my sinuses, and watery stuff filled my eyes. The last time I felt that way was at the end of *Beaches* when somebody died and Bette Midler sang "Wind Beneath My Wings."

I explained the letter, the confrontation, and the impending clash. Tom just nodded like I'd told him it was going to snow. He turned around, told me to grab a few minutes alone in his office, and said he was going to use my office to make a phone call.

Minutes later I found him in my office. He hadn't called any high-priced lawyer or any reporter. He had called his longtime confidant Doug Holladay to reassure himself that his intended plan was the right one. He was going to walk into Winn's office, reiterate his arguments from their meetings the previous week and the previous month, and then tell Winn how sad and disappointed he was that Craig hadn't called him directly to discuss the change in plans.

Morgan and I walked into Winn's office, where the now-agitated trinity sat nervously plotting their next moves. Morgan took my recently evacuated chair, while I retreated to the far corner next to Cristal. I sat silently, petting the panting dog as Morgan turned to Winn.

Winn looked at Morgan like they'd never met.

"Craig, there is nothing you have that I want," Morgan began. "Last Thursday we sat right here, and I said I was happy to leave. You *insisted* that wasn't the right thing to do. We talked about the conditions under which I would stay. When we left, I said, 'Think about it,' and you said, 'No, this is the right thing. You have to stay.' I don't know what happened between then and now, but it is clear that things have changed. I still don't want anything you have. If you want me to step down, I will."

Step down? Winn mused to himself. What did Morgan really *mean* by that? Would stepping down mean constructive termination? Would constructive termination mean Morgan would get two years of salary like his contract required? Was *step down* a euphemism? Was he resigning again? Under what circumstances?

Winn said nothing. He just nodded his head. More than anything, he looked like he wanted a fight. But to fight he needed a target, and Morgan wasn't giving him anything to hit. He was like a dancing shadow or a guy who had gone fetal. It was disarming, and it made his case infuriatingly harder to advance.

Morgan thought he held the confidential support of 90 percent of the management team. He had attended to each of them for months as they complained and criticized and generally grumbled about Winn. But it remained unclear how many of those executives would desert him to kiss Winn's feet. Technically, only the board could vote to remove Tom Morgan as CEO. As chairman, Winn was limited in his power. But as the primary shareholder, who, combined with Scatena, controlled more than 50 percent of the stock, Winn carried a big stick.

In fact, even Scatena and Kicklighter had privately expressed serious reservations about Winn and his veracity. Scatena told Morgan that at one point he was going to insist both he and Winn leave. The general had told Winn he didn't know if he wanted to stay with Winn or with Value America at all. But in this moment, they both cowered behind the master.

As the drama in Charlottesville unfolded, Winn's draft press release was reaching key board members. "Shit!" said one with a slow southern drawl. "Damn!" said another. "What the ——?" was uttered by several others. The board that had wanted to be part of the dot.com revolution was being drawn into a revolution of a different sort.

Down the hall, a determined Tom Starnes had made a decision of his own. Starnes had spent the whole summer trying to get the government relationship on track after Winn's anti-eFed decree. Over that time, he'd occasionally talked with Tim Driscoll, the longshoreman–venture capitalist who'd disappeared from Value America's radar after the IPO. Value America, Driscoll felt, tried to stiff him out of his $1 million fee, and Driscoll now hated Winn passionately. When Driscoll started calling, Starnes provided him with tidbits about Winn's dealings or hyperboles or tirades. Driscoll knew in general terms about the Citibank and FedEx deals, about the tension Winn introduced into the office. As much as Driscoll hated Winn, however, he'd stayed on the periphery of the action.

Starnes, however, had endured enough of Craig's havoc and was ready to pull Tim Driscoll in to ensure that Morgan remained CEO. Over the course of the next sixty minutes, Starnes gave Driscoll as many details as he could remember about Winn's tyrannical rule in the post-IPO days. As the facts piled up, Driscoll leaned back in his chair, ran his free hand through his puff of salt-and-pepper hair, and somehow knew the $8 million he'd invested in the company was gone, zippo, dead, unless he stepped back in and tried to right the situation.

Driscoll hung up with Starnes and called an investment buddy of his in New York. "Tell me," Driscoll said without a hello, "if Winn leaves Value America, what happens to the stock?"

The investment banker didn't hesitate a second. "It doubles."

"Why?"

"Because the Street doesn't trust Winn, his exaggerations, or his track record."

"Thanks."

Driscoll was back in the game. He had to be. There were invest-ments and a reputation to protect.

Back inside the chairman's office, Morgan cracked the iceberg. "It's out of my hands now, Craig. I faxed the press release to Gary LeClair, and I believe he's sent it to Fred [Smith] and others. I have no intention of fighting you for anything, Craig. Don't worry about it."

Winn's eyes shot all colors of hatred at Tom. So that's the way he was going to play — humiliating Winn to his own elite board. Winn couldn't figure out what Morgan *really* wanted. What was Morgan's price? What would it take to make him leave quietly?

The damn press release was the smoking gun, if interpreted the wrong way. What the release suggested, Winn knew, was that he was taking back control of the company in contravention of Morgan. The re-lease showed a new management team, a new strategic approach, what some people could construe to be . . . a coup.

Morgan stood up and waited for the other three men to stand so he could shake their hands and bid them farewell. They didn't move. With a sad nod to the floor, Morgan walked out. I hurried after him. Cristal leapt up to follow us, but Winn growled her name and she whimpered back to her coiled position in the corner.

Morgan marched through the conference room to his office, and I drifted down the hall to Starnes's office in hopes of finding solace. Starnes furtively recounted his phone call with Driscoll and asked me if I would be willing to relay my experiences through Driscoll to the board.

I remembered Driscoll's name. It had emanated from the emperor's lips like a curse in many days past. Winn made him sound like a troll — a greedy, untrustworthy, and *Democrat* troll at that. But these were des-perate hours, and I was willing to do desperate things — including talk-ing to a troll — if it meant the board would hear at least some of the truth that was Value America.

Hours after I'd left to read my letter to Winn and crew, I stumbled back to Kim's office. In a tidal wave of emotion and disbelief, I relayed the morning's episodes right up to the last conversation with Starnes. "Give me the number," she said. "I'm calling Driscoll now."

I had never feared Kim would shrink into the background, either too scared to say what she believed or worried about what others would think. She'd made up her mind. Winn needed to go.

In his office, door shut, Tom Morgan mulled over his next steps. Everything was happening much faster than he'd expected. This turn of events was not entirely unexpected, it was just dizzying. Fred Smith was on the phone again.

"I've got my own damn company to run," Smith hollered. "Now I've got a bunch of yahoos tearing each other apart in the middle of the Virginia countryside." So much for the retail revolution.

None of the outside members of the board could figure out *why now?* At the Value America board meeting eleven days earlier, Winn and Morgan had virtually cooed over one another. The two had announced a smooth, pleasant separation. Now they were in some sort of damn lovers' quarrel. Why hadn't anyone else given a damn enough to tell the board what the hell was happening? Now it was all dissolving into a huge mess that *they* were going to have to clean up.

As with an impending divorce, the only thing that made sense was a trial separation. Winn and Morgan agreed Morgan should take an immediate two-week vacation. Key board members thought the break was a good idea as well.

Kim and I sat in her office commiserating about the pathetic state of our newly joined life. Although she never once said it, the obvious question was "I left AOL for this?" Kim's entire Value America experience had been based on insight and information from a Winn-weary financial community. She'd been waging a lonely battle on the front lines against cynical and angry analysts, irate investors and traders, and endless anti-Winn tirades. As such, she was ready to load up, aim some truth at the back of Winn's head, and pull the trigger. Her calculus was simple: no Winn, no problems.

Kim grabbed the phone, called Tim Driscoll, and said, "Hi, Tim? This is Kimberly Kuo. I used to work at AOL. Now I'm heading up investor relations at Value America. Tom Starnes said you might be interested in how the financial community views Craig Winn." Kim had her points scribbled in a long list in front of her. Point by point she analytically detailed all the conversations from the Value America "Give Me Love Now" tour to the scores of analyst and investor conversations she'd logged in her few weeks with the company.

As Kim relayed damning quotes, Tom Starnes was down the hall charting other executives he could line up to inform the board about the dysfunctional realities of Value America. I wandered back to my office, perched by my small window, absorbed the mid-afternoon sun, and re-flected on what in the hee-haw just happened.

Outside my office Glenda Dorchak was buzzing to no one in partic-ular about what a spectacular success Comdex had been. People were "lining up" at the Value America booth. She was a featured speaker on a panel with . . . gasp . . . Lou Dobbs! Value America's presence had been "huge," "enormous," "remarkable." She wasn't in the building more than forty seconds before Winn emerged to greet her. I thought he was going to give his former adversary a hug. I averted my eyes; that was something I didn't need to see.

Glenda Dorchak was suddenly *very* important to Winn. In fact, she now tipped the scales of power. Three months before, she had fought to retain her beloved president title. She'd fought for a prime seat during the big board meeting earlier in the summer. Indeed, she'd fought to be part of any board call she ever heard about. It mattered less what she said than that she was *there*. Now, to the board, there was the chairman — Winn — the CEO — Morgan — and the president — her.

Dorchak had worked hard to create a team of loyal followers, all of whom diligently kept her informed of every muttering and maneuver-ing throughout the company. Her intelligence sources now told her Morgan was effectively gone and maneuvering was under way to take out Winn as well. Well, if Winn was gone and if Morgan was gone, she was the only logical choice to take over the company. That suited her just fine.

The rest of the afternoon and into the dreary evening, the various factions in the executive office complex schemed behind closed doors. Starnes and Kim were the generals of the anti-Winn movement. Dor-chak and team were studying their options. Winn, Scatena, and Kick-lighter assumed they were in the driver's seat: After all, two of the men controlled more than 50 percent of the company, and the other was a for-mer three-star general. What on earth could hurt them?

As darkness fell, all Kim and I wanted to do was dine with Heather and Scott, drink a lot, and beg them not to hate us forever — after all, we were *family!*

As I gathered up my things, looking at the Robert Kennedy 1968 poster that leaned against my wall, I mulled over all the Value-able memories of the past eight months. Suddenly, my door flew open and a tired but grinning Winn entered. "Hi there!" he said, beaming.

I was positively in the twilight zone. It took me a moment to wipe the stupefied look off my face. Thanks to years of training in the conniving political world, I assumed there was another agenda. There was. It just took Craig a few minutes of awkward chitchat to get to it.

"Listen, I understand how upset you are by this whole thing. I was extremely angry about the press release matter, but I forgive you. The important thing now is to move forward."

"OK."

"So, let's just do that." Winn thrust out a stiff, open hand for me to grasp. I offered a limp and clammy mitt.

As he rose to leave, he nonchalantly tilted his head and addressed his real agenda. "Oh, by the way," he began, "could you please give me all the copies you and Kim might have of that release? And do you think you could get me Tom's copy as well?"

As quickly as I could formulate a strategic response, I said, "Tom Starnes or Tom Morgan?"

Craig looked panicked. Starnes had a copy, too? "Morgan's, I think that's it."

"Yeah, right. I'll see what I can do."

I handed a couple copies of the release over to him. He left, twisting them in his hands. Kim, however, had already made twelve copies, faxed one to her dad, given one to Heather, one to Scott, sent one to our house in Arlington, and who knows where else. Try as Winn might, there was no way to suppress the damage contained in that release.

Dinner with the family was, to put it mildly, a somber affair. Heather and Scott waxed nostalgic about their former life in Colorado Springs, their house by the Garden of the Gods. They had once told us they *hated* their jobs, but maybe absence and Internet insanity had changed their perspective.

As we were driving home, Kim's cell phone rang. Driscoll was checking up on her — and he'd found good news. "Well," he said, "you've got good references. Bob Pittman likes you, and so do a bunch of other bigwigs at AOL. Don't worry about this shit. Anything happens, you'll have no trouble landing on your feet. Anything happens, we'll double your salary and hire you here to work in venture capital."

Kim liked this guy!

"Listen, you willing to talk to Mike Steed about this stuff?" he pressed on.

She was and she did. Over the course of the next two days, Kim talked to Mike Steed, Fred Smith, Gerry Roche, and Tom Casey — all decisive powers on the board. Her AOL credibility and the stories she relayed about Winn — and the financial community's distaste for him — were all backed by meticulous notes, numbers, and disinterested observers. Every other senior executive — Glenda, Tom Starnes, John Steele, and departed executives Dean Johnson and Jerry Goode — told the board the company would be best served without Winn. It wasn't betrayal, it was exhaustion.

With Morgan ensconced in his McLean, Virginia, home and maintaining relative silence, I called Doug Holladay to find out what Morgan was thinking. Would he, I asked Holladay, even consider coming back to Value America to run it?

Holladay didn't know.

The board didn't know either. Did Morgan want to stay? Did he want to go? Roche, Smith, and LeClair didn't know if Morgan wanted severance or incentive. They also didn't feel it was their responsibility to convince him to stay. They waited for his calls. The calls never came.

Morgan didn't know what he wanted. He'd always assumed the answer to his ultimatum was that since Winn owned more than one-third of the company, Morgan would be forced to leave. Now things weren't so clear. Of course, Winn could start a proxy fight and simply use the power of his shares to get his way. But even he probably realized how suicidal that might be.

Morgan's biggest concern was that the well was now too poisoned. Winn had said too many negative things about him to executives, board members and others. Leading would be difficult if not impossible. And as much as anything, Morgan was exhausted. He had never mentioned his weariness publicly. But his mind, his emotions, his body were ravaged by eight months of constant turmoil. He needed to get away. Far, far away. He hoped that didn't mean abandoning friends in trouble, but they were all professionals and would be fine no matter what happened to him. He tried very hard to convince himself of that.

By Friday, November 19, Winn was deep into examining the business he'd created. Things were an even bigger mess than he'd assumed. The technology implementations were not going smoothly. The company was burning $15 million a month on advertising and wasn't getting many new customers. Even the custom stores weren't performing as well as he'd hoped.

More alarming to Winn was the overall state of e-commerce. The market was too cluttered. There were more than one thousand unique e-commerce sites selling everything from discounted caskets to discounted cars to discounted pet products. For the first time since he'd founded the company in 1995, Winn stood back to assess the competitive marketplace. He surfed through competitors' sites. He read through industry magazines. He tried to see Value America objectively. His conclusions startled even him.

Winn saw only two options for Value America. It had to be sold or radically repositioned. The former would certainly have short-term payoffs. With the stock at about $15 a share and figuring a conservative 30 percent premium, the company would sell for about $800 million. His personal take would be somewhere north of $250 million. It wasn't a billion, but it was enough money to lavish on toys, stone walls, and baubles for his wife for many, many years. With that kind of money, he could also endow a foundation, start a nonprofit, and run for office. But for Winn, there was always a pull beyond bank-account figures. There were Greg Dorn and Neal Harris and Richard Gerhardt, and Rex Scatena and the fact that he had *birthed* this angel. He had to see it through to a successful finish — and that would require heavy, heavy lifting.

Winn had rewarded his longtime acquaintance Wolf Schmitt with a board seat, and now Wolf was important to Winn's plans. The former Rubbermaid CEO was now out of a job, having merged Rubbermaid with Newell to form a larger plastics conglomerate. Without having to resort to a proxy fight, Winn could count his board votes — Rex Scatena, Wolf Schmitt, Gary LeClair, Roy Keith, Gerry Roche, and Fred Smith. Assuming he lost Casey, Steed, Savoy, and Bennett, he was still in fine shape.

Schmitt was also Winn's choice to be Morgan's interim replacement until Value America named a new full-time CEO. Lacking an excuse not to, Schmitt agreed to oversee the completely new Value America management structure. Winn would remain chairman, Wolf would be CEO, and an executive committee of the company's executive vice presidents — John Steele, Neal Harris, Glenda Dorchak (who was demoted under the plan), Paul Ewert, and Tom Starnes — would help manage the company under Schmitt. Winn contemplated raising one of those EVPs to CEO, but he preferred to test their loyalty and fortitude first.

Winn vetted his leadership proposal with key board members and received generally positive feedback. Like the consummate politico he longed to be, Winn worked the phones and said whatever necessary to secure the votes he needed to regain power and remake his company into what it should be. It would take time, but he would repair the damage Morgan had done.

As Winn maneuvered behind the scenes, a *Fortune* reporter called to check out big changes she'd heard mumblings about. Might Wolf Schmitt somehow be involved? I could neither confirm nor deny. Apart from Winn, no one in the company had a clue what was happening or, more important, what was going to happen next. The reporter warned me that Schmitt was widely viewed as one of the worst CEOs in American history. Schmitt had apparently taken the helm at Rubbermaid when it was voted one of the five strongest brands in America. It had strong revenue, robust profits, was a generous corporate citizen, cared for its employees — the quintessential American success story. But within a year of his taking control, Schmitt's Rubbermaid was nose-diving. His temper tantrums were as legendary as his foolish decisions. Employees left the company in droves, and Schmitt was ultimately forced to sell to the much weaker Newell. My *Fortune* reporter volunteered to share the stinging articles *Fortune* had written about Schmitt just to give me a glimpse of what we were in for.

As Winn continued selling his new plan to board members, they continued their own investigations and were discovering some very unhappy things about him. All the items Morgan confronted Winn with on November 11 were supplemented by other specific examples of serious problems, such as misleading reporters and overstating facts like the number of returns, direct-marketing efficiency, custom-store efficiency, number of brands in the store, and on and on.

On Monday evening, November 21, Winn flew Schmitt in from Ohio on the Hawker to become Value America's interim CEO and to sit next to Winn on the pivotal board call the next evening.

The next morning, Tuesday, November 22, Winn arranged for senior executives to meet with Schmitt and debrief him on the state of the company. Sitting in Tom Morgan's vacant office, Schmitt interviewed a dozen key executives in an attempt to understand the condition of the company. In his naïveté, Schmitt was shocked that the Value America Craig Winn had described to him and the Value America executives portrayed didn't jibe. In fact, the two interpretations bore little resemblance to each other. The Value America Schmitt *thought* he was inheriting was poised to do billions of dollars in business with Falwell, Citibank, Visa, and FedEx. It was supposed to have achieved a massive systems integration that rendered it the most technologically advanced e-commerce company in the world. The executives were supposedly thrilled about the company's future. But after six hours of discussions, Schmitt walked into Craig Winn's office to tell him his company was a house of cards and that he had no interest in becoming CEO — interim or otherwise.

It was now 4:45 P.M., and Craig Winn didn't have a plan. The board call was starting in fifteen minutes. The plan he'd been selling to board members had just walked into his office and announced he didn't want anything to do with Value America.

Winn flipped out. As he bounced from wall to wall to ceiling to floor, he shrieked at Wolf. How could Schmitt do this to him? How stupid could he possibly be? Value America *was* exactly as Winn had described it. If anyone told him otherwise, they were lying, sniveling bastards. Then it occurred to Winn: Morgan probably put the executives up to it! Morgan was leading the coup — right now!

Winn had no time to devise a completely new plan, so he returned to the plan of the previous weekend, in which he would be interim CEO and run the company until a replacement could be found.

Meanwhile, Value America board member and Global Crossing vice chairman Tom Casey called me from California. He'd heard rumors about Value America and Craig Winn and wanted to know if I could confirm any of them. I asked what they were. He briefly mentioned the New York Saks meeting, the Citibank exaggerations, the Robbie Stephens speech, the Falwell loan, and the Bloomberg press call. Each item was, I informed him, true. Winn did, however, have reasons that justified each questionable action.

At 4:55, Gerry Roche called and asked the same questions. I gave him the same answers.

The board conference call commenced minutes later. Winn, still shaken by Schmitt's rejection and wondering what Schmitt had heard, introduced his plan to the board. For Value America to succeed, he told them, it would have to execute precisely and intelligently. The only person able to do that was him. For thirty minutes he described his plan — with exactly the same conviction he had the week before when he described the previous plan to the board.

The board was seeing firsthand what others had pointed out before: Winn couldn't help selling. No matter what the idea was, no matter what the product was, he sold it with conviction. The problem for Value America's board, however, was that Value America needed more than a good salesman. It needed a real leader.

Mike Steed leapt like a lion. "No way will I approve Craig Winn returning as CEO. No way."

Other board members more placidly asked what happened to the previous plan to have Schmitt take over? Schmitt relayed his conversations with executives and detailed the real tribulations the company faced. Value America was, in his opinion, a house of cards. When asked what he recommended be done, Schmitt didn't hesitate. "I believe Tom Morgan needs to return as CEO."

Winn nearly bit through his lip.

The board concurred with Schmitt and promptly got Morgan on the telephone. Describing to Morgan all that transpired, Fred Smith first asked Winn whether he'd be willing to work with Tom Morgan again. Winn said he'd be happy to. Smith then asked Morgan whether he'd be willing to return as CEO with Craig Winn as chairman.

Morgan, at home in northern Virginia with his family, listened to Fred's account and repeated what he had told Craig Winn eleven days before. There was no way he could ever work with Craig Winn again. That left little room for discussion. The board thanked Morgan for his contributions and bid him farewell. And with that, post–Value America life began in earnest for Tom Morgan. He turned to his family and said, "Well, anyone got the *Post* classifieds around?" A weight had been lifted.

After Morgan clicked off the call, Winn unleashed his fury, deriding Morgan as stupid, arrogant, conniving, and duplicitous.

Steed roared back at Winn. "How *dare* you insult Morgan after he was a gentleman to you? You arrogant . . ."

Winn tried to back off, but the board had had enough.

Gerry Roche chimed in that he could not support Winn returning as CEO. The other directors echoed his sentiment.

Winn stared at the phone, utterly stunned. Smith told Winn the board wanted the situation resolved immediately. If Morgan refused to return, Winn couldn't be trusted as CEO, and Schmitt wouldn't take over, who was left to be Value America's CEO?

Winn considered the only four candidates available — John Steele, Neal Harris, Paul Ewert, and Glenda Dorchak.

Harris and Ewert were immediately scratched because they weren't well known enough.

John Steele, Winn said, was consumed with operations that were key to ensuring the technology was sound. And frankly, to this point, no one was impressed with how that process was going.

That left Glenda Dorchak. Gerry Roche enthusiastically supported her. They'd spent time together during board meetings, and Roche liked her. He'd heard good things about her.

Winn, hearing the conversation turn toward Dorchak, rushed to head her off at the pass. Dorchak, he told them, was incredibly insecure and couldn't be trusted. She was acceptable at driving numbers but was a terrible manager.

The board barely acknowledged Winn's comments. Instead, they ordered him to ask Dorchak if she was willing to be CEO and if Steele would be COO.

Winn wobbled out of the room, grasping for a worthy strategic tactic to take back control of this debacle.

Kim and I sat in Kim's office, which happened to be next to the conference room. After days of talking and planning and wondering, we knew Value America's future was being decided a mere thirty-five feet away.

Suddenly we heard Winn. I spun around, thinking he was behind me. Instead, he was talking loudly in the conference room. The filament-thin walls didn't offer much soundproofing.

We heard Winn ask Dorchak if she wanted to be CEO. There was a pause, and then she said she'd be happy to. But, she added, she could do it *only* if she had Winn's *full* support. She needed a veritable cheerleader. Winn would, he promised, be there every step of the way. He would rally the troops behind her, and, most important, help guide her decisions and plans for the company. Next, he asked John Steele if he would agree to be COO. Steele cooed for a minute about how much he'd have to learn and how he wasn't sure he was worthy. Then he eagerly gave his affirmative.

Meanwhile, Schmitt remained in Winn's office, sharing his experiences inside the company. One board member asked Schmitt if he would become chairman. If Schmitt was chairman and Dorchak was CEO, then Value America could present an entirely new face to the world. After a moment's consideration, Schmitt agreed. It was actually, he told them, the perfect solution. As chairman, he wouldn't be responsible for day-to-day operations but could still actively try to resurrect Value America.

Winn strutted proudly back into his office with Dorchak and Steele. Winn had quickly realized that thrusting Dorchak into the CEO position could be the perfect solution to his problem. He would remain a virtual CEO, completely dominate her, and achieve everything he had originally planned. An eager grin swept over his face. He was going to survive.

Dorchak had, Winn gleefully informed the board, agreed to become CEO. In addition, John Steele had agreed to become COO. Winn was pleased, he announced, to be working closely with them both in his role as chairman.

Fred Smith announced wryly that the board had made another decision. If Winn agreed, Wolf Schmitt would become chairman of Value America, and Winn would become chairman of the board's executive committee.

Winn's breathing mechanisms locked up again. What happened to *his* plan? He looked blankly at the phone, then around the room, then back down at the speakerphone. His ability to process was gone. Every one of his plans was failing. Now Smith was asking him to step down as chairman — *Fred Smith.* "OK," he whispered. "OK."

Almost before the words left his mouth, Winn started looking around for a way to take his words back. He hadn't meant it. He really hadn't. It was a mistake. It was . . . too late. The board accepted the new plan unanimously.

Kim and I heard rumblings in the hallway and poked our heads out to see what was happening. Winn, Kicklighter, Scatena, and Harris

walked slowly out into the hallway overlooking both Winn's office —
now his *old* office — and the atrium.

Once outside the building Winn stared into the spacious window of
his old office. The men around him stared too. Our general counsel, Biff
Pusey, summoned Kim and me into Winn's old office. There, Glenda
Dorchak and Wolf Schmitt were concluding a big gooey hug. Looking
out the window, I saw Winn standing and looking up at us.

Glenda excitedly told me the new leadership was all about "quality
growth" and the "path to profitability." I was ordered to craft a press release that captured the new joy inside Value America. Kim sat across
from me, barely able to contain her tears. Disbelieving, I scribbled notes
and silently retreated to my office. One final glance out Winn's office
window revealed him lifting Cristal into the back of his big Yukon.

In my office I stared blankly at my computer screen, unable to collect
coherent thoughts for a press release about joy and growth and leadership. Dorchak interrupted my coma by announcing she was treating the
executive team to dinner.

There, at the Outback Steakhouse at 9:00 P.M., squeezed around a
crowded table with Biff Pusey, Kim, Tom Starnes, John Steele, and me,
Glenda Dorchak held up one hand to bid everyone silent. "I have something important to say. My goal here is to make everyone at this table
very, very rich. If we pull together, we can really do it. We'll all be rich."

Epilogue

The death of a company, unlike the death of a person, is hard to pin-point. When exactly did Value America die? For me it died the night both Winn and Morgan left the company. On that night, both the visionary's hope and the executioner's ability were lost.

Bright and early the next morning, November 23, a press release rolled out: "Value America Announces Change to Focus on Profitability."

Value America, Inc. (NASDAQ: VUSA), the Internet super-store, announced a change in its management team designed to focus on quality growth and a drive to profitability.

Glenda Dorchak, who joined the company as President in October 1998 after 23 years at IBM, will become Value America's new CEO. "Value America's innovative business model is becoming a viable and exciting business," said Dorchak. "As we advance toward profitability, we are determined to focus on providing the highest-quality customer experience, increasing the depth of products in our store and solidifying our standing as e-commerce's inventoryless pioneer."

... Wolf Schmitt, retired Chairman and CEO of Rubber-maid, Inc. and current Value America director, has been named the new Chairman of the Board ...

Craig Winn, the company's innovative founder and e-tailing pioneer, will serve as Chairman of the Board's Executive Committee and will consult with Schmitt on strategic direction and brand relationships.

> The company also announced that Tom Morgan, former
> CEO, will be leaving the company for personal reasons, return-
> ing to be with his family in Northern Virginia.

Kim and I were scheduled to drive to New York to be with my family for Thanksgiving. But family was something we couldn't face. We needed diversion. We needed entertainment. We needed someplace calm and staid following the Internet madness. We needed Vegas. We needed to escape the Babylon of our daily lives for the Neverland of our dreams.

People go to Las Vegas for a lot of reasons. They go for glitz and glamour. Easy money is a big draw, sex always a hope. They go to see a couple bleached-blond guys with funny accents and white leather suits stick their heads in tigers' mouths, secretly longing for one of those cats to finally chomp. Normal people don't "retreat" to Las Vegas. Retreat to a monastery? Appealing to some. Retreat to the beach or the mountains? In a heartbeat. But retreat to Las Vegas? Ridiculous. Still, I knew mountains and monasteries would have sent me into shock. After my bout with e-commerce hell, Vegas had a pace brisk enough to keep me from flat-lining. And isolated enough to keep me sane.

We were supposed to do the Internet shuffle — get in, change the world, get rich, and get out. But we discovered the prevailing wisdom was flawed. The Internet *is* a tremendous force for change, but the industry chews up more folks than it blesses.

Sprawled in my chair at Caesars Palace, I stared up trancelike at the huge OMNIMAX dome, a 180-degree overhead version of IMAX. A film called *Alaska* came on. There, between zoom-ins on polar bears mating and stomach-churning aerial mountain shots, was a snippet of the great Alaska gold rush of the 1890s.

Suddenly, the screen was filled with larger-than-life pictures of starving, freezing fools dressed for fall, scrabbling through the Chilkoot Pass at 14,000 feet in a blizzard, still fantasizing about the gold they were going to find. But their faces wore an expression a shade different from a billionaire's grin. It was raw terror.

In just a few years, the narrator informed us, more than one hundred thousand people ventured near the Arctic Circle in search of their chunk of gold. Of those hundred thousand–plus, only a handful ever found anything of any worth. A few thousand covered the cost of their trip. Most came back cold and penniless. Thousands froze to death.

The truth hit me over the head like a gold miner's shovel. Despite the hype, headlines, and hysteria, this was just a gold rush we were in, not a gold mine we had found. We might look like hip, chic, cutting-edge, new-economy Internet workers, but in fact, a lot of us were kin to those poor, freezing fools in Alaska who had staked everything on turning up a glittering chunk of gold.

It was strange that at Thanksgiving, the time for rejoicing with one's family, the Value America family had disintegrated. Winn was alone with his family, insulated by the expanse of Winndom. Morgan and his family were enjoying a final weekend of rest on their Charlottesville farm, which was about to go on the market. General Kicklighter was disconsolate in northern Virginia with his family. Glenda spent the day plotting with her comrades in their country-club neighborhood west of town. Dean was roaming greener pastures.

Value America was comatose. All that was left were the spasms.

Kim and I returned from Vegas and spent a night in our Arlington, Virginia, house prior to returning to Charlottesville. There, sitting on our back porch, was our new Weber grill. It had, five months late, arrived. Sitting next to it was a Styrofoam box that made a sloshing noise when I moved it — my ice cream. At least the grill worked nicely.

On Wednesday, November 30, we finally got the OK to announce the Citibank relationship. The release itself said nothing other than that Value America was offering Citibank cardmembers special online and offline benefits. There were no financial terms disclosed. Citibank had actually wanted Value America to announce the deal as "provisional," but we talked them out of it at the last minute. After he'd spent months and months hyping the "billions and billions" of dollars the Citibank relationship would bring Value America, Winn's quote about the relationship was written for him by Dorchak. She had originally told me that she didn't want Winn's name anywhere on the release. Only a last-minute appeal to her softer side led her to relent and not stiff him totally.

To analysts, investors, potential brand partners, and reporters, the release was almost comical. We were flooded with calls asking if the Citibank release was real or just a teaser for a real release. It was, we were forced to admit, all there was. Value America's stock continued to sink.

The problems on the business side mounted. Customer-service issues that had visited us earlier in the summer decided to move in. Neither SAP nor Siebel, nor any of the other smaller technology "upgrades," had been fully debugged. Orders were lost, customer information was missing, and hundreds and hundreds of calls and e-mails daily inundated the executive suite and every other phone number people could find for Value America. All the messages said the same thing, that they'd ordered products from Value America at least a month before and still hadn't heard anything. But their credit cards had been billed already, and they were incurring interest on purchases they didn't know if they'd ever get. Even Value America employees were sending each other notices on whether Buy.com, Amazon.com, or eToys had the best deals. Everyone knew not to order from Value America.

The e-mails and calls complaining about Value America weren't stopping at Value America. Those same people were calling consumer-affairs reporters for major newspapers and television stations. They were also calling the Better Business Bureau, attorneys, and anyone else they could think of.

By the middle of December, Glenda Dorchak was leading near-constant meetings with key executives to come up with a go-ahead strategy for the company. Much to Tom Starnes's chagrin, she was, even more emphatically than Winn before her, uninterested in either government or business markets. She was intent on making Value America successful in the consumer marketplace and on reshaping the company to achieve that desire.

Winn, meanwhile, was working on two fronts. First, he was trying to convince the board that Value America needed a wholesale change in orientation that was as sweeping as what Dorchak and Wolf envisioned but that took advantage of the brand relationships and inventoryless model he had dreamed up exactly five years before. He and Rex wrote to the board:

Value America's unique ability to present manufacturing brands, specialty retail brands or credit card brands in unique custom marketplaces with their own unique departments makes our infrastructure functional, credible and *very* valuable. Of particular importance, as an infrastructure company, demand generation would become the burden of the strategic partner. There would be no advertising expense. The company would simply earn a fee on gross revenue and services. As a result, we would become a Business to Consumer and Business to Business version of Ebay.

Second, even as he argued for a change to the business model, Winn tried to convince the board that Value America needed to be acquired. There was no way, Winn argued, for the company to succeed and win on its own. The losses were too great, the competition was too fierce. The world had changed. The day of the Internet-only companies had come and gone. What Value America needed was a strategic partner that could give it the kind of grown-up help it needed.

For us to achieve profitability, Value America must have inspired and engaged strategic leadership and flawless managerial execution. The company must form and capitalize upon strategic alliances and operate in a manner worthy of their trust. A careful reading of these materials by every Board member is essential if we are to make the best informed decision. Accordingly, in light of the company's current stock price, its current and projected financial performance and its current cash position, we firmly believe that it is in the best interests of the company's shareholders to immediately commence a process to find a strategic partner for the company.

The board quickly rejected Winn's plans and accepted Glenda's. Value America would eliminate multimedia product presentations, custom stores, and thirty-five product categories. All told, 304 people would also be eliminated.

It was the anti-IPO. Eight and a half months earlier, employees had streamed into bars on April 7, anticipating the IPO that would make them rich. Now, on December 28, they streamed into a companywide meeting at the DoubleTree Hotel, anticipating their pending unemployment.

It was the biggest Internet layoff on record, and it came on the next to last day of the twentieth century. Amid the barrage of phone calls from investors and the media, Kim and I learned from Heather and

Scott that they had been let go. Kim hung up on whoever she was trying to spin, stood to face her sister, and hugged Heather as both dissolved into tears. "I hate this place," Kim sputtered. "I hate this company, I hate these people."

My job for the rest of that day was to escort Glenda Dorchak to the University of Virginia media center, where she was interviewed by CNBC, CNN, and CNNfn. Value America, the news headlines trumpeted, was the world's first dot.bomb.

Dorchak, meanwhile, was most worried about her New Year's Eve plans in Scottsdale, scheduled to kick off that evening. She had arranged to have three centuries of different alcoholic beverages to serve. There would be eighteenth-century port, nineteenth-century red wine, and twentieth-century white. To ensure that she'd make her party in time, Glenda did what seemed to come naturally to newly minted Value America executives: She arranged for a $25,000 charter to jet her to Scottsdale so she could partake of her gourmet food and wine.

Kim and I jettisoned our New Year's plans and instead hung out with Heather, Scott, and all our other laid-off friends. As Y2K passed and the world didn't end, we popped a bottle of nice bubbly and listened to the fireworks over downtown Charlottesville. We counted ten different booms. It was a Value America kind of millennium celebration — long on hype, short on returns.

Value America continued to spasm through 2000. Things imploded far faster than they had been built. As the company struggled to close 1999's fourth quarter, it was virtually impossible to determine how much money it had lost and how many orders had been placed. More and more orders were lost, reports couldn't be found, and hundreds of incorrect or duplicate items had been shipped. The SAP and Siebel implementations were still full of bugs. Virtually everyone was on their computers that first week in January checking monster.com and hotjobs.com for new employment leads. Houses were being placed on the market, and even Amigo's, the old standby Mexican restaurant where I accepted my offer, was offering a 10 percent discount for remaining — and former — Value America employees.

Glenda Dorchak, meanwhile, scrambled to remake the entire company so that it didn't look, smell, taste, or feel anything like Craig Winn's. She tasked the creative team to come up with new logos and a new storefront design. Value America, she decreed, was not Value

America anymore. Instead, it was going to become VA.com, an alternative Web address we owned. It didn't seem to matter that VA.com suggested either that we were part of Veterans Affairs or the state of Virginia. Glenda had control now and was hell-bent on making sure that the company reflected her wishes and her desires.

When word went out in early February that everyone was required to attend a VA.com meeting at the DoubleTree, panic hit. People started backing up their hard drives or making arrangements to pilfer their laptops. Little did they know they were instead to be treated to one of Dorchak's IBM colleagues who doubled as an inspirational speaker. "Mr. Smile," as we came to know him, told everyone that they needed to smile a lot, keep their resumes sharp, and always, always, ask themselves how they were doing. Mr. Smile, it seemed, perpetually asked himself, "How am I doing? How am I feeling? How am I doing? How am I feeling?"

As VA.com employees asked themselves that question, the answer was invariably, "Lousy, horrible, dreadful, awful." Dozens of employees left in January, dozens more in February. Kim and I were among those who left in February. We didn't have anywhere else to go. We just needed to get ourselves out of Value America. We'd been married for five months. We needed a life again.

Although we tried to forget its existence, Value America kept twitching. A month after we left, Value America finally announced the "successful implementation" of the SAP software. The "successful conversion" to Siebel happened in April.

Throughout the spring and early summer, Glenda and Value America did what Glenda and Value America knew how to do — take out lots and lots and lots of newspaper advertisements. Unfortunately, virtually no one responded to the advertisements anymore. Value America by any name was an e-commerce leper.

Then came the grand announcement that VA.com raised $90 million, but again, it was a lot of hype. They did raise commitments of $30 million from some past investors, but some didn't end up paying.

One day in June, as I pondered my next move, I got Value America's annual report in the mail. Flipping through it and the financials, I was surprised to read that Glenda Dorchak had been awarded a $500,000 bonus, $200,000 in loan forgiveness, and a $100,000 raise for her seven months as Value America CEO. I was even more surprised when only ten weeks later, on August 11, 2000, Value America declared bankruptcy and laid off an additional 185 employees. By November 2000, Value America's assets — its technology infrastructure and about fifty remaining employees — were purchased by struggling computer distributor Merisel for less than $2 million. Value America had spent more than $100 million on their systems; Merisel was the only interested bidder. Within months, Merisel shut down the last remaining Charlottesville outpost and fired all remaining Value America employees.

Value America was hardly alone in its demise. As rapidly as e-commerce had arrived in 1998, it disappeared in 2000. Company after company followed the same death script: "restructurings" that would help "focus on profitability" led to explorations of "strategic alternatives," which led to "further layoffs" and finally to bankruptcy. It didn't matter if the company sold toys or lingerie, luxury items or pet food, they started to disappear one by one. Public and private interest in e-commerce evaporated. There was a problem, it seemed, with companies that had no proven way to make money and lots of proven ways to lose it. Only Amazon.com remained on something of a sure footing. But even that was relative; its stock had declined from a $118 high to about $15.

At the end of December 2000, I returned to Charlottesville to visit Winn. At midnight, when I left, the route west out of D.C. was almost deserted, as was Route 29 south to Charlottesville. I hadn't been back to Charlottesville since I left the company in February. Kim and I endured exactly ninety days after Winn and Morgan left the company — I promised Glenda Dorchak I'd stay that long to help with the transition. Now I was heading back to see what was left and to meet Winn face-to-face for the first time in a year.

On a night so cold even the cows were looking for a bonfire, I saw all the same signs Michelle Morgan had told me to look for on my first drive down to Charlottesville — the Hearth and Home outlet store, the "frish sider" sign, the "country Chinese diner." I drove past the airport and wondered what became of the maroon Hawker. The light turned red as I approached Insurance Lane, which led to my first Value America office. Wrenching the wheel to the left, I made the quick dash up the hill and into my former office complex. The weather-beaten Value

America sign was still posted outside my office window. On all the doors were signs that read PASSKEY ENTRY ONLY — AUTHORIZED PERSONNEL ONLY. Value America's old executive offices had become undertaker central — the place where lawyers and bankers fought to divvy up Value America's remaining cash and equipment in an attempt to pay off as many creditors as possible. I drove around the building a few times, wondering whether I could somehow steal the old sign. I couldn't figure out where to put the purloined sign — and besides, it might be bad luck.

I stayed up most of the night at the DoubleTree Hotel, wondering what Craig and I would say to each other the next day. We'd talked on and off over the previous week. He was, he informed me, writing a novel about the Value America experience. It was going to be a study of the character needed to build a revolutionary company and the lack of character on the part of those who destroyed it.

After a few hours tossing in the darkness, I roused myself and headed to Winndom for my 7:00 A.M. meeting. Driving past the reservoir and the small country homes, I soon arrived at the main entrance — a twenty-foot-high cast-iron gate sandwiched between two great brick walls. I sat in the middle of the road looking at the imperious five-foot gray concrete eagles perched atop the gate staring at me. I decided to try the back entrance. There, across from an old cemetery, was the small, unmarked path lined with someday-to-be-great trees and small NO TRESPASSING signs. It wound me back into Winndom, where I was to meet Craig Winn at his carriage house.

Opening the door and walking past his collection of John Deere tractors (there was still no combine), I heard Cristal's great barks from atop the stairs I had last climbed to attend the John McCain fund-raiser. There, standing next to Cristal, was Winn. I climbed the stairs as he stood with arms folded, smiling benevolently down at me. Shaking his hand, I glanced around the cavernous cedar-lined room he had transformed into his office. Two great stuffed turkeys seemed to fly out of the wall behind his desk. Turkeys were, he reminded me, birds of nobility.

I sat down in one of the oversize sofas, and he plopped down opposite me. For the next seven and a half hours we talked. He led me back into his wonderful world, where Value America was still as great as the hour he first conceived of it.

Value America's problems, Winn told me, came about because he wasn't involved enough in the business after it went public. His greatest mistake, he said, was leaving the company in the hands of others whom he thought he could trust. He wasn't necessarily bitter toward them, but he was bitter about the outcome. His great vision had been scuttled by others. Still, he marveled, how great those custom stores and Citibank and FedEx deals *would have been* had things been run properly. He was right about much of it. His vision for an inventoryless e-commerce company was still spectacular. Management hadn't been what it could have been. Wall Street's ever-changing rules and questionable ethics had helped create a *Lord of the Flies* environment. Saks had struggled to come up with an e-commerce strategy of its own. EFed struggled in its e-government applications. Citibank and FedEx could have been great. Listening to him, I found myself swept up again in the possibilities and reminded anew of why I had jumped at Value America: No one can sell like Craig Winn.

At the end of our day together, Winn walked me down to my car and gave me a hug. There wasn't any way, he said, he could endure the pain of building a business ever again — unless, of course, the world changed dramatically. But what, he asked, were the chances of that happening?

Acknowledgments

I've always loved reading acknowledgments — not because I've ever been in many but because it is fun to see who the author thanks and how. After writing this book, I wonder how some authors can keep their acknowledgments to fewer than a dozen pages. However, I've been instructed that these words have to be especially brief.

There are dozens of people who have helped every step of the way. From interviews to ideas to edits, countless people gave greatly of their time and talent to help me make this book what it could be. To all, my thanks extend far beyond these pages.

A few people, however, deserve special thanks. My wife, Kimberly, is first. She is my partner, my most trusted friend, and the person whom I most want to impress. She is also a ruthless editor. I thank her heartily for not divorcing me after I persuaded her to leave AOL for Value America, for not shooting me when a large chunk of her family was fired from Value America, and for not having someone else shoot me during the stressful moments of writing this book.

My next thanks go to my two daughters, Laura and Rachel. I always want to be the kind of dad and man I am in your eyes.

Infinite thanks to my parents for things too many to mention. Oh, Dad, you *are* next.

This is a project born of a grand vision by someone I believe to be a good and decent man — Craig Winn. I thank him for the idea that was Value America and for the countless hours he spent with me not only at Value America but on the phone and in person while I labored through this book.

Without Tom Morgan's help and friendship this book would, similarly, be just an idea. I have learned so much from him about business, management, and leadership. But most important, I have learned from him about grace, forgiveness, and faith.

It is still my hope that one day Tom and Craig will take the time to sit down and break bread.

My agents, Glenn Hartley and Lynn Chu, are brilliant, reliable, and loyal. They are also dear friends.

Enormous thanks to Michael Pietsch and Ryan Harbage at Little, Brown. Michael is already a legend. Nothing I could write about him would be nearly as good as what so many others have written. It was a privilege to learn from and be edited by him. Ryan is a young editor with spectacular talents — it was a joy working with him. Similarly, thanks to Pamela Marshall, Geoff Shandler, and Karen Auerbach at Little, Brown for helping to make this book something far greater than I thought it could be.

Finally, to everyone at Value America, it was an amazing joy to work with all of you. We tried to do something great. That is a reward in and of itself.